D0050680

In God We Still Trust
© 2010 by Dr. Richard G. Lee

All rights reserved. No portion of this book may be reproduced, stored in a retrieval system, or transmitted in any form or by any means—electronic, mechanical, photocopy, recording, scanning, or other—except for brief quotations in critical reviews or articles, without the prior written permission of the publisher.

Published in Nashville, Tennessee, by Thomas Nelson®. Thomas Nelson is a registered trademark of Thomas Nelson, Inc.

Cover design: Koechel Peterson Design, Minneapolis, MN
Interior design: Kristy Morell
Managing Editor: Lisa Stilwell

Thomas Nelson, Inc., titles may be purchased in bulk for educational, business, fund-raising, or sales promotional use. For information, please e-mail SpecialMarkets@ThomasNelson.com.

Scripture quotations are taken from the NEW KING JAMES VERSION. © 1982, 1992 by Thomas Nelson, Inc. Used by permission. All rights reserved.

Scripture quotations marked NIV are from the HOLY BIBLE: NEW INTERNATIONAL VERSION®. © 1973, 1978, 1984 by International Bible Society. Used by permission of Zondervan Publishing House. All rights reserved.

Scripture quotations marked KJV are from the KING JAMES VERSION.

ISBN-13: 978-1-4041-8965-2

Printed in Singapore

10 11 12 13 14 TWP 5 4 3 2 1

www.thomasnelson.com

2017

To:

Aunt Lynnie

From:

Love,
Debbie

On the occasion of:

Happy Birthday!!

IN GOD
WE *Still* TRUST

A 365-Day Devotional

Dr. Richard G. Lee

THOMAS NELSON
Since 1798

NASHVILLE DALLAS MEXICO CITY RIO DE JANEIRO BEIJING

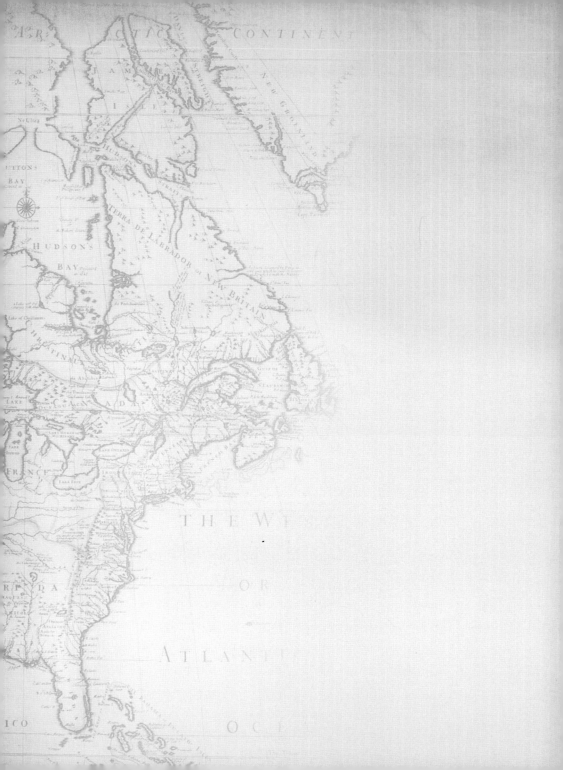

January

Praying for Our Nation

If My people who are called by My name will humble themselves, and pray and seek My face, and turn from their wicked ways, then I will hear from heaven, and will forgive their sin and heal their land.

2 CHRONICLES 7:14

From our nation's earliest days, God's promise in 2 Chronicles 7 that He will hear the cry of a humbled people has motivated America's leaders to call citizens to prayer. In 1775, as it began the process of forming a new nation, the Continental Congress called for a day of prayer. At critical junctures during the Civil War, President Abraham Lincoln called for the nation to fast and pray. And in 1952 President Truman signed a bill establishing an annual National Day of Prayer.

Second Chronicles helps establish a model of national spiritual renewal. The book recounts how a succession of righteous kings in Judah led to reforms that brought the people back to true faith in God. Second Chronicles 16:9 assures us that God will "show Himself strong" toward those who place their trust in Him.

★ ★ Patriot's Prayer ★ ★

Lord, I am very aware of our nation's need to repent and return to You. I am also very aware that such repentance must begin in every heart, including mine. Today I ask You to reveal to me the sins hidden in my heart and accept my plea for forgiveness.

★ ★ Patriot's Promise ★ ★

God promises that "If we confess our sins, He is faithful and just to forgive us our sins and to cleanse us from all unrighteousness" (1 John 1:9).

The men of Judah . . . remained loyal to their king.

2 SAMUEL 20:2

Patriotism Defined

Noah Webster's *An American Dictionary of the English Language*, 1828:
> *patriotism,* n. Love of one's country; the passion which aims to serve one's country, either in defending it from invasion, or protecting its rights and maintaining its laws and institutions in vigor and purity. Patriotism is the characteristic of a good citizen, the noblest passion that animates a man in the character of a citizen.

Merriam-Webster's Collegiate Dictionary, Eleventh Edition, copyright © 2004:
> *patriotism,* n. Love for or devotion to one's country.

Note how the definitions have changed. With its objective actions, Noah Webster's patriotism is very different from the vague, subjective patriotism of one who only feels love for his country. True patriotism is not just an emotional feeling; it is action.

Webster's original definition starts with a love for country, but moves to specific actions: service to country, defense of country, protection of the rights of country, maintenance of the laws and institutions of country, and preservation of religion and morality in public and private life. This kind of patriotism puts the needs of the country above personal or partisan desires, as well as above the favor of foreign nations.

★ ★ Patriot's Prayer ★ ★

I love my country, Lord, and I ask You to protect us from harm. Be with those men and women in each branch of service. Guard us all in Your Name.

★ ★ Patriot's Promise ★ ★

Hear God's promise: "The LORD commanded us to observe all these statutes, to fear the Lord our God, for our good always, that He might preserve us alive, as it is this day" (Deuteronomy 6:24).

True History or Consummate Fraud?

> If Christ is not risen, your faith is futile.
>
> 1 CORINTHIANS 15:17

Hear the confident declaration of American statesman Daniel Webster (1782–1852):

> The Gospel is either true history, or it is a consummate fraud; it is either a reality or an imposition. Christ was what He professed to be, or He was an imposter. There is no other alternative. His spotless life in His earnest enforcement of the truth—His suffering in its defense, forbid us to suppose that He was suffering an illusion of a heated brain. Every act of His pure and holy life shows that He was the author of truth, the advocate of truth, the earnest defender of truth, and the uncompromising sufferer for truth. Now, considering the purity of His doctrines, the simplicity of His life, and the sublimity of His death, is it possible that He would have died for an illusion? In all His preaching the Savior made no popular appeals. His discourses were always directed to the individual. Christ and His apostles sought to impress upon every man the conviction that he must stand or fall alone—he must live for himself, and die for himself, and give up his account to the omniscient God as though he were the only dependent creature in the universe. The Gospel leaves the individual sinner alone with himself and his God.

★ ★ Patriot's Prayer ★ ★

Gracious Father, thank You for sending Jesus to die for sinners, myself among them.

★ ★ Patriot's Promise ★ ★

In Isaiah 9:6, God promised to send His Son: "His name will be called Wonderful, Counselor, Mighty God, Everlasting Father, Prince of Peace." Promise fulfilled!

January 3

4

The word of the LORD endures forever.

1 PETER 1:25

Investing in Eternity

Elias Boudinot Jr. (1740–1821) was an American lawyer and statesman from Elizabeth, New Jersey. An energetic patriot, he was elected a delegate to the Continental Congress from 1777 to 1784, serving as its president from 1782 until 1783. He then served three terms in Congress and ten years as Director of the Mint. Boudinot supported many civic and educational causes during his life, including serving as one of Princeton's trustees for nearly half a century.

Boudinot was elected president of the American Bible Society at its founding in 1816. In accepting the office, he wrote that this was "the greatest honor" that could have been conferred upon him "this side of the grave." He had an unwavering faith that God had called the men of the society to the work of making Bibles available in America. His $10,000 gift, at a time when an annual salary of $400 was considered good, essentially enabled the formation and organization of the American Bible Society, which still sponsors the work of Bible translation and distribution around the world.

★ ★ Patriot's Prayer ★ ★
Help me, Father, to remember—as Elias Boudinot did—that the most significant work I can do on this earth is work I do for You. The things of this world will fade away, but work done for Your kingdom will last for eternity.

★ ★ Patriot's Promise ★ ★
In 1 Samuel 2:30, God says, "Those who honor Me I will honor," and we honor Him by being committed to living by His principles each day and by giving our time, talents, and treasures to His kingdom work.

5

"The God Who Made the Peanut"

There is a God in heaven who reveals secrets.

DANIEL 2:28

Chemist George Washington Carver (1864–1943) gained international fame in the field of agriculture due to his research into crops like peanuts, soybeans, pecans, and sweet potatoes that could be alternatives to soil-depleting cotton. He wanted poor farmers to grow soil-enriching crops so they would be able to provide food for their family as well as marketable products, thereby improving their quality of life.

In 1921 (when it was unusual for an African-American to be called as an expert), Carver spoke in favor of a peanut tariff before the Ways and Means Committee of the US House of Representatives. After he detailed the potential uses of the peanut and other new crops to improve the economy of the South, the Chairman of the Committee had a question:

"Dr. Carver, how did you learn all of these things?"

Carver answered: "From an old book."

"What book?"

Carver replied, "The Bible."

The senator inquired, "Does the Bible tell about peanuts?"

"No, sir," Dr. Carver replied, "but it tells about the God who made the peanut. I asked Him to show me what to do with the peanut, and He did."

★ ★ Patriot's Prayer ★ ★

Almighty God, help me today to be guided by Your hand. Only You know those things that are a mystery to me. Please reveal to me what You would have me know so I can serve You today.

★ ★ Patriot's Promise ★ ★

Daniel 2:22 says, "He reveals deep and secret things; He knows what is in the darkness, and light dwells with Him."

In Him we live and move and have our being.

ACTS 17:28

God's Co-Worker

Agricultural chemist George Washington Carver (1864–1943) discovered three hundred uses for peanuts and hundreds more uses for soybeans, pecans, and sweet potatoes. Read his thoughts about God:

> As a very small boy exploring the almost virgin woods of the old Carver place, I had the impression someone had just been there ahead of me. Things were so orderly, so clean, so harmoniously beautiful. A few years later in this same woods . . . I was practically overwhelmed with the sense of some Great Presence. Not only had someone been there. Someone was there. . . .
>
> Years later when I read in the Scriptures, "In Him we live and move and have our being," I knew what the writer meant. Never since have I been without this consciousness of the Creator speaking to me. . . . The out-of-doors has been to me more and more a great cathedral in which God could be continuously spoken to and heard from. . . .
>
> Man, who needed a purpose, a mission, to keep him alive, had one. He could be . . . God's co-worker. . . . My purpose alone must be God's purpose—to increase the welfare and happiness of His people. . . . Why, then, should we who believe in Christ be so surprised at what God can do with a willing man in a laboratory?

★ ★ Patriot's Prayer ★ ★

Lord, show me the specific purpose that You have for me today.

★ ★ Patriot's Promise ★ ★

"The LORD God took the man and put him in the garden of Eden to tend and keep it" (Genesis 2:15)—this assignment is the promise of a purposeful life.

A Vital Connection

The LORD your God is He who goes with you, to fight for you against your enemies, to save you.

DEUTERONOMY 20:4

As Franklin D. Roosevelt's 1939 State of the Union underscores, until recent years America's leaders understood the vital connection between religion and democracy. With Hitler on the move in Europe, President Roosevelt said this:

> Storms from abroad directly challenge three institutions indispensable to Americans, now as always. The first is religion. It is the source of the other two—democracy and international good faith.
>
> Religion, by teaching man his relationship to God, gives the individual a sense of his own dignity and teaches him to respect himself by respecting his neighbors.
>
> Democracy, the practice of self-government, is a covenant among free men to respect the rights and liberties of their fellows.
>
> International good faith, a sister of democracy, springs from the will of civilized nations of men to respect the rights and liberties of other nations of men. . . .
>
> There comes a time in the affairs of men when they must prepare to defend, not their homes alone, but the tenets of faith and humanity on which their churches, their governments, and their very civilization are founded. The defense of religion, of democracy, and of good faith among nations is all the same fight. To save one we must now make up our minds to save all.

★ ★ **Patriot's Prayer** ★ ★

Father, may I always defend the faith—today and every day.

★ ★ **Patriot's Promise** ★ ★

"Watch therefore, and pray always that you may be counted worthy to escape all these things that will come to pass, and to stand before the Son of Man" (Luke 21:36).

O Lord, the hope of Israel . . .

Jeremiah 17:13

Words of Truth

The Sea of Galilee—like life itself—is known for unexpected storms. Winds gust, waves crash, and fishermen fear for their well-being. Likewise, settling a new land, establishing a new nation, and experimenting with a new form of government meant unexpected storms for American colonists.

No matter the place or the course, storms of life happen, and we do well to have an anchor to keep from drifting off course or even capsizing. The founders of the State of Rhode Island knew that well. On the state seal appears a picture of an anchor. Above it, this motto:

IN GOD WE HOPE

★ ★ Patriot's Prayer ★ ★

You are my anchor, heavenly Father. Sometimes I feel like I am on a tumultuous sea, being tossed to and fro and having no real sense of direction. But I know that You are there with me, You have me in Your hand, and that You are guiding me safely to shore. Thank You, Lord, that I can hope in You.

★ ★ Patriot's Promise ★ ★

Psalm 33:18 is one of God's many promises that gives us hope: "Behold, the eye of the Lord is on those who fear Him, on those who hope in His mercy."

Revival Fires

So the people of Nineveh believed God.

JONAH 3:5

A chaplain in the Confederate Army, William W. Bennett published a first-hand account of the spiritual renewal that swept through every corps, division, brigade, and regiment in General Robert E. Lee's Army of Northern Virginia:

> Up to January 1865, it was estimated that nearly 150,000 soldiers had been converted during the progress of the war, and it was believed that fully one-third of all the soldiers in the field were praying men and members of some branch of the Christian church.

★ ★ Patriot's Prayer ★ ★

What amazing good came out of the tragedy of the Civil War! Use me today as an instrument of Your saving power, Lord, whether people are dealing with tragedy or the everyday. I want my life to be an open book to those who are searching for You. Let people see Jesus in me and may my words be Spirit led.

★ ★ Patriot's Promise ★ ★

David told the Lord, "I will teach transgressors Your ways, and sinners shall be converted to You" (Psalm 51:13). He trusted in God's promise that if we tell people about His ways, they will be converted—and you and I can too.

For to me, to live is Christ, and to die is gain.

PHILIPPIANS 1:21

"To Live Is Christ"

The apostle Paul's letter to believers in Philippi is a note of thanks for their help during his time of need. He also lovingly urged the members of the church there to center their actions and thoughts on the pursuit of the Person and power of Christ. Paul's central point was simple: only in Christ are real unity and genuine joy possible. With Christ as our model of humility and service, we believers can enjoy a oneness of purpose, attitude, goal, and labor. Paul then reminded the Philippians that their ultimate citizenship is in heaven.

However, the words of Adlai Stevenson (1900–1965), who served as the US ambassador to the United Nations from 1961 to 1965, remind us of the privilege of being an American citizen:

> "When an American says that he loves his country, he means not only that he loves the New England hills, the prairies glistening in the sun, the wide and rising plains, the great mountains, and the sea. He means that he loves an inner air, an inner light in which freedom lives and in which a man can draw the breath of self-respect."

★ ★ Patriot's Prayer ★ ★

Lord, I thank You for the unspeakable joy I have discovered in the Christian life, joy that can supersede circumstances. Help me this day to encourage people in my life to look to You to find hope for a better tomorrow even in the midst of difficult times.

★ ★ Patriot's Promise ★ ★

Psalm 84:11 is the promise that "no good thing will [the Lord] withhold from those who walk uprightly."

Liberty, a Gift from the Creator

Have we not all one Father?

MALACHI 2:10

Founding Father and one of the three authors of the *Federalist Papers*, Alexander Hamilton (January 11, 1755–July 12, 1804) wrote this concerning the nature of liberty:

> The fundamental source of all your errors, sophisms, and false reasonings is a total ignorance of the natural rights of mankind. Were you once to become acquainted with these, you could never entertain a thought that all men are not, by nature, entitled to a parity of privileges. You would be convinced that natural liberty is a gift of the beneficent Creator to the whole human race; and that civil liberty is founded in that and cannot be wrested from any people, without the most manifest violation of justice.

★ ★ Patriot's Prayer ★ ★

I praise You, Righteous Father, for giving me the liberties that I enjoy each day. May I never take for granted that You grant us our freedoms only by Your grace.

★ ★ Patriot's Promise ★ ★

We have been set free in Christ. As Galatians 4:7 promises, we are no longer slaves, but heirs of God.

Therefore the children of Israel could not stand before their enemies.

JOSHUA 7:12

The Loss of Virtue

Samuel Adams, the great American patriot accused by King George III of being "the chief rabble-rouser" of American independence, wrote the following in a letter to James Warren, the president of the Provincial Congress of Massachusetts, in 1779:

> A general dissolution of principles and manners will more surely overthrow the liberties of America than the whole force of the common enemy. While the people are virtuous they cannot be subdued; but when once they lose their virtue, they will be ready to surrender their liberties to the first external or internal invader. How necessary then is it for those who are determined to transmit the blessings of liberty as a fair inheritance to posterity, to associate on public principles in support of public virtue.

★ ★ Patriot's Prayer ★ ★

Grant us strength, dear Father, that we may be able to provide the blessings of liberty to our children and to our children's children. Help us all to understand what virtue means and to live virtuously every day. Let us also teach the principles of virtue as we live our lives.

★ ★ Patriot's Promise ★ ★

God said that He will never leave us or forsake us, but if we leave Him, what then? In Joshua 7, God's people turned their backs on God and did not obey Him. Only when we are in God's perfect will, only when we have forsaken sin, will we have the privilege of His presence with us.

13

Quiet Commitment

Entreat me not to leave you, or to turn back from following after you; for wherever you go, I will go; and wherever you lodge, I will lodge; your people shall be my people, and your God, my God.

RUTH 1:16

Like Ruth of the Old Testament, women of steadfast loyalty and faith have been key to America's strength. One such woman was Ruth Bell Graham, wife of America's beloved twentieth-century spiritual leader Dr. Billy Graham. Throughout their life together, Dr. Graham often emphasized how vital his wife was to his own success, noting that "my work through the years would have been impossible without her encouragement and support."

For her own part, Mrs. Graham's quiet commitment to her God and to her family reflected the determination of her biblical namesake to follow the God of Israel. Mrs. Graham once explained, "I must faithfully, patiently, lovingly, and happily do my part—then quietly wait for God to do His." That same faithfulness was what led the widowed and desolate Ruth to become the wife of Boaz and a member of the line of Jesus Christ.

★ ★ Patriot's Prayer ★ ★

Father in heaven, thank You for the many godly women who have played such an important role in the shaping of America. I pray for every mother and daughter to exemplify Christ in their daily living, at home and in public, just as Ruth of old did.

★ ★ Patriot's Promise ★ ★

The influence of a godly life will last for generations to come: "The LORD your God, He is God, the faithful God who keeps covenant and mercy for a thousand generations with those who love Him and keep His commandments" (Deuteronomy 7:9).

Remember the Sabbath day, to keep it holy.

Exodus 20:8

A Church for Each Parish

In 1665, the Legislature of New York Colony issued this decree:
Whereas, the public worship of God is much discredited for want of painful [serious] and able ministers to instruct the people in the true religion, it is ordered that a church shall be built in each parish, capable of holding two hundred persons; that ministers of every church shall preach every Sunday, and pray for the king, queen, the Duke of York, and the royal family; and to marry persons after legal publication of license . . .

Sunday is not to be profaned by traveling, by laborers, or vicious persons . . . Church wardens [are] to report twice a year all misdemeanors, such as swearing, profaneness, Sabbath-breaking, drunkenness, fornication, adultery, and all such abominable sins.

★ ★ Patriot's Prayer ★ ★

I would like to make a new commitment to You today, Lord, to be more faithful to Your church, specifically to my local church and its work. Also, give me the desire to see churches built in our nation and around the world and show me how I may be a part of it.

★ ★ Patriot's Promise ★ ★

Hear the charge of Hebrews 10:24–25: "Let us consider one another in order to stir up love and good works, not forsaking the assembling of ourselves together, as is the manner of some, but exhorting one another, and so much the more as you see the Day approaching." God promises that we will find love and ways to serve Him in our local church. In fact, He asks that we serve Him there more and more because the coming of the Lord is near.

Courage, Dignity, and Love

Behave courageously, and the LORD will be with the good.

2 CHRONICLES 19:11

Hear these words from Martin Luther King Jr. (January 15, 1929–April 4, 1968), a pivotal leader of the civil rights movement:

> If you will protest courageously, and yet with dignity and Christian love, when the history books are written in future generations, the historians will have to pause and say, "There lived a great people—a black people—who injected new meaning and dignity into the veins of civilization."

★ ★ Patriot's Prayer ★ ★

Gracious Father, give me courage and boldness to speak up about my faith in You. Keep me from sounding arrogant or condemning. Instead, help me show love for the people You put in my path today, people You created and love. Put Your Word in my heart that I will know what to say in every situation. And, Lord, please bless my efforts to win someone to You today.

★ ★ Patriot's Promise ★ ★

Consider this charge to share your testimony with the world: "I will declare Your name to My brethren; in the midst of the assembly I will praise You" (Psalm 22:22). God promises us that "My word that goes forth from My mouth; it shall not return to Me void" (Isaiah 55:11). If we share an account of our journey of faith—our testimony—to others and take a stand for God, He will do the rest for their salvation.

Set in order the things that are lacking, and appoint elders in every city as I commanded you.

TITUS 1:5

As a young pastor, Titus faced the difficult assignment of setting in order the church at Crete. Paul advised him to appoint elders, men of proven spiritual character in their homes and businesses, to do the work of the church. In addition, Paul discussed in his letter to Titus that men and women, young and old, all have vital functions to fulfill in the church if they are to be living examples of the doctrine they profess.

Consider the wisdom of this statement attributed to Dr. Martin Luther King Jr., the great civil rights leader of the twentieth century: "Our lives begin to end the day we become silent about things that matter." If King did not say it, he certainly lived it. Likewise, Paul told Titus that he could not be silent about the greatest matter in human history: "the grace of God that brings salvation has appeared to all men" (2:11). Paul charged Titus to "speak these things, exhort, and rebuke with all authority" (2:15).

★ ★ Patriot's Prayer ★ ★

Father in heaven, please grant me wisdom and courage to speak about Your great and gracious plan of salvation. Keep from me a spirit of fear or timidity. And, by the power of Your Spirit, go before me to soften hearts and open minds to Your truth.

★ ★ Patriot's Promise ★ ★

"My soul finds rest in God alone; my salvation comes from him. He alone is my rock and my salvation; he is my fortress, I will never be shaken" (Psalm 62:1–2 NIV).

A More Just Society

You shall love your neighbor as yourself.

MARK 12:31

The civil rights movement of the 1950s and 1960s was led primarily by Dr. Martin Luther King Jr., who had become pastor of Dexter Avenue Baptist Church in Montgomery, Alabama, in 1954. At that time, American society was characterized by inequality, oppression, and segregation of black citizens, fueled by hatred, prejudice, and hostility. Refusing to stoop to such hatred and succumb to any bitterness, Dr. King connected his deep love for God and for his fellowman with the powerful determination to gain equal civil rights for African-Americans.

Dr. King rose to national prominence as the leader of the movement through nonviolent, mass demonstrations. The first was the Montgomery (Alabama) bus boycott in 1956, which started after Rosa Parks was arrested for refusing to give her seat on a bus to a white man. The movement produced scores of men and women who risked, and some who gave, their lives to secure a more just and more inclusive society.

★ ★ Patriot's Prayer ★ ★

Enable me, Father, to love those who treat me wrongly. Give me a heart of Your grace and forgiveness, and enable me to live by the Golden Rule. Teach me to live selflessly, bless us with unity despite our differences, and, again, grant us Your grace to live this way.

★ ★ Patriot's Promise ★ ★

"Now the Lord is the Spirit; and where the Spirit of the Lord is, there is liberty" (2 Corinthians 3:17).

I have chosen . . . to undo the heavy burdens, to let the oppressed go free.

Isaiah 58:6

Free at Last!

Our actions must be guided by the deepest principles of our Christian faith. Love must be our regulating ideal. Once again we must hear the words of Jesus echoing across the centuries: 'Love your enemies'. . ."

These are the words of Dr. Martin Luther King, leader of the American Civil Rights Movement, who pursued his dream of a color-blind society through lectures, nonviolent marches, and protests. He suffered harassment, threats, beatings, having his house bombed, and incarceration—but he kept marching for justice, equality, and peace. During the 1963 March on Washington, at the Lincoln Memorial, King delivered his famous "I have a dream" speech before 200,000 to 300,000 marchers: "I look to a day when people will not be judged by the color of their skin, but by the content of their character." The speech, which beautifully and forcefully articulated the hopes and aspirations of the civil rights movement, was rooted in two cherished national treasures: the Bible and the American Constitution.

Dr. King was assassinated before he could see victory over inequality. His tombstone proclaims his dream: "Free at last. Free at last. Thank God Almighty, I'm free at last."

★ ★ Patriot's Prayer ★ ★
Lord, thank You for Dr. King and others who have given their lives to liberate those in bondage.

★ ★ Patriot's Promise ★ ★
"Ask the Lord for rain . . . He will give them showers of rain" (Zechariah 10:1).

A Recurring Theme

> Holy, holy, holy is the LORD Almighty; the
> whole earth is full of his glory.
>
> ISAIAH 6:3 NIV

Dr. James Kennedy, influential pastor of Coral Ridge Presbyterian Church in Florida, shared this observation:

In reading over the Constitutions of all fifty of our states, I discovered . . . there is in all fifty, without exception, an appeal or a prayer to the Almighty God of the universe. . . . Through all fifty state Constitutions, without exception, there runs this same appeal and reference to God who is the Creator of our liberties and the preserver of our freedoms.

★ ★ Patriot's Prayer ★ ★

God, I lift Your name high above every name in heaven and on earth. I give you praise for who You are. I give You thanks for the saving work You have done. And I thank You, too, for our Founding Fathers and the insight they had as they planned and prayed for this nation.

★ ★ Patriot's Promise ★ ★

According to Isaiah 59:2, "your iniquities have separated you from your God; and your sins have hidden His face from you, so that He will not hear." When we sin, we do not have access to God. He only hears the prayers of those whose hearts are pure.

January 19

> Whoever desires to become great among you shall be your servant.
>
> JESUS IN MARK 10:43

The Godly Use of Power

In his January 20, 1989 inaugural address, George H. W. Bush said this:

We meet on democracy's front porch, a good place to talk as neighbors and as friends. For this is a day when our nation is made whole, when our differences, for a moment, are suspended.

And my first act as President is a prayer. I ask you to bow your heads:

Heavenly Father, we bow our heads and thank You for Your love. Accept our thanks for the peace that yields this day and the shared faith that makes its continuance likely. Make us strong to do Your work, willing to heed and hear Your will, and write on our hearts these words: "Use power to help people." For we are given power not to advance our own purposes, nor to make a great show in the world, nor a name. There is but one just use of power, and it is to serve people. Help us to remember it, Lord. Amen.

★ ★ Patriot's Prayer ★ ★

Help me, dear Lord, to always remember that I am here on this earth as Your servant, called to reach out to others with Your truth, mercy, and love. Give me strength to do Your work and keep me faithful to heed Your will.

★ ★ Patriot's Promise ★ ★

Hear the truth Jesus taught about those who love others: "Inasmuch as you did it to one of the least of these My brethren, you did it to Me" (Matthew 25:40). He will bless the acts of love we extend to those He puts in our path.

21

What Lies Ahead

Our light affliction . . . is working for us a far more exceeding and eternal weight of glory.

2 CORINTHIANS 4:17

Thomas "Stonewall" Jackson (January 21, 1824–May 10, 1863), the revered Civil War general whose death was a severe setback for the Confederacy, wrote the following in a letter to his wife:

> Don't trouble yourself . . . these things are earthly and transitory. There are real and glorious blessings, I trust, in reserve for us, beyond this life. It is best for us to keep our eyes fixed upon the throne of God. . . . It is gratifying to be beloved, and to have our conduct approved by our fellowmen; but this is not worthy to be compared with the glory that is in reservation for us, in the presence of the glorified Redeemer . . . knowing that there awaits us "a far more exceeding and eternal weight of glory."

★ ★ Patriot's Prayer ★ ★

Lord, at times, people can be so cruel. Please guard my family from hurtful tongues and spiteful words. Make our hearts so rooted in You that we will love people—and one another—no matter how they treat us.

★ ★ Patriot's Promise ★ ★

Hear words of blessing spoken by Boaz long ago: "The LORD repay your work, and a full reward be given you by the LORD God of Israel, under whose wings you have come for refuge" (Ruth 2:12). Inherent in the benediction is the promise that God will generously reward our service to Him.

God . . . gives life to all things.

1 Timothy 6:13

"The Transcendent Right to Life"

Ronald Reagan, the 40th president of the United States (1981–1989), stated: Abraham Lincoln recognized that we could not survive as a free land when some men could decide that others were not fit to be free and should therefore be slaves. Likewise, we cannot survive as a free nation when some men decide that others are not fit to live and should be abandoned to abortion or infanticide.

Hear is what Mr. Lincoln said:

My administration is dedicated to the preservation of America as a free land, and there is no cause more important for preserving that freedom than affirming the transcendent right to life of all human beings, the right without which no other rights have any meaning.

★ ★ Patriot's Prayer ★ ★

Lord, I come humbly before Your throne today asking that You forgive me. I have not stood up or worked for the preservation of life the way that I, as a Christian, should. Compel those of us who call Jesus "Lord" to defend the right to life. By Your Spirit, open the eyes of the people of this country to the fact that all life—that of the unborn, the elderly, the middle-aged, the young, those with special needs—is precious.

★ ★ Patriot's Promise ★ ★

Leviticus 17:11 tells us that all life is in the blood, and God's own Son shed His blood that we might know life in relationship with God for eternity.

23

"Sail On, O Ship of State!"

On Mount Zion there shall be deliverance.

OBADIAH 17

Henry Wadsworth Longfellow (1807–1882) was one of the the most widely known American poets in his day. Reflecting his fervent abolitionist convictions, "The Building of a Ship" speaks of his fear that the slavery issue would destroy the nation.

> Thou, too, sail on, O Ship of State!
>> Sail on, O Union, strong and great!
>> Humanity with all its fears,
>> With all the hopes of future years,
>> Is hanging breathless on thy fate! . . .
> Our hearts, our hopes, are all with thee,
>> Our hearts, our hopes, our prayers, our tears,
>> Our faith triumphant o'er our fears,
>> Are all with thee,—are all with thee!

In January 1941, President Franklin D. Roosevelt included the first five lines of Longfellow's poem in a handwritten letter to English Prime Minister Winston Churchill and said the verse "applies to you people as it does to us." Deeply moved, Churchill saw the letter as a symbol of the two countries' growing partnership. "Give us the tools," he told the president, "and we will finish the job!"

★ ★ Patriot's Prayer ★ ★

Thank You, Father, for those who have gone before us, who have stood strong and brave against that which is wrong and evil in Your sight. Help us do the same as we hold in our hands the hopes of future Americans.

★ ★ Patriot's Promise ★ ★

Psalm 33 says, "The LORD brings the counsel of the nations to nothing; He makes the plans of the peoples of no effect. . . . Blessed is the nation whose God is the LORD" (vv. 10, 12).

January 23

★ ★
★ 24 ★
★ ★

You . . . turn justice to wormwood.

AMOS 5:7

"Where Justice Is Denied"

Hear these words from Frederick Douglass (1818–1895), an abolitionist, orator, author, statesman, and one of the most prominent figures in African-American and American history:

> Where justice is denied, where poverty is enforced, where ignorance prevails, and where any one class is made to feel that society is an organized conspiracy to oppress, rob, and degrade them, neither persons nor property will be safe.

★ ★ Patriot's Prayer ★ ★
Allow me to see where I am unfair, Lord, and help me to correct any mistakes that I may make against another. Make my life an expression of Your Word and may others see Jesus in me every day.

★ ★ Patriot's Promise ★ ★
Job 13:10 tells us that if we show partiality, God will rebuke us. The Lord shows mercy to those who ask for it. We are to do the same or else face God's rebuke. God promised that if we are fair to others, He will be fair to us. He loves people and so should we.

25

January 24

"The Last Best Hope of Man"

It is good that one should hope.

LAMENTATIONS 3:26

On January 25, 1974, Ronald Reagan gave his famous "Shining City Upon a Hill" speech and concluded by saying this:

> We cannot escape our destiny, nor should we try to do so. The leadership of the free world was thrust upon us two centuries ago in that little hall of Philadelphia. In the days following World War II, when the economic strength and power of America was all that stood between the world and the return to the dark ages, Pope Pius XII said, "The American people have a great genius for splendid and unselfish actions. Into the hands of America God has placed the destinies of an afflicted mankind."

We were indeed—and we are today—the last best hope of man on earth.

★ ★ Patriot's Prayer ★ ★

Lord, hope is something that is difficult to have these days. Fill my heart and head with hope grounded in You and Your Truth and, consequently, enthusiasm for the future. Let me be unselfish and generous to my fellowman and an encouragement to those who need hope.

★ ★ Patriot's Promise ★ ★

"Be of good courage, and He shall strengthen your heart, all you who hope in the LORD." Psalm 31:24 is very clear: Hope brings courage and courage brings strength. When we have a zeal and passion for Him, the Lord God says, we can face anything.

If anyone wills to do [God's] will, he shall know concerning the doctrine, whether it is from God.

JOHN 7:17

Simon Greenleaf (1783–1853) served as the Royall Professor of Law at Harvard and contributed extensively to the school's development. In correspondence with the American Bible Society, he wrote this:

> Of the Divine character of the Bible, I think no man who deals honestly with his own mind and heart can entertain a reasonable doubt. For myself, I must say, that having for many years made the evidences of Christianity the subject of close study, the result has been a firm and increasing conviction of the authenticity and plenary inspiration of the Bible. It is indeed the Word of God.

★ ★ Patriot's Prayer ★ ★

Father, thank You for the Bible that enables me to read and digest the very words that You have spoken. May I be ever vigilant to pay heed to the standards and examples You have set before us. Fill me with Your Holy Spirit that He may increase my understanding of Your Word.

★ ★ Patriot's Promise ★ ★

In a promise about the power of the Scriptures, 1 John 5:13 says, "These things I have written to you who believe in the name of the Son of God, that you may know that you have eternal life, and that you may continue to believe in the name of the Son of God." The Bible gives us confidence in salvation through Christ and the reality of heaven.

27

The Four Freedoms

They have seduced My people, saying,
"'Peace!' when there is no peace.

EZEKIEL 13:10

In January 1941, with Germany, Italy, and Japan already waging war on four continents, President Franklin D. Roosevelt urged Americans that if democracy were to survive, mobilization was necessary to rid the world of dictatorships and military rule. He then described "four essential human freedoms" that the United States hoped to secure for the world community:

The first is freedom of speech and expression—everywhere in the world.

The second is freedom of every person to worship God in his own way—everywhere in the world.

The third is freedom from want—which, translated into world terms, means economic understandings which will secure to every nation a healthy peacetime life for its inhabitants—everywhere in the world.

The fourth is freedom from fear—which, translated into world terms, means a worldwide reduction of armaments to such a point and in such a thorough fashion that no nation will be in a position to commit an act of physical aggression against any neighbor— anywhere in the world.

That is no vision of a distant millennium. It is a definite basis for a kind of world attainable in our own time and generation. . . .

Freedom means the supremacy of human rights everywhere. . . .

To that high concept there can be no end save victory.

★ ★ Patriot's Prayer ★ ★

Father, use Your people to make these four human freedoms a reality around the world.

★ ★ Patriot's Promise ★ ★

"Whatever is born of God overcomes the world. And this is the victory that has overcome the world—our faith" (1 John 5:4).

[May you receive Onesimus] no longer as a slave but more than a slave—a beloved brother . . . both in the flesh and in the Lord. If then you count me as a partner, receive him as you would me.

PHILEMON 1:16–17

This briefest of Paul's epistles is a model of loving concern for the forgiveness of a slave who would otherwise face the death sentence for running away from his master. With much tact and tenderness, Paul asked Philemon to receive his slave Onesimus back with the same gentleness he would receive Paul himself, and Paul was confident that brotherly love and godly forgiveness would prevail in Philemon's heart.

Paul never suggested that Philemon had committed a sin in owning Onesimus. Pro-slavery advocates used this fact to defend slavery before the Civil War. Abolitionists, however, argued that referring to slaves as "brothers" undercut the social distinctions inherent in slavery and that although Paul did not directly condemn slavery, the spirit of his words embodies the principle of love, which motivates Christian action against slavery's oppression and its violation of the concept of justice as well as of the dignity, value, and equality of every human person.

★ ★ Patriot's Prayer ★ ★

Lord, teach me to forgive others as You have forgiven me. Show me any wickedness, pride, or prejudice within me. Grant me the ability to see every person—regardless of heritage, race, gender, or character—as You see them. Every person I meet—every person You created—is an object of Your love.

★ ★ Patriot's Promise ★ ★

Hear the promise of God's love for everyone in Peter's words: "God does not show favoritism but accepts men from every nation who fear him and do what is right" (Acts 10:34–35 NIV).

January 28

A Reawakening

The desire of our soul is for Your name and for
the remembrance of You.

ISAIAH 26:8

President Harry S. Truman held office during the end of World War II. In this 1946 speech, he reminded Americans of what we fought for and how to preserve it:

> We have just come through a decade in which forces of evil in various parts of the world have been lined up in a bitter fight to banish from the face of the earth . . . religion and democracy. For these forces of evil have long realized that both religion and democracy are founded on one basic principle, the worth and dignity of the individual man and woman. Dictatorship, on the other hand, has always rejected that principle. Dictatorship, by whatever name, is founded on the doctrine that the individual amounts to nothing; that the State is the only thing that counts; and that men and women and children were put on earth solely for the purpose of serving the State . . .
>
> If men and nations would but live by the precepts of the ancient prophets and the teachings of the Sermon on the Mount, problems which now seem so difficult would soon disappear. . . .
>
> This is a supreme opportunity for the Church to continue to fulfill its mission on earth. . . . Oh, for an Isaiah or a Saint Paul to reawaken this sick world to its moral responsibilities!

★ ★ Patriot's Prayer ★ ★

Lord, help me seek first Your kingdom—and use me to help our nation do likewise.

★ ★ Patriot's Promise ★ ★

"Seek first the kingdom of God and His righteousness, and all these things shall be added to you" (Matthew 6:33).

When the righteous are in
authority, the people rejoice.

PROVERBS 29:2

The Bible and American Presidents (Part 1)

Presidents who have honored God and relied on His Word have profoundly impacted our country.

It is impossible to rightly govern the world without God and the Bible.

ATTRIBUTED TO GEORGE WASHINGTON, FIRST PRESIDENT

The first and almost the only book deserving of universal attention is the Bible. I speak as a man of the world . . . and I say to you, "Search the Scriptures."

JOHN QUINCY ADAMS, SIXTH PRESIDENT

That book, sir, is the Rock on which our Republic rests.

ANDREW JACKSON, SEVENTH PRESIDENT

In regard for this Great Book, I have this to say, it is the best gift God has given to man. All the good the Savior gave to the world was communicated through this book.

ABRAHAM LINCOLN, SIXTEENTH PRESIDENT

If you take out of your statutes, your constitution, your family life all that is taken from the Sacred Book, what would there be left to bind society together?

BENJAMIN HARRISON, TWENTY-THIRD PRESIDENT

The Bible is the one supreme source of revelation of the meaning of life, the nature of God, and spiritual nature and needs of men. . . . America was born a Christian nation. America was born to exemplify that devotion to the elements of righteousness which are derived from the revelations of Holy Scripture.

WOODROW WILSON, TWENTY-EIGHTH PRESIDENT

★ ★ **Patriot's Prayer** ★ ★

Almighty Father, grant us leaders who serve You by serving this country.

★ ★ **Patriot's Promise** ★ ★

"The word of the LORD is proven" (Psalm 18:30).

The Bible and American Presidents (Part 2)

The foundations of our society and our government rest so much on the teachings of the Bible that it would be difficult to support them if faith in these teachings would cease to be practically universal in our country.

CALVIN COOLIDGE, THIRTIETH PRESIDENT

We cannot read the history of our rise and development as a nation without reckoning with the place the Bible has occupied in shaping the advances of the Republic. Where we have been the truest and most consistent in obeying its precepts, we have attained the greatest measure of contentment and prosperity.

FRANKLIN D. ROOSEVELT, THIRTY-SECOND PRESIDENT

The fundamental basis of this nation's laws was given to Moses on the Mount. The fundamental basis of our Bill of Rights comes from the teachings we get from Exodus and Saint Matthew, from Isaiah and Saint Paul. . . . If we don't have a proper fundamental moral background, we will finally end up with a totalitarian government which does not believe in rights for anybody except the State!

HARRY S. TRUMAN, THIRTY-THIRD PRESIDENT

Inside the Bible's pages lie all the answers to all of the problems man has ever known. . . . The Bible can touch our hearts, order our minds, and refresh our souls.

RONALD REAGAN, FORTIETH PRESIDENT

★ ★ Patriot's Prayer ★ ★

Almighty Father, grant this nation leaders who will make decisions based upon the principles and teachings found in Your Word.

★ ★ Patriot's Promise ★ ★

Psalm 119:160 says, "The entirety of Your word is truth, and every one of Your righteous judgments endures forever." Godly leaders who seek wisdom from Scripture will bring God's blessing to our nation.

February

Acknowledging God

You who are near, acknowledge My might.

ISAIAH 33:13

While there have been revisions to state constitutions over the years, forty-three states acknowledge God or a higher power in their preambles, and the other seven states acknowledge God in their religious freedom provisions.

The following is a short sample from various state constitutions:

Connecticut's 1818 Preamble: "The People of Connecticut, acknowledging with gratitude the good Providence of God in permitting them to enjoy a free government ..."

Maine's 1820 Preamble: "We the People of Maine ... acknowledging with grateful hearts the goodness of the Sovereign Ruler of the Universe in affording us an opportunity ... and imploring His aid and direction in its accomplishment ..."

Massachusetts' 1780 Preamble: "We, therefore, the people of Massachusetts, acknowledging with grateful hearts, the goodness of the Great Legislator of the Universe, in affording us, in the course of His Providence, an opportunity ... and devoutly imploring His direction ..."

New York's 1846 Preamble: "We, the people of the State of New York, grateful to Almighty God for our freedom, in order to secure its blessings ..."

★ ★ Patriot's Prayer ★ ★

Today, Lord, I acknowledge You as the source of opportunity and blessings. I also ask Your aid and direction this day and always.

★ ★ Patriot's Promise ★ ★

The promise of Psalm 5:12 is straightforward: "You, O LORD, will bless the righteous; with favor You will surround him as with a shield."

February 1

The good shepherd lays down his life for the sheep.

JOHN 10:11

Faithful to the End

Shortly before 1 a.m. on February 2, 1943, the American transport ship *Dorchester* was steaming through the icy North Atlantic from Newfoundland toward an American base in Greenland, carrying 902 service men, merchant seamen, and civilian workers when a German torpedo struck the starboard side. The blast killed scores of men, and many more were seriously wounded.

Through the pandemonium, four Army chaplains—George L. Fox, Methodist; Alexander D. Goode, Jewish; John P. Washington, Roman Catholic; and Clark V. Poling, Dutch Reformed—brought hope to the men struggling to survive. They could be heard encouraging the frightened, praying for the dying, and guiding the disoriented toward the lifeboats.

Men jumped into lifeboats, overcrowding them to the point of capsizing. Other rafts drifted away before soldiers could get in. As men reached topside, the chaplains began distributing life jackets. When no more were available, the chaplains astonished onlookers, taking off their own and giving them to four frightened young men.

Then in the darkness, singing and shouting biblical encouragement, the four chaplains linked arms and grasped the railing of the ship as it slipped into the ocean. William Bednar said that, as he floated among dead comrades, "Their voices . . . were the only thing that kept me going."

Of the men aboard the *Dorchester*, 672 died, including the chaplains. Their heroic conduct offered a vision of greatness that stunned America.

★ ★ Patriot's Prayer ★ ★
Lord, use me to show others the selflessness of Christian love.

★ ★ Patriot's Promise ★ ★
"Greater love has no one than this, than to lay down one's life for his friends" (John 15:13). When we give our lives in service or sacrifice, Jesus calls us "friend."

35

"Duty to God"

The Boy Scouts of America believes that no member can grow into the best kind of citizen without recognizing an obligation to God. Accordingly, youth members and adult volunteer leaders obligate themselves to do their duty to God and live in accordance with the Scout Oath and the Scout Law. But it hasn't been without its share of legal battles.

In *Welsh v. Boy Scouts of America* (1993), the US Court of Appeals for the Seventh Circuit ruled that the Boy Scouts could keep the phrase *duty to God* in their oath and that, as a private organization, they have the right to exclude anyone who refuses to take the oath:

> The leadership of many in our government is a testimonial to the success of Boy Scout activities. In recent years, single-parent families, gang activity, availability of drugs and other factors have increased the dire need for support structures like the Scouts. When the government, in this instance through the courts, seeks to regulate the membership of an organization like the Boy Scouts in a way that scuttles its founding principles, we run the risk of undermining one of the seedbeds of virtue that cultivate the sorts of citizens our nation so desperately needs.

Cases in 1995 and 1998 upheld the "duty to God" requirements for Scouts as well as leaders.

★ ★ Patriot's Prayer ★ ★

God, may I uphold with my life the importance of doing one's "duty to God." Guide me and use me for Your kingdom work.

★ ★ Patriot's Promise ★ ★

"Serve the LORD your God, and He will bless your bread and your water" (Exodus 23:25).

> [God] has shone in our hearts to give the light of the knowledge of the glory of God in the face of Jesus Christ.
>
> 2 CORINTHIANS 4:6

Answers from the Bible

John McLean (1785–1861), a US Postmaster General and justice of the US Supreme Court, wrote this:

> No one can estimate or describe the salutary influence of the Bible. What would the world be without it? Compare the dark places of the earth, where the light of the Gospel has not penetrated, with those where it has been proclaimed and embraced in all its purity. Life and immortality are brought to light by the Scriptures. Aside from Revelation, darkness rests upon the world and upon the future. There is no ray of light to shine upon our pathway; there is no star of hope. We begin our speculations as to our destiny in conjecture, and they end in uncertainty. We know not that there is a God, a heaven, or a hell, or any day of general account, when the wicked and the righteous shall be judged. The Bible has shed a glorious light upon the world. It shows us that in the coming day we must answer for the deeds done in the body. It has opened us to a new and living way, so plainly marked out that no one can mistake it.

★ ★ Patriot's Prayer ★ ★

Dear God, thank You for the understanding I gain as Your Word shines the light of Your truth in my life.

★ ★ Patriot's Promise ★ ★

Psalm 18:28 gives us this wonderful assurance: "You will light my lamp; the LORD my God will enlighten my darkness."

The Nation's Guiding Principle

> I will never leave you nor forsake you.
>
> JESUS IN HEBREWS 13:5

Hear President John F. Kennedy in a February 1961 speech: No man who enters upon the office to which I have succeeded can fail to recognize how every president of the United States has placed special reliance upon his faith in God. Every president has taken comfort and courage when told . . . that the Lord "will be with thee. He will not fail thee nor forsake thee. Fear not—neither be thou dismayed". . . Each of our presidents in his own way has placed a special trust in God. Those who were strongest intellectually were also strongest spiritually. . . .

Let us . . . lead this land that we love, joining in the prayer of General George Washington in 1783, "that God would have you in His holy protection, that He would incline the hearts of the citizens . . . to entertain a brotherly love and affection one for another . . . and finally that He would most graciously be pleased to dispose us all to do justice, to love mercy, and to demean ourselves with . . . the characteristics of the Divine Author of our blessed religion, without an humble imitation of whose example we can never hope to be a happy nation."

The guiding principle and prayer of this nation has been, is now, and shall ever be "In God We Trust."

★ ★ Patriot's Prayer ★ ★

Dear God, I put my trust in You. You are my Rock and my Deliverer.

★ ★ Patriot's Promise ★ ★

"Hezekiah trusted in the LORD God of Israel . . . [and] kept His commandments. . . . The LORD was with him; he prospered wherever he went" (2 Kings 18:5–7).

February 5

To those who are defiled and unbelieving nothing is pure; but even their mind and conscience are defiled.

TITUS 1:15

A Serious Imbalance

General Omar Bradley was one of the main US Army field commanders in North Africa and Europe during World War II. Later, he was the first officer assigned to the post of Chairman of the Joint Chiefs of Staff. In 1948, he stated this powerful insight, "We have grasped the mystery of the atom and rejected the Sermon on the Mount. . . . The world has achieved brilliance without conscience. Ours is a world of nuclear giants and ethical infants."

★ ★ Patriot's Prayer ★ ★
Dear God, may I shine the light of morality in the world today.

★ ★ Patriot's Promise ★ ★
Colossians 2:8 gives us a warning—"Beware lest anyone cheat you through philosophy and empty deceit, according to the tradition of men, according to the basic principles of the world, and not according to Christ." We cannot rely upon philosophy and tradition to show us truth. Instead, we must continually gauge the world's message through the lens of the Bible to see how it compares to the Lord's ultimate truth. When we do, God promises that we will be "complete in Him" (v. 10).

Christ Reigns Supreme

We have a great High Priest who has passed through the heavens, Jesus the Son of God.

HEBREWS 4:14

In the early church many believers who had stepped out of Judaism into Christianity found themselves persecuted by nonbelieving Jews, prompting the writer of Hebrews to address the superiority of Christ over Judaism. Christ is superior to angels, the Aaronic priesthood, and the Law. In short, he argued, there is infinitely more to be gained by following Christ than to be lost by yielding up the Jewish traditions.

The recipients of the book of Hebrews faced persecution, even death, for their Christian confession, and it is worth noting that the marching song of the Union Army during the Civil War included the line "as Christ died to make men holy, let us die to make men free." Although that phrase was later changed to "let us live to make men free," for the soldiers who placed their lives on the line to end slavery and preserve the Union, the original wording was absolutely correct.

★ ★ Patriot's Prayer ★ ★

Dear Christ, there is none like You. May every one of us who follows You boldly proclaim that You and You alone are the Way, the Truth, and the Life for all mankind (John 14:6). My hope is not based in the religions of the world and the men who create them, but in You, my High Priest, my Savior, my Lord.

★ ★ Patriot's Promise ★ ★

Our great High Priest understands our weaknesses and intercedes for us: "Now He who searches the hearts knows what the mind of the Spirit is, because He makes intercession for the saints according to the will of God" (Romans 8:27). What a promise!

For the weapons of our warfare
are . . . mighty in God.

2 Corinthians 10:4

A Nation's Most Powerful Resource

Dwight David Eisenhower, the thirty-fourth president of the United States (1953–1961), signed into law the Congressional Act, Joint Resolution 243, which added the phrase "one Nation under God" to the Pledge of Allegiance. He explained why:

> In this way we are reaffirming the transcendence of religious faith in America's heritage and future; in this way we shall constantly strengthen those spiritual weapons which forever will be our country's most powerful resource in peace and war.

★ ★ Patriot's Prayer ★ ★

No weapon formed against You, God, will stand. That truth helps me trust that You will look after me and keep my family and me from all harm. After all, the battles we see with our eyes are not the only battles that rage. So I ask you to protect me and those I love, as both earthly and heavenly battles rage.

★ ★ Patriot's Promise ★ ★

The promise of Isaiah 54:17—"No weapon formed against you shall prosper"—is, like all God's promises, a source of hope, security, and comfort.

41

"Ask Not"

As for me and my house, we will serve the LORD.

JOSHUA 24:15

With Americans fearing war, President John F. Kennedy spoke these inspirational words in his 1961 inaugural address:

The torch has been passed to a new generation of Americans, born in this century, tempered by war, disciplined by a hard and bitter peace, proud of our ancient heritage and unwilling to witness or permit the slow undoing of those human rights to which this nation has always been committed. . . .

Let every nation know, whether it wishes us well or ill, that we shall pay any price, bear any burden, meet any hardship, support any friend, oppose any foe, to assure the survival and the success of liberty. . . .

In the long history of the world, only a few generations have been granted the role of defending freedom in its hour of maximum danger. . . . The energy, the faith, the devotion which we bring to this endeavor will light our country and all who serve it—and the glow from that fire can truly light the world. And so, my fellow Americans: ask not what your country can do for you—ask what you can do for your country. . . .

With a good conscience our only sure reward, with history the final judge of our deeds, let us go forth to lead the land we love, asking His blessing and His help, but knowing that here on earth God's work must truly be our own.

★ ★ Patriot's Prayer ★ ★

Lord of my heart, may Your desires take root, that they may be my heartfelt desires as well. Let your work become my own.

★ ★ Patriot's Promise ★ ★

"Delight yourself also in the LORD, and He shall give you the desires of your heart" (Psalm 37:4).

February 9

42

Blessed is the nation whose God is the LORD.

PSALM 33:12

The Goal of Government

When the first settlers arrived in America, the influence of the Bible on their lives came with them. For many, their Christian faith was as much a part of who they were as their brave spirit was, and their faith impacted everything they did. This fact stands out boldly as one sees, again and again, Scripture reflected in the individual colonies' statements of the goal of their government. The Rhode Island Charter of 1683, for instance, begins this way: "We submit our person, lives, and estates unto our Lord Jesus Christ, the King of kings and Lord of lords, and to all those perfect and most absolute laws of His given us in His Holy Word."

In fact, from the first colony at Jamestown to the Pennsylvania Charter of Privileges granted to William Penn in 1701—where "all persons who . . . profess to believe in Jesus Christ, the Savior of the world, shall be capable . . . to serve this government in any capacity, both legislatively and executively" —the Bible was considered the rule of life in the colonies.

★ ★ Patriot's Prayer ★ ★
Lord, please keep my mind fixed on You and my thoughts grounded in Your Word so that You can use me to encourage my family, friends, and co-workers today. Help me to be aware of what I say and the way I say it—before I say it.

★ ★ Patriot's Promise ★ ★
"The Helper, the Holy Spirit . . . will teach you all things, and bring to your remembrance all things that I said to you" (John 14:26).

Reverence for the Word

William Cullen Bryant (1794–1878), known as the Father of American Poets and a long-time editor of the *New York Evening Post*, wrote the following about the Bible:

> The sacredness of the Bible awes me, and I approach it with the same sort of reverential feeling that an ancient Hebrew might be supposed to feel who was about to touch the ark of God with unhallowed hands.

★ ★ Patriot's Prayer ★ ★

Lord, may Your Word be my revered guide through both the good times and the bad times of my life.

★ ★ Patriot's Promise ★ ★

In the promise of Revelation 22:18, the apostle John spoke on God's behalf and let us know the serious consequences of adding to His Word: "I testify to everyone who hears the words of the prophecy of this book: If anyone adds to these things, God will add to him the plagues that are written in this book."

He who doubts is like a wave of the sea driven and tossed by the wind.

JAMES 1:6

Abraham Lincoln on Skepticism

A close friend of Abe Lincoln, Joshua Speed published *Reminiscences of Abraham Lincoln*, which includes a story from 1864 when he visited Lincoln:

> When I knew [Mr. Lincoln], in early life, he was a skeptic. He had tried hard to be a believer, but his reason could not grasp and solve the great problem of redemption as taught. He was very cautious never to give expression to any thought or sentiment that would grate harshly upon a Christian's ear. For a sincere Christian, he had great respect. . . . But this was a subject we never discussed.
>
> The only evidence I have of any change, was in the summer before he was killed. I was invited out to the Soldier's Home to spend the night. As I entered the room, near night, he was sitting near a window intently reading his Bible.
>
> Approaching him I said, "I am glad to see you so profitably engaged."
>
> "Yes," said he, "I am profitably engaged."
>
> "Well," said I, "if you have recovered from your skepticism, I am sorry to say that I have not."
>
> Looking me earnestly in the face and placing his hand on my shoulder, he said, "You are wrong, Speed. Take all of this book upon reason that you can, and the balance on faith, and you will live and die a happier and better man."

★ ★ Patriot's Prayer ★ ★

Father, grow my faith as I regularly read my Bible and pray.

★ ★ Patriot's Promise ★ ★

"Blessed are those who have not seen and yet have believed" (John 20:29).

February 12

Finding Hope in Suffering

Do not think it strange concerning the fiery trial which is to try you, as though some strange thing happened to you; but rejoice to the extent that you partake of Christ's sufferings, that when His glory is revealed, you may also be glad with exceeding joy.

1 PETER 4:12–13

The apostle Peter wrote these words to persecuted believers, encouraging them to persevere for the person and message of Christ. Peter provided them with a divine perspective on their trials so that they could endure them without wavering in their faith. Having been born again to a living hope, they are to imitate the Holy One who Himself suffered and to rely on His strong presence when they suffer.

As commander of the Allied forces in Europe during World War II and later president of the United States, Dwight D. Eisenhower also knew a great deal about the strength of men and women in difficult times. He said, "The spirit of man is more important than mere physical strength, and the spiritual fiber of a nation than its wealth. The Bible is endorsed by the ages. Our civilization is built upon its words. In no other book is there such a collection of inspired wisdom, reality, and hope."

★ ★ Patriot's Prayer ★ ★

Lord, give me wisdom when I suffer so that I may not only endure, but that I may also face those trials with a divine perspective. Grant my spirit strength to trust in Your sovereign will for my life.

★ ★ Patriot's Promise ★ ★

"The sufferings of this present time are not worthy to be compared with the glory which shall be revealed in us" (Romans 8:18).

Let each man have his own wife.

1 CORINTHIANS 7:2

One Man, One Woman

In the 1885 Utah Territory case of *Murphy v. Ramsey*, the US Supreme Court recognized the fundamental importance of the traditional institution of marriage:

> Every person who has a husband or wife living ... and marries another ... is guilty of polygamy, and shall be punished.... For certainly no legislation can be supposed more wholesome and necessary in the founding of a free, self-governing commonwealth, fit to take rank as one of the coordinate States of the Union, than that which seeks to establish it on the basis of the idea of the family, as consisting in and springing from the union for life of one man and one woman in the holy estate of matrimony; the sure foundation of all that is stable and noble in our civilization; the best guaranty of that reverent morality which is the source of all beneficent progress in social and political improvement.

★ ★ Patriot's Prayer ★ ★

Lord, thank You for designing marriage, and I ask You to bless mine. Give me patience, wisdom, and a soft heart toward my spouse and may I not harbor grudges against him/her. Enable me to be a positive influence on all my family members.

★ ★ Patriot's Promise ★ ★

This is a sweet promise from God: "A man shall leave his father and mother and be joined to his wife, and the two shall become one flesh" (Ephesians 5:31).

"A Christian Nation"

> They were unfaithful to the God of their fathers.
>
> 1 CHRONICLES 5:25

In the 1892 case *The Church of the Holy Trinity v. United States*, the US Supreme Court determined that an English minister was not a foreign laborer. The court considered America's Christian identity to be a strong support for concluding that Congress could not have intended to prohibit foreign ministers.

In the court's opinion, Justice David Josiah Brewer stated that the United States was a "Christian nation." The court had already demonstrated the religious character of the country with a remarkable list of eighty-seven examples taken from pre-Constitutional documents, historical practice, colonial charters, and the like, all of which reveal religious roots. The court made these statements:

> This is a religious people. . . . From the discovery of this continent to the present hour, there is a single voice making this affirmation. . . . There is no dissonance in these declarations. There is a universal language pervading them all, having one meaning; they affirm and reaffirm that this is a religious nation. These are not individual sayings . . . they speak the voice of the entire people.

Brewer later clarified his position on the US being a "Christian nation": many American traditions are rooted in Christianity, but Christianity should not receive legal privileges or be established to the exclusion of other religions or to the exclusion of irreligion.

★ ★ Patriot's Prayer ★ ★

Dear God, thank You for this nation. Renew our commitment to You, Lord, that we may continue to know Your blessing.

★ ★ Patriot's Promise ★ ★

"Because you . . . keep and do [these commands], . . . the LORD your God will keep with you the covenant and the mercy which He swore to your fathers" (Deuteronomy 7:12).

Your word I have hidden in my heart, that I might not sin against You.

Psalm 119:11

The Faith of the Founders

Much has been written in recent years to try to dismiss the fact that America was founded upon the biblical principles of Judeo-Christianity, but all the revisionism in the world cannot change the facts. Anyone who examines the original writings, personal correspondence, biographies, and public statements of the individuals who were instrumental in the founding of America will find an abundance of quotations showing the profound extent to which their thinking and their lives were influenced by a Christian worldview.

That is not to say that all of the Founding Fathers were Christians. Such is not the case, but even those who were not Christians were deeply influenced by the principles of Christianity. We can easily get so distracted, wondering whether Benjamin Franklin or Thomas Jefferson ever put their personal faith in Jesus Christ, that we will easily miss the important fact that almost all the Founders thought from a biblical perspective, whether or not they believed.

★ ★ Patriot's Prayer ★ ★

Father, please open the eyes of the people who have been blinded by those who would like to shut You out of the history books. Our children need to know the truth. May we as Christians speak that truth boldly and sing Your praises without timidity.

★ ★ Patriot's Promise ★ ★

"Let us not grow weary while doing good, for in due season we shall reap if we do not lose heart" (Galatians 6:9).

49

God's Covenant People

You are the light of the world. A city that is set on a hill cannot be hidden.

MATTHEW 5:14

Peter Bulkley (1583–1659) was the Puritan leader who founded the city of Concord, Massachusetts. In *The Gospel Covenant*, a book of his sermons, he reminded us believers of our high calling:

> We are as a city set upon a hill, in the open view of all the earth. . . . We profess ourselves to be a people in covenant with God, and therefore . . . the Lord our God . . . will cry shame upon us if we walk contrary to the covenant which we have promised to walk in. If we open the mouths of men against our profession, by reason of the scandalousness of our lives, we [of all men] shall have the greater sin.

★ ★ Patriot's Prayer ★ ★

O Lord, my God, help me live in a manner that is pleasing to You. May people know that You are the one true God—and my Lord—from the example of my life.

★ ★ Patriot's Promise ★ ★

"All the paths of the LORD are mercy and truth, to such as keep His covenant and His testimonies" (Psalm 25:10).

No prophecy of Scripture is of any private inter-
pretation, for prophecy never came by the will
of man, but holy men of God spoke as they were
moved by the Holy Spirit.

2 Peter 1:20–21

Guard Against False Teachers

In his second epistle Peter warned believers about the false teachers whose
heresies could seduce them into erroneous beliefs and immoral practices. He
stressed the need for diligent study of God's Word if they were to grow in the grace
and knowledge of Jesus Christ. That knowledge— the preventative as well as the
antidote for spiritual error—comes only from the infallible Word of God, penned
by men, but authored by the Holy Spirit.

The apostle also urged his readers to keep a close watch over their personal
lives. The false teachers were sensual, arrogant, greedy, and covetous, whereas the
Christian life demands the pursuit of godliness, virtue, patience, and brotherly
kindness. Benjamin Franklin had a similar warning for his fellow citizens: "A great
empire, like a great cake, is most easily diminished from its edges." We in America
today would do well to remember Franklin's warning to guard the core principles
of this nation. We are a nation that has, throughout our history, stood united in
principle and purpose. If America is to continue to stand for that which is right, it
is incumbent upon her citizens to stand together in strength, virtue, and kindness.

★ ★ Patriot's Prayer ★ ★
Lord God, thank You for Your Word of truth. And, Holy Spirit, guard my life
from heresies and error. Remind me that my strength lies in hiding Your Word in
my heart that I may not sin against You.

★ ★ Patriot's Promise ★ ★
"Your word is a lamp to my feet and a light to my path" (Psalm 119:105).

51

Protecting the Foundations

If the foundations are destroyed, what can the righteous do?

PSALM 11:3

Jedidiah Morse (1761–1826) was a pioneer American educator, clergyman, geographer, and the father of Samuel Morse, inventor of the telegraph and Morse Code. Jedidiah studied for the ministry at Yale and, in 1789, accepted a call to the First Church of Charlestown, Massachusetts. He was highly alarmed by how far away the clergy had moved from doctrinal orthodoxy and by the influence of European rationalism. In a 1799 sermon "If the foundations be destroyed, what can the righteous do?" he said the following:

> Our dangers are of two kinds, those which affect our religion, and those which affect our government. They are, however, so closely allied that they cannot, with propriety, be separated....
>
> To the kindly influence of Christianity we owe that degree of civil freedom, and political and social happiness which mankind now enjoys. In proportion as the genuine effects of Christianity are diminished in any nation ... in the same proportion will the people of that nation recede from the blessings of genuine freedom, and approximate the miseries of complete despotism.... It follows, that all efforts made to destroy the foundations of our holy religion, ultimately tend to the subversion also of our political freedom and happiness. Whenever the pillars of Christianity shall be overthrown, our present republican forms of government, and all the blessings which flow from them, must fall with them.

★ ★ Patriot's Prayer ★ ★

God Almighty, forgive my apathy toward spiritual things. Put in my heart a new and lasting passion for You.

★ ★ Patriot's Promise ★ ★

"I will heal their backsliding, I will love them freely, for My anger has turned away from him" (Hosea 14:4).

February 19

The heavens declare the glory of God.

PSALM 19:1

An American Hero

Between 1957 and 1975, a heated part of the Cold War between the Soviet Union and the United States was competition in the realm of space exploration, because of its potential military and technological applications, as well as its morale-boosting social benefits. The Soviets took the lead in the "Space Race" when they were the first to achieve a manned orbit of the earth in 1961. But on February 20, 1962, atop an Atlas rocket, Colonel John Glenn piloted the first American manned orbital mission aboard Friendship 7, circling the globe three times. Taking this step toward fulfilling America's political and scientific hopes and dreams, Glenn returned to Earth as virtually every American's hero.

In 1998, NASA invited John Glenn to join the space shuttle Discovery crew. On October 29, 1998, he became the oldest human, at the age of 77, to venture into space, a vivid reminder of the heroic spirit that has fueled space exploration.

As Glenn observed the heavens and Earth from the windows of Discovery, he said, "To look out at this kind of creation out here and not believe in God is to me impossible. It just strengthens my faith. I wish there were words to describe what it's like."

★ ★ Patriot's Prayer ★ ★
Heavenly Father, there truly are no words to describe how awesome You are. I acknowledge You today as Creator of this magnificent universe.

★ ★ Patriot's Promise ★ ★
Psalm 90:2 proclaims, "Before the mountains were brought forth, or ever You had formed the earth and the world, even from everlasting to everlasting, You are God." Know that the Creator of the universe will keep you in His care.

February 20

The American Moses

I will send you to Pharaoh that you may bring My people, the children of Israel, out of Egypt.

EXODUS 3:10

Major General Henry Lee said about George Washington, "First in war, first in peace, and first in the hearts of his countrymen." He was surely that and more. Emerging as the most significant leader in the founding of the United States, he was the essential man, the American Moses, the Father of the Country. At the three major crossroads in the establishment of the nation, he led our troops to victory in the Revolutionary War, he superintended the Constitutional Convention, and he was unanimously elected as the first president.

How can such greatness be embodied in one man? Washington was surrounded by a host of other courageous leaders, brilliant thinkers, passionate orators, and gifted writers—Franklin, Jefferson, Patrick Henry, John and Samuel Adams, Hamilton, Madison—almost all of whom were far more educated than he. Yet Washington always led the way.

While much has often been made of his physical stature (he stood six feet two inches when the average man stood five feet seven inches) and his courage, charisma, energy, vision, and calm demeanor, it was his high moral character that most historical sources commonly cite as the reason for his emergence as the supreme leader. Combine his sterling character and his genius in the area of leadership, and here was a man who could be trusted to lead.

★ ★ Patriot's Prayer ★ ★

Lord, may I walk according to the Holy Spirit today. May my conduct reflect Your goodness.

★ ★ Patriot's Promise ★ ★

"Judge me, O LORD, according to my righteousness, and according to my integrity within me" (Psalm 7:8).

Those who honor me I will honor.

1 SAMUEL 2:30

Asking God's Aid for a Good Cause

On July 2, 1776, as the Continental Congress was meeting in Philadelphia to declare independence, Commander-in-Chief George Washington was gathering his troops on Long Island to meet the British in battle in and around New York City. That day he wrote in the General Orders to his men these memorable words declaring that we, as a nation, serve under God:

> The time is now near at hand which must probably determine whether Americans are to be freemen or slaves....The fate of unborn millions will now depend, under God, on the courage and conduct of this army. Our cruel and unrelenting enemy leaves us no choice but a brave resistance, or the most abject submission; this is all we can expect.
>
> We have therefore to resolve to conquer or die ...
>
> Let us therefore rely upon the goodness of the cause, and the aid of the Supreme Being, in whose hands victory is, to animate and encourage us to great and noble actions. The eyes of all our countrymen are now upon us, and we shall have their blessings and praises, if happily we are the Instruments of saving them from the tyranny meditated against them. Let us therefore ... show the whole world that a freeman contending for liberty on his own ground is superior to any slavish mercenary on earth.

★ ★ Patriot's Prayer ★ ★

Father, help me contend for Your kingdom with the courage and passion that Washington urged his men to have as they fought for America's freedom.

★ ★ Patriot's Promise ★ ★

"We are receiving a kingdom which cannot be shaken" (Hebrews 12:28).

55

The Foundation for Morality

Let your "Yes" be "Yes," and your "No," "No. "

JESUS IN MATTHEW 5:37

In his 1796 farewell address, President George Washington (February 22, 1732–December 14, 1799) spoke about the essential connection between religion and morality:

> Of all the dispositions and habits which lead to political prosperity, religion and morality are indispensable supports. In vain would that man claim the tribute of patriotism who should labor to subvert these great pillars of human happiness—these firmest props of the duties of men and citizens.... Let it simply be asked, "Where is the security for property, for reputation, for life, if the sense of religious obligation desert the oaths which are the instruments of investigation in courts of justice?" And let us with caution indulge the supposition that morality can be maintained without religion.... Reason and experience both forbid us to expect that national morality can prevail in exclusion of religious principle.

★ ★ Patriot's Prayer ★ ★

Lord, the virtue and the morality of this nation need to be grounded in biblical, Christian faith. Thank You for those in this nation who stand strong for these Judeo-Christian principles. Show us how You would have us be active and effective salt and light in America today.

★ ★ Patriot's Promise ★ ★

Imagine putting into practice this truth: "Above all these [virtues] put on love, which is the bond of perfection" (Colossians 3:14). Love for our brothers and sisters, for our fellow citizens, that is rooted in God's love would bind us together as a nation.

I pray that you may prosper in all things.

3 John 2

Staying True

Considered one of the greatest orators in American history, Daniel Webster (1782–1852) is served as a US congressman and senator as well as secretary of state for three different presidents. The following is from a speech given before the Historical Society of New York on February 23, 1852:

> If we and our posterity shall be true to the Christian religion, if we and they shall live always in the fear of God, and shall respect His commandments, if we and they shall maintain just moral sentiments and such conscientious convictions of duty as shall control the heart and life, we may have the highest hopes of the future fortunes of our country. . . .
>
> But if we and our posterity reject religious institutions and authority, violate the rules of eternal justice, trifle with the injunctions of morality, and recklessly destroy the political constitution which holds us together, no man can tell how sudden a catastrophe may overwhelm us.

★ ★ Patriot's Prayer ★ ★

Almighty God, forgive us for rejecting Your principles and authority. Forgive our nation for straying from the very foundation upon which we were founded and established. We have been reckless with the freedoms You have entrusted to us. Please heal our nation and restore our land.

★ ★ Patriot's Promise ★ ★

Proverbs 22:9 says, "He who has a generous eye will be blessed." Such generosity involves sharing time, love, charity, and finances: it calls for us to be good stewards of the very nation God has blessed us with.

February 24

Eternal Hope

> Let Your mercy, O LORD, be upon us, just as we hope in You.
>
> PSALM 33:22

The author of the following and the twentieth president of the United States (1881), James Garfield was assassinated after serving only four months in office:

> The world's history is a Divine poem, of which the history of every nation is a canto and every man a word. Its strains have been pealing along down the centuries, and though there have been mingled the discords of warring cannons and dying men, yet to the Christian philosopher and historian—the humble listener—there has been a Divine melody running through the song which speaks of hope and halcyon days to come.

★ ★ Patriot's Prayer ★ ★

Heavenly Father, have mercy on me, for I know Your mercies are new every morning, and they never fail. Help me learn from my history. May I repeat the good and never repeat those actions that were not pleasing to You.

★ ★ Patriot's Promise ★ ★

Job 4:6 says, "Is not your reverence your confidence? And the integrity of your ways your hope?" God promises that our honesty, honor, and reliability will bring blessings.

Go therefore and make disciples
of all the nations.

Jesus in Matthew 28:19

John Eliot, "Apostle to the Indians"

The 1628 Massachusetts Bay Company charter stated that one of the chief purposes of establishing a colony in New England was "to win the natives of the country to the knowledge and obedience of the only true God and Savior of mankind." During the colony's earliest years, however, the Puritans just tried to survive in the American wilderness.

In 1637, the Puritans became involved in an intertribal war between the Narragansett and Pequot Indians. In 1675 and 1676, a bitter armed conflict broke out in which over 600 colonists and 3,000 Native Americans died. Surprisingly, the Pequot war triggered the earliest Puritan missions to the Indians. John Eliot began learning the Algonquian language from captured Indians. Learning Christian truths in their own language, many Indians put their faith in Christ. Leaving their nomadic and pagan lives, they formed villages that became "praying Indian towns." In these self-governing communities, the Indians often made strict biblical laws punishing such former practices as wife beating, polygamy, lying, and stealing.

John Eliot translated the entire Bible into Algonquian. In 1663, it became the first Bible printed in America. Eliot also composed an Indian primer, an Indian grammar, and an Indian psalter, rounding out his legacy of disciple-making tools.

★ ★ Patriot's Prayer ★ ★
Father, thank You for those who go into all the world and preach the gospel. Show me how You would have me obey that command—and empower me to do so.

★ ★ Patriot's Promise ★ ★
"Let your light so shine before men, that they may see your good works and glorify your Father in heaven" (Matthew 5:16).

The Faith of Our Founding Fathers

The just shall live by his faith.

HABAKKUK 2:4

George H. W. Bush served as the forty-first president of the United States. The following words reflect his Christian faith:

The great faith that led our nation's Founding Fathers to pursue this bold experience in self-government has sustained us in uncertain and perilous times; it has given us strength and inspiration to this very day.

Like them, we do very well to recall our "firm reliance on the protection of Divine Providence," to give thanks for the freedom and prosperity this nation enjoys, and to pray for continued help and guidance from our wise and loving Creator.

★ ★ Patriot's Prayer ★ ★

Almighty Father, use me to preserve the faith in You that our Founding Fathers had. Let the words of my mouth be totally directed by You, and may I be filled with Your Holy Spirit so that I will point others to You, their wise and loving Creator.

★ ★ Patriot's Promise ★ ★

Hear the promise of Psalm 55:22—"Cast your burden on the LORD, and He shall sustain you." God will take care of us when we depend on Him.

He who . . . has founded His strata in the earth . . . the LORD is His name.

AMOS 9:6

Hear the conviction in this statement by James Dwight Dana (1813–1895), a famous geologist, mineralogist, and zoologist who became the president of the Geological Society of America as well as the American Association for the Advance of Science:

> That grand old Book of God still stands; and this old earth, the more its leaves are turned over and pondered, the more it will sustain and illustrate the Sacred Word.

★ ★ Patriot's Prayer ★ ★

Mighty God, I thank You that I can be confident that the more we know of Your Creation the more we can be assured that Your Word is true.

★ ★ Patriot's Promise ★ ★

In Genesis 9:15, God made this vow: "The waters shall never again become a flood to destroy all flesh." Our Creator God has promised to never be the Destroyer again.

March

The wind goes toward the south . . . The wind whirls about continually, and comes again on its circuit.

ECCLESIASTES 1:6

Support for Science

First nicknamed the "Pathfinder of the Seas" for having charted the ocean and wind currents while serving in the US Navy, Matthew Maury (1806–1873) was considered the "Father of Modern Oceanography and Naval Meteorology" and later the "Scientist of the Seas." He wrote the following:

> I have always found in my scientific studies, that, when I could get the Bible to say anything on the subject, it afforded me a firm platform to stand upon and a round in the ladder by which I could safely ascend.
>
> As our knowledge of nature and her laws has increased, so has our knowledge of many passages of the Bible improved.
>
> The Bible called the earth "the round world," yet for ages it was . . . heresy for Christian men to say that the world is round; and, finally, sailors circumnavigated the globe and proved the Bible to be right, and saved Christian men of science from the stake.
>
> And as for the general system of circulation which I have been so long endeavoring to describe, the Bible tells it all in a single sentence: "The wind goeth toward the South . . . and returneth again to his circuits."

★ ★ Patriot's Prayer ★ ★

Your Word is amazing, Lord. It is truth, righteous and powerful. You have created all things, You know all things, and You see all things. You have redeemed me.

★ ★ Patriot's Promise ★ ★

"[God's] kingdom is the one which shall not be destroyed, and His dominion shall endure to the end. He delivers and rescues, and He works signs and wonders in heaven and on earth" (Daniel 6:26–27).

March 1

"The Word and the Works of God"

Benjamin Silliman (1779–1864), an American physicist, chemist, and geologist, founded and edited the *American Journal of Science and Arts*. Hear his perspective on science and Scripture:

> The relation of geology, as well as astronomy, to the Bible, when both are well understood, is that of perfect harmony. The Bible nowhere limits the age of the globe, while its chronology assigns a recent origin to the human race; and geology not only confirms that Genesis presents a true statement of the progress of the terrestrial arrangements and of the introduction of living beings in the order in which their fossil remains are found entombed in the strata.

The Word and the works of God cannot conflict, and the more they are studied the more perfect will their harmony appear.

★ ★ Patriot's Prayer ★ ★

Thank You, Jesus, that You have made the heavens and the earth and all that is in them. Help me do my part to be a respectful and effective steward of what You have given us human beings to care for.

★ ★ Patriot's Promise ★ ★

"In the beginning was the Word, and the Word was with God, and the Word was God. He was in the beginning with God. All things were made through Him, and without Him nothing was made that was made" (John 1:1–3). Jesus was . . . and is . . . and always will be.

The LORD . . . formed [the earth] to establish it.

JEREMIAH 33:2

The Signature of the Creator

Charles Stine (1882–1954) served as the Director of Research for the E. I. Dupont Company, a leader in the development of significant new products and patents, most of which were connected with propellant powder, high explosives, dyes, artificial leather, and paints. Consider this scientist's observation:

> The world about us, far more intricate than any watch, filled with checks and balances of a hundred varieties, marvelous beyond even the imagination of the most skilled scientific investigator, this beautiful and intricate creation, bears the signature of its Creator, graven in its works.

★ ★ Patriot's Prayer ★ ★

This world is a fascinating creation, Father. It is difficult for me to grasp the intricacies of Your craftsmanship in what I see around me, and I can't begin to comprehend the vastness of this universe.

★ ★ Patriot's Promise ★ ★

Isaiah 40:28 says this of our amazing God: "The everlasting God, the LORD, the Creator of the ends of the earth, neither faints nor is weary. His understanding is unsearchable." How wonderful to know that God has promised that He will be there always!

March 3

Godly Leaders

The wall was finished . . . in fifty-two days. . . . When all our enemies heard of it . . . they perceived that this work was done by our God.

NEHEMIAH 6:15–16

Scripture's unifying theme is God's unchanging covenant with His people. When Israel stayed true to God's Word and His will, He blessed the nation with prosperity. When the people disobeyed God, they faced some stiff consequences. Then, in Nehemiah 9, after Ezra read the law, the people confessed their sin and boldly reaffirmed their loyalty to God's covenant.

On March 4, 1933, in his first inaugural address and at the beginning of the Great Depression, President Franklin D. Roosevelt spoke a bold word of encouragement to his fellow citizens: "Let me assert my firm belief that the only thing we have to fear is fear itself. . . . We face arduous days that lie before us in the warm courage of national unity; with the clear consciousness of seeking old and precious moral values." Beseeching God's blessing, the president added, "May He protect each and every one of us! May He guide me in the days to come!" FDR's leadership would be a decisive factor in keeping America's resolve strong throughout the years of the Depression and the world war that followed.

★ ★ Patriot's Prayer ★ ★

Dear Lord, provide us godly men and women to lead our nation into unity and peace. May these leaders enable America to rebuild her broken walls of righteousness, that our land might once again prosper under Your blessings and care.

★ ★ Patriot's Promise ★ ★

God recognizes godly leaders and is willing to bless any nation willing to follow them: "He who walks righteously and speaks uprightly, he who despises the gain of oppressions . . . he will dwell on high; his place of defense will be the fortress of rocks; bread will be given him, his water will be sure" (Isaiah 33:15–16).

Let Your hand become my help,
for I have chosen Your precepts.

PSALM 119:173

"The Loving Devotion of a Free People"

In his inaugural address on March 5, 1877, Rutherford B. Hayes, the nineteenth president of the United States (1877–1881), stated the following:

> Looking for the guidance of that Divine Hand by which the destinies of nations and individuals are shaped, I call upon you, Senators, Representatives, judges, fellow citizens, here and everywhere, to unite with me in an earnest effort to secure to our country the blessings, not only of material property, but of justice, peace, and union—a union depending not upon the constraint of force but upon the loving devotion of a free people; and that all things may be so ordered and settled upon the best and surest foundations that peace and happiness, truth and justice, religion and piety, may be established among us for all generations.

★ ★ Patriot's Prayer ★ ★

Almighty God, may we listen to Your voice so that You will pour Your blessings down upon us, so that our blessed nation will be a guiding light to all nations.

★ ★ Patriot's Promise ★ ★

God promises that if we give, blessings will be given to us in such a volume that, figuratively speaking, they will have to be pressed down into a container and shaken together, and still they will overflow (Luke 6:38).

March 5

Guarding Truth

In [Jesus] dwells all the fullness of the Godhead bodily; and you are complete in Him, who is the head of all principality and power.

COLOSSIANS 2:9–10

In Colossians—perhaps the most Christ-centered book in the Bible—the apostle Paul refuted a threatening heresy that devalued Christ by explaining that believers are risen with Christ, and are to put off the old man and put on the new, which will result in holiness in all relationships. Paul stressed the preeminence of Christ and the completeness of the salvation He provides. Paul countered false teaching with his presentation of Jesus. A proper view of Christ is always the most powerful antidote to heresy.

Just as the Colossians needed to guard the truth of the gospel, so we need to guard our country. President Calvin Coolidge (1923–1929) said:

The issues of the world must be met and met squarely. The forces of evil do not disdain preparation, they are always prepared and always preparing. . . . The welfare of America, the cause of civilization will forever require the contribution, of some part of the life, of all our citizens, to the natural, the necessary, and the inevitable demand for the defense of the right and the truth.

★ ★ **Patriot's Prayer** ★ ★

In a world, Lord, where many are enemies of the Cross, let me speak the gospel truth in love, so Your gospel may be known and untruth dispelled.

★ ★ **Patriot's Promise** ★ ★

"When they bring you to the synagogues and magistrates and authorities, do not worry about . . . what you should say. For the Holy Spirit will teach you in that very hour what you ought to say" (Luke 12:11–12).

His hand shall be against every man, and every man's hand against him.

GENESIS 16:12

The Barbary Pirates

Based in Morocco, Algeria, Tunisia, and Libya, the Barbary pirates operated from the time of the Crusades until the early nineteenth century. These Muslim pirates often raided European coastal towns, capturing an estimated 1 million to 1.25 million Europeans as slaves from the sixteenth to the nineteenth century. France, England, and Spain each lost thousands of ships, and long stretches of coast in Spain and Italy were almost completely abandoned.

In 1783, America won its freedom from the British monarchy, and in 1784, Moroccan pirates seized their first US ship. Algeria seized two more ships in 1785. Why was the Libyan government hostile to American ships? The ambassador to Britain explained:

> It was written in their Koran, that all nations which had not acknowledged the Prophet were sinners, whom it was the right and duty of the faithful to plunder and enslave; and that every mussulman who was slain in this warfare was sure to go to paradise.

After some serious debate, the US boldly chose to fight the pirates of Barbary, and the US Navy was born in March 1794. Six frigates were authorized, and this new military presence helped lead to the two Barbary Wars (1801–1805 and 1815). The tiny US Navy broke a ring of international terrorism dating back more than one hundred and fifty years.

★ ★ Patriot's Prayer ★ ★
Abba Father, thank You for the brave men and women of the US armed forces. Guide and protect them as they serve our country.

★ ★ Patriot's Promise ★ ★
"If you indeed obey [the angel's] voice and do all that I [God] speak, then I will be an enemy to your enemies" (Exodus 23:22).

69

Search the Scriptures

[The Bereans] received the word with all readiness, and searched the Scriptures daily.

ACTS 17:11

John Quincy Adams (1767–1848) served as the sixth president of the United States. Hear his exhortation to the American people:

> I speak as a man of the world to men of the world; and I say to you, Search the Scriptures! The Bible is the book of all others, to be read at all ages, and in all conditions of human life; not to be read once or twice or thrice through, and then laid aside, but to be read in small portions of one or two chapters every day, and never to be intermitted, unless by some overruling necessity.

★ ★ Patriot's Prayer ★ ★

Father, I love Your Word and the way it speaks to my heart. Reading its words puts joy in my heart and gives me a peace that truly does go beyond my understanding.

★ ★ Patriot's Promise ★ ★

Psalm 119:105 reminds us that God's Word "is a lamp to my feet and a light to my path." We who have the Word of God never have to wander in the darkness of uncertainty or indecision.

Greater love has no one than this, than to lay down one's life for his friends.

JOHN 15:13

Freedom's Cost

A wise person once said, "Freedom is never free."

Nathan Hale (1755–1776) was a schoolteacher when the Revolutionary War broke out in April 1775. After hearing about the siege of Boston in a letter from a friend, Hale joined his five brothers in the fight for independence.

Hale fought under General George Washington in New York as British General William Howe began a military buildup on Long Island. When Washington asked for a volunteer to go on a spy mission behind enemy lines, Hale stepped forward. For a week he gathered information on the position of British troops, but he was captured while returning to the American side. Because of the incriminating papers Hale possessed, the British knew he was a spy. Howe ordered the twenty-year-old Hale to be hanged the following day without a trial.

Patriot Nathan Hale was hanged on September 22, 1776. Before he gave his life for his country, he made a short speech, ending with these famous and inspiring words: "I only regret that I have but one life to lose for my country."

As John Quincy Adams said, "You will never know how much it has cost my generation to preserve your freedom. I hope you will make good use of it." We must do all we can to protect the freedoms that generations past have entrusted to us.

★ ★ Patriot's Prayer ★ ★

Almighty God, may we as a nation be ever grateful for the men and women who have given—or are today giving—their lives to give us freedom.

★ ★ Patriot's Promise ★ ★

"The LORD . . . executes justice for the oppressed" (Psalm 146:7).

71

"Enlightenment and Salvation"

I thank my God . . . that the sharing of your faith may become effective by the acknowledgment of every good thing which is in you in Christ Jesus.

PHILEMON 4, 6

Hear the confidence of Rutherford B. Hayes, the nineteenth president of the United States (1877–1881):

I am a firm believer in the Divine teachings, perfect example, and atoning sacrifice of Jesus Christ. I believe also in the Holy Scriptures as the revealed Word of God to the world for its enlightenment and salvation.

★ ★ Patriot's Prayer ★ ★

O God, help me learn more about Jesus and His life so that, by Your Spirit, I can be more like Him. Give me boldness to share Jesus with others so that they, too, will accept Him as their Savior.

★ ★ Patriot's Promise ★ ★

Jesus said, "I have given you an example, that you should do as I have done to you," and then He made this wonderful promise: "If you know these things, blessed are you if you do them" (John 13:15, 17). Jesus is our example, and if we follow His example, we will surely be blessed individually and collectively as a nation.

Let the words of my mouth and the meditation of my heart be acceptable in Your sight, O LORD, my strength and my Redeemer.

PSALM 19:14

The Joy of Worship

The book of Psalms is a profoundly rich and personal guide to worship, praise, prayer, meditation, and even instruction about God. Containing some of the most beautiful poetry ever penned, Psalms can help us express our deepest needs, thoughts, and desires to our heavenly Father—in times of great joy as well as times of great sorrow.

Fanny Crosby (1820–1915), one of America's most beloved hymn writers, no doubt received much inspiration and tutoring in song from time spent in the book of Psalms. Blind from infancy, she nevertheless went on to pen more than 8,000 songs of praise to God, including such classic hymns as "Near the Cross," "Praise Him, Praise Him," and "To God Be the Glory." The chorus of one of her most well-known hymns, "Blessed Assurance," sums up the theme of Psalms:

> This is my story, this is my song,
> Praising my Savior all the day long;
> This is my story, this is my song,
> Praising my Savior all the day long.

★ ★ Patriot's Prayer ★ ★

Lord of heaven, today I will speak of Your great mercy and grace toward those who love You, I will sing of Your goodness and grace, and I will show my love for You in acts of worship that glorify Your name.

★ ★ Patriot's Promise ★ ★

God is "holy, enthroned in the praises of [His people] Israel" (Psalm 22:3). As we praise and worship Him, we are assured of His presence among us.

73

A Necessity of American Life

The proconsul believed, when he saw what had been done, being astonished at the teaching of the Lord.

ACTS 13:12

Herbert Hoover (1874–1964) served as the thirty-first president of the United States from 1929 through 1933. He wrote this:

The whole inspiration of our civilization springs from the teachings of Christ and the lessons of the prophets. To read the Bible for these fundamentals is a necessity of American life.

★ ★ Patriot's Prayer ★ ★

Precious Lord, I am encumbered with a huge weight of concern for friends who do not know You. I pray that You will allow the Holy Spirit to come upon them and convict their hearts of unbelief. If it is Your will, use me to lead them to Christ or at least plant the seed that someone else will cultivate, a seed that will eventually bear the fruit of their giving their hearts to You.

★ ★ Patriot's Promise ★ ★

The promise in Romans 10:9 is very straightforward: "If you confess with your mouth the Lord Jesus and believe in your heart that God has raised Him from the dead, you will be saved."

The LORD has anointed Me . . . to give them beauty for ashes.

ISAIAH 61:1, 3

A New Birth of Freedom

Abraham Lincoln's second inaugural address in March 1865 came at one of the darkest moments of the Civil War. Consider what he said:

> Both [North and South] read the same Bible, and pray to the same God; and each invokes His aid against the other. It may seem strange that any men should dare to ask a just God's assistance in wringing their bread from the sweat of other men's faces; but let us judge not that we be not judged. The prayers of both could not be answered; that of neither has been answered fully. The Almighty has His own purposes.

In the end, over three million Americans fought in the Civil War, and over 600,000 people died. The war meant the end of slavery and ushered in a new political and economic order. The era of Southern plantation aristocracy was over, the powers of the federal government expanded, and the days of big industry and business began. The clash over federal rights and state rights came down to a struggle over the meaning of freedom in America. Perhaps in his Gettysburg Address in 1863, Lincoln was prophetic when he said the war was about a "new birth of freedom."

★ ★ Patriot's Prayer ★ ★
Father, thank You for creating all people to live free. Thank You for breaking the bonds of slavery in this country and giving all men and women the opportunity to pursue their dreams.

★ ★ Patriot's Promise ★ ★
"Stand fast therefore in the liberty by which Christ has made us free, and do not be entangled again with a yoke of bondage" (Galatians 5:1).

March 13

Promised Blessings

All these men who have seen My glory and the signs which I did in Egypt and in the wilderness, and have put Me to the test . . . and have not heeded My voice, they certainly shall not see the land of which I swore to their fathers, nor shall any of those who rejected Me see it.

NUMBERS 14:22–23

America's rich history is filled with accounts of men and women who left the comfort and familiarity of their homes and families in search of greater freedom and opportunity. With hearts set on adventure, these early pioneers braved hardships and hazards to claim their personal "promised land." And that choice required courage, determination, and faith in God.

The book of Numbers recounts a similar grand adventure, of God preparing His own people to conquer the land of milk and honey that He had promised them generations earlier. Before they can succeed, however, the people of Israel must deal with the fear and doubt that grip them. God required—and He requires it today—that those called by His Name put their faith in Him alone. Numbers shows the process by which He brought His people to that place of trust and led them into a place of blessing.

★ ★ Patriot's Prayer ★ ★

Heavenly Father, may I trust this day in You and You alone. I don't want fear and doubt to keep me from the promised land of resting in Your care and knowing Your blessings.

★ ★ Patriot's Promise ★ ★

"Trust in the LORD with all your heart, and lean not on your own understanding; in all your ways acknowledge Him, and He shall direct your paths" (Proverbs 3:5–6).

Teach [God's statutes] to your children.

Deuteronomy 4:9

The First Amendment and Common Sense

In the 1952 case *Zorach v. Clauson*, the Supreme Court upheld the New York City school district practice of releasing students during school hours for religious instruction:

> The First Amendment ... does not say that in every respect there shall be a separation of Church and State. Rather ... there shall be no concert or union or dependency one on the other. That is the common sense of the matter. Otherwise the state and religion would be aliens to each other. ...
>
> Municipalities would not be permitted to render police or fire protection to religious groups. ... Prayers in our legislative halls; the appeals to the Almighty in the messages of the Chief Executive; the proclamation making Thanksgiving Day a holiday; "so help me God" in our courtroom oaths—these and all other references to the Almighty that run through our laws, our public rituals, our ceremonies, would be flouting the First Amendment. ...
>
> When the state ... cooperates with religious authorities by adjusting the schedule of public events ... it follows the best of our traditions. For it then respects the religious nature of our people and accommodates the public service to their spiritual needs. To hold that it may not would be to find in the Constitution a requirement that the government show a callous indifference to religious groups. That would be preferring those who believe in no religion over those who do believe. ... We cannot read into the Bill of Rights such a philosophy of hostility to religion.

★ ★ Patriot's Prayer ★ ★
Omnipotent God, clarify our leaders' understanding of the First Amendment.

★ ★ Patriot's Promise ★ ★
Severe punishment awaits "whoever causes one of these little ones who believe in Me to sin" (Matthew 18:6).

March 15

Honor the Creator

Remember now your Creator in the days of your youth.

ECCLESIASTES 12:1

The fourth president of the United States and "Chief Architect of the Constitution," James Madison (March 16, 1751–June 28, 1836) wrote the following: The religion then of every man must be left to the conviction and conscience of every man; and it is the right of every man to exercise it as these may dictate. This right is in its nature an unalienable right. It is unalienable, because the opinions of men, depending only on the evidence contemplated by their own minds cannot follow the dictates of other men: It is unalienable also, because what is here a right toward men, is a duty toward the Creator. It is the duty of every man to render to the Creator such homage and such only as he believes to be acceptable to him. This duty is precedent, both in order of time and in degree of obligation, to the claims of civil society. Before any man can be considered as a member of civil society, he must be considered as a subject of the Governor of the Universe.

★ ★ Patriot's Prayer ★ ★

Lord, may I honor You in my life today. Help me to live according to Your principles: may my duty to You, my God, and to my country be evident in all I say and do.

★ ★ Patriot's Promise ★ ★

Hear Ecclesiastes 12:13 (NIV): "Fear God and keep his commandments, for this is the whole duty of man." Following God gives meaning and purpose to life.

That which we have seen and heard we declare to you, that you also may have fellowship with us; and truly our fellowship is with the Father and with His Son Jesus Christ. And these things we write to you that your joy may be full.

1 JOHN 1:3–4

Remembering the Past for a Brighter Future

The apostle John wrote these opening words in a letter designed to encourage believers to stand against false doctrine and walk in the knowledge of the truth. John listed the criteria for, and the characteristics of, fellowship with God and showed that those who abide in Christ, remembering that He died and rose again, will one day partake in the fullness of Christian joy.

Just as the apostle reminded his readers of the marvelous work Christ has done for us, enabling us to become children of God, President Woodrow Wilson reminded Americans that "a nation that does not remember what it was yesterday, does not know what it is today, nor what it is trying to do. We are trying to do a futile thing if we do not know where we came from or what we have been about."

★ ★ Patriot's Prayer ★ ★

Lord, let me not forget where You have brought me from and where I might be were it not for Your mercy. For sometimes I seem to forget, so please remind me, dear Lord.

★ ★ Patriot's Promise ★ ★

"Now may the God of hope fill you with all joy and peace in believing, that you may abound in hope by the power of the Holy Spirit" (Romans 15:13).

March 17

The Fundamentals

In the late nineteenth and early twentieth centuries, conservative evangelical Christians began to reject the growing influence of modernism, especially the movement toward a social, humanistic gospel. Relying on *The Fundamentals,* written by prominent pastors and scholars in the 1910s, these believers actively affirmed basic Christian beliefs being questioned by the church's growing liberalism.

The first formulation of these beliefs can be traced to the Niagara Bible Conference (1878–1897). In 1910, the General Assembly of the Presbyterian Church outlined these "five fundamentals":

1. Inerrancy of the Scriptures
2. The virgin birth and the deity of Jesus Christ (Isaiah 7:14)
3. The doctrine of substitutionary atonement by God's grace and through human faith (Hebrews 9)
4. The bodily resurrection of Jesus (Matthew 28)
5. The authenticity of Christ's miracles (or, alternatively, His premillennial second coming)

Many strongly conservative churches combined their religious views with social and political action. The movement's plain and powerful teaching revived the American church. Bible schools, colleges, seminaries, missionary agencies, homes for troubled youths, homes for the aged, and the Christian school movement have followed, as have the Christian publishing, radio, and television industries. These efforts remain a major force in religious America.

★ ★ Patriot's Prayer ★ ★

Lord, may whatever I say and do today magnify Your name and lift up Jesus.

★ ★ Patriot's Promise ★ ★

"Those who turn many to righteousness [shall shine] like the stars forever and ever" (Daniel 12:3).

> This Book of the Law shall not depart from your mouth.
>
> JOSHUA 1:8

The Faith of Our Forefathers

Most historians do not limit the "Founding Fathers" to the 55 delegates to the Constitutional Convention, but this core group of men represents the religious roots and thought of those who shaped the political foundations of our nation. As a matter of public record, the delegates included 28 Episcopalians, 8 Presbyterians, 7 Congregationalists, 2 Lutherans, 2 Dutch Reformed, 2 Methodists, 2 Roman Catholics, 1 unknown, and 3 deists (those who believe in an impersonal God who gave the world its initial impetus but then left it to run its course). A full 93 percent of the convention's members were members of Christian churches, and all were deeply influenced by a biblical view of mankind and government.

The Declaration of Independence, for instance, identified the source of all authority and rights as "Their Creator" and then clearly stated that individual human rights are God-given, not manmade. Therefore, the argument continues, no king or established religion would ever stand in the way of human liberty or dignity—an assertion uniquely Judeo-Christian and key to the republic we have today.

★ ★ Patriot's Prayer ★ ★

I praise You, the Creator of the world and the Author of history. I am humbled by Your power and blessed by Your presence in my life and Your care for this nation.

★ ★ Patriot's Promise ★ ★

"Let all the earth fear the LORD; let all the inhabitants of the world stand in awe of Him. For He spoke, and it was done; He commanded, and it stood fast" (Psalm 33:8–9). Created to worship the Lord and enjoy Him forever, we are blessed when we praise Him.

March 19

Freedom and the Soul of Man

My soul thirsts for You; My flesh longs for You.

PSALM 63:1

Whittaker Chambers (1901–1961) was once a Soviet spy before he turned from communism and defected to the West. His life experiences taught him about freedom:

Freedom is a need of the soul, and nothing else. It is in striving toward God that the soul strives continually after a condition of freedom. God alone is the inciter and guarantor of freedom. He is the only guarantor.

External freedom is only an aspect of interior freedom. Political freedom, as the Western world has known it, is only a political reading of the Bible. Religion and freedom are indivisible. Without freedom the soul dies. Without the soul there is no justification for freedom.

★ ★ Patriot's Prayer ★ ★

Thank You, Father, that You have granted us freedom of the soul through the sacrifice of Your Son and freedom in our nation through the sacrifice of our forefathers. May I remember the high cost of these freedoms every day.

★ ★ Patriot's Promise ★ ★

In Isaiah 45:22, God tells us, "Look to Me, and be saved, all you ends of the earth! For I am God, and there is no other." Our freedom can only come from God above. As long as we look to Him, our freedom will be assured.

March 20

Whoever transgresses and does not abide in the doctrine of Christ does not have God. He who abides in the doctrine of Christ has both the Father and the Son. If anyone comes to you and does not bring this doctrine, do not receive him into your house nor greet him.

2 JOHN 9–10

Avoiding False Teachers

The apostle John warned of the danger of false teachers who deny the incarnation of God in Christ Jesus. Believers are to reach out and embrace others with Christian love, but that love must be discerning. We do not want to open the door to false teaching. In this letter to "the elect lady and her children" (v. 1), John insisted that they—and we—deny even the slightest assistance to itinerant teachers who promote an erroneous view of Christ.

The apostle would have concurred with Elias Boudinot, a Founding Father and president of the Continental Congress from 1782–1783, who said, "Good government generally begins in the family, and if the moral character of a people once degenerate, their political character must soon follow." The principle is clear: If you allow a bit of evil into the home or heresy into the church, it will spread out into the world.

★ ★ Patriot's Prayer ★ ★
Holy Spirit, guide my mind, protect my heart, and guard Your church from those who would teach a gospel other than Yours. Reveal to me whether or not a teacher is from You.

★ ★ Patriot's Promise ★ ★
God's Word will help us discern truth from falsehood: "[The Bereans] received the word with all readiness, and searched the Scriptures daily to find out whether these things were so" (Acts 17:11).

Last Words

I am not ashamed of the gospel.

ROMANS 1:16 NIV

Hear in their last wills and testaments the faith of the Founding Fathers:
We recognize no sovereign but God, and no King but Jesus!

JOHN HANCOCK AND JOHN ADAMS

My only hope of salvation is in the infinite, transcendent love of God manifested to the world by the death of His Son upon the cross. Nothing but His blood will wash away my sins. I rely exclusively upon it. Come, Lord Jesus! Come quickly!

BENJAMIN RUSH, SIGNER OF THE DECLARATION OF INDEPENDENCE

The general principles upon which the Fathers achieved independence were the general principles of Christianity. . . . Those general principles of Christianity are as eternal and immutable as the existence and attributes of God.

JOHN ADAMS, SECOND PRESIDENT

Without morals a republic cannot subsist any length of time; they therefore who are decrying the Christian religion, whose morality is so sublime and pure . . . are undermining the solid foundation of morals, the best security for the duration of free governments.

CHARLES CARROLL, SIGNER OF THE DECLARATION OF INDEPENDENCE

Providence has given to our people the choice of their rulers, and it is the duty, as well as the privilege and interest of our Christian nation, to select and prefer Christians for their rulers.

JOHN JAY, FIRST CHIEF JUSTICE OF THE SUPREME COURT

★ ★ Patriot's Prayer ★ ★

Lord, thank You for Americans—yesterday and today—who walk in Your ways.

★ ★ Patriot's Promise ★ ★

"Walk in the ways of your heart, and in the sight of your eyes; but know that for all these God will bring you into judgment" (Ecclesiastes 11:9).

March 22

> Having been justified by faith, we have peace with God through our Lord Jesus Christ.
>
> ROMANS 5:1

As for Me!

Patrick Henry (1736–1799) was one of the most passionate and fiery advocates of the American Revolution. Many have compared him to an Old Testament prophet in his powerful denunciations of corruption in government officials and his defense of the colonists' rights. Elected to the Virginia legislature in 1775, he rallied Virginia, the largest of the thirteen colonies, into military preparedness.

Rebellion against unjust taxes had begun, and the British had posted troops throughout the colonies and warships in the harbors. On March 23, 1775, during the Second Virginia Convention's debates on whether to declare independence or negotiate with the British, Patrick Henry called upon his countrymen to trust God:

> Sirs, we shall not fight our battles alone. There is a just God who presides over the destinies of nations, and who will raise up friends to fight our battles for us. The battle, sir, is not to the strong alone; it is to the vigilant, the active, the brave.

Hear his passionate conclusion:

> Is life so dear, or peace so sweet, as to be purchased at the price of chains and slavery? Forbid it, Almighty God! I know not what course others may take; but as for me, give me liberty or give me death!

★ ★ Patriot's Prayer ★ ★

Lord Jesus, Prince of Peace, guide our nation's leaders and we, its citizens, to be ambassadors of Your peace.

★ ★ Patriot's Promise ★ ★

"My peace I give to you . . . Let not your heart be troubled, neither let it be afraid" (John 14:27).

Whose Side?

> The LORD will make you the head and not the tail; . . . if you heed the commandments of the LORD your God, which I command you today, and are careful to observe them.
>
> DEUTERONOMY 28:13

Known as "The Father of the American Space Program" and often said to be the preeminent rocket scientist of the twentieth century, Wernher von Braun (1912–1977) became director of NASA. He stated the following:

In this age of space flight, when we use the modern tools of science to advance into new regions of human activity, the Bible—this grandiose, stirring history of the gradual revelation and unfolding of the moral law—remains in every way an up-to-date book.

Our knowledge and use of the laws of nature that enable us to fly to the Moon also enable us to destroy our home planet with the atom bomb. Science itself does not address the question whether we should use the power at our disposal for good or for evil.

The guidelines of what we ought to do are furnished in the moral law of God. It is no longer enough that we pray that God may be with us on our side. We must learn to pray that we may be on God's side.

★ ★ Patriot's Prayer ★ ★

Today, Lord, I pray that, whatever we do as a people and a nation, we live, work, and govern according to Your Word. Today, may we as a nation clearly and unquestionably demonstrate that we are on Your side.

★ ★ Patriot's Promise ★ ★

Psalm 118:26 reads, "Blessed is he who comes in the name of the LORD!" As you serve the Lord in your day-to-day life, you will know His blessing.

Woe to him who strives with his Maker!

Isaiah 45:9

The Designer of the Universe

One-time director of NASA and "The Father of the American Space Program," Wernher von Braun stated the following in a May 1974 article:

> One cannot be exposed to the law and order of the universe without concluding that there must be design and purpose behind it all. . . . The better we understand the intricacies of the universe and all it harbors, the more reason we have found to marvel at the inherent design upon which it is based. . . .
>
> To be forced to believe only one conclusion—that everything in the universe happened by chance—would violate the very objectivity of science itself. . . . What random process could produce the brains of a man or the system of the human eye? . . .
>
> [Evolutionists] challenge science to prove the existence of God. But must we really light a candle to see the sun? . . . They say they cannot visualize a Designer. Well, can a physicist visualize an electron? . . . What strange rationale makes some physicists accept the inconceivable electron as real while refusing to accept the reality of a Designer on the grounds that they cannot conceive Him?

★ ★ Patriot's Prayer ★ ★

All praise to You, Almighty God and Creator of this Universe, whom the human mind cannot fully comprehend. It is good to serve an infinite and all-wise God.

★ ★ Patriot's Promise ★ ★

Jeremiah 33:3 says, "Call to Me, and I will answer you, and show you great and mighty things, which you do not know." Accept this invitation and come to know God better.

March 25

Our Sacred Duty

You shall walk after the LORD your God and fear Him, and keep His commandments and obey His voice; you shall serve Him and hold fast to Him.

DEUTERONOMY 13:4

According to the Declaration of Independence, the American colonists were determined to defend "the laws of nature and of nature's God." This phrase defines the key principle upon which the Founders stood. *The laws of nature* meant the will of God for man as revealed to man's reason. However, because man is fallen and his reason does not always comprehend this law, God gave us the Bible to make His law absolutely clear.

The churches in the colonies became a voice of freedom, stirring the fires of liberty by telling the colonists that the British government was usurping their God-given rights and that the king and Parliament were violating the laws of God. The Founding Fathers were convinced that it was their sacred duty to start a revolution in order to uphold the law of God against the unjust and oppressive laws of men. This fight for political liberty was seen as a sacred cause because civil liberty is an unalienable right, according to God's natural law.

★ ★ Patriot's Prayer ★ ★

Heavenly Father, may I value my political freedom as a gift from You. May I not take for granted the opportunity I have to know You, follow You, and serve You.

★ ★ Patriot's Promise ★ ★

"This is the will of God, that by doing good you may put to silence the ignorance of foolish men—as free, yet not using liberty as a cloak for vice, but as bondservants of God" (1 Peter 2:15–16).

Blessed is the man . . .
[whose] delight is in the law of the LORD.

PSALM 1:1–2

God Alone

Tom Campbell Clark served as an associate justice of the US Supreme Court from 1949 through 1967. As the following statement illustrates, he understood our nation's heritage:

> The Founding Fathers believed devoutly that there was a God and that the unalienable rights of man were rooted—not in the state, nor the legislature, nor in any other human power—but in God alone.

★ ★ Patriot's Prayer ★ ★

I know, dear Lord, that You alone are the source of my unalienable rights. I put my trust in You alone.

★ ★ Patriot's Promise ★ ★

Written by David, Psalm 62:5 reads, "My soul, wait silently for God alone, for my expectation is from Him." There was never a time in King David's life when God did not exceed his expectations. Whenever David waited upon God, He always came through—just as He does for you.

89

Loyalty

So Jonathan said to David, "Whatever you yourself desire, I will do it for you."

1 SAMUEL 20:4

Few accounts in the Bible paint a picture of loyalty the way the story of Jonathan and David's friendship does. Despite the attempts of King Saul—his father—to kill David, Jonathan pledges his loyalty to David. Jonathan is loyal to his principles and his friend in the face of the greatest opposition.

During the Revolutionary War, there were far more Loyalists (American colonists who remained loyal to the British monarchy) than one might think. According to historian Robert Calhoun, "best estimates put the proportion of adult white male Loyalists somewhere between 15 and 20 percent [approximately 500,000 men]. Approximately half the colonists of European ancestry tried to avoid involvement in the struggle. The Patriots received active support from perhaps 40 to 45 percent of the white populace, and at most no more than a bare majority." Some of the Loyalists returned to Europe, but many remained in the colonies fighting against the Founding Fathers and influencing others to follow in their steps. In spite of this opposition, the Patriots continued to fight for what they believed was God's will.

★ ★ Patriot's Prayer ★ ★

Help me, dear Lord, to always be loyal to You first and above all else.

★ ★ Patriot's Promise ★ ★

If we are loyal to God our Father, He can use our lives as a positive influence on generations to come: "He shall bring forth your righteousness as the light, and your justice as the noonday" (Psalm 37:6).

Do not remove the ancient landmark which your fathers have set.

PROVERBS 22:28

First Amendment Wrongs or First Amendment Rights?

In 1962 and 1963 the Supreme Court struck down the inclusion of religious activities, such as prayer and Bible reading, in public schools. The basis for this dramatic reversal of policy was the Court's controversial reinterpretation of the phrase *separation of church and state*. The First Amendment simply states: "Congress shall make no law respecting an establishment of religion or prohibit the free exercise thereof." The court interpreted this as a prohibition of religious activities in public and delivered far-reaching decisions to remove:

- Student prayer: "Prayer in its public school system breaches the constitution's wall of separation between Church and State." *Engle v. Vitale,* 1962
- School Bible readings: "No state law or school board may require that passages from the Bible be read ... at the beginning of each school day." *Abington v. Schempp,* 1963
- The Ten Commandments: "If the posted copies of the Ten Commandments are to have any effect at all, it will be to induce the schoolchildren to read, meditate upon, perhaps to venerate and obey the Commandments ... this ... is not a permissible state objective." *Stone v. Graham,* 1980
- Benedictions and invocations: "Religious invocation ... conveyed the message that district had given its endorsement to prayer and religion, so that school district was properly [prohibited] from including invocation." *Graham v. Central,* 1985; *Kay v. Douglas,* 1986; *Jager v. Douglas,* 1989; *Lee v. Weisman,* 1992

★ ★ Patriot's Prayer ★ ★

Father, use us to restore Your truth in our schools and in public places.

★ ★ Patriot's Promise ★ ★

"The LORD is our help and our shield" (Psalm 33:20).

March 29

Forgetting God

> Is this not the fast that I have chosen: to loose the bonds of wickedness . . . to let the oppressed go free . . . ?
>
> ISAIAH 58:6

In anguish over the ravages of civil war, President Abraham Lincoln declared a National Fast Day on March 30, 1863:

> We have been the recipients of the choicest bounties of Heaven; we have been preserved these many years in peace and prosperity; we have grown in numbers, wealth, and power as no other nation has ever grown. But we have forgotten God. We have forgotten the gracious hand which preserved us in peace and multiplied and enriched and strengthened us, and we have vainly imagined, in the deceitfulness of our hearts, that all these blessings were produced by some superior wisdom and virtue of our own. Intoxicated with unbroken success, we have become too self-sufficient to feel the necessity of redeeming and preserving grace, too proud to pray to the God that made us.
>
> It behooves us, then, to humble ourselves before the offended Power, to confess our national sins, and to pray for clemency and forgiveness.

★ ★ Patriot's Prayer ★ ★

Heavenly Father, look upon our nation with mercy and forgiveness. We, as a people, have fallen far away from You. Help us, Lord, return to Your eternal truths that have held this nation together for more than two hundred years.

★ ★ Patriot's Promise ★ ★

According to the hope-filled promise of 2 Chronicles 7:14, if we humble ourselves—on the local, the state, and the national level—God will be faithful to forgive our sins and restore our nation. Returning to our nation's foundational Judeo-Christian principles will mean a fresh experience of God's mercy, forgiveness, and faithfulness.

The people wept very bitterly
[over their sinful ways].

EZRA 10:1

Sins Forgiven

Peter Cartwright (1785–1872) was a Methodist circuit rider and evangelist in Tennessee, Kentucky, and surrounding states during the Second Great Awakening. He preached nearly 15,000 sermons and himself baptized twelve thousand people. Here is what he said about his own conversion:

> I went with weeping multitudes and bowed before the preaching stand and earnestly prayed for mercy. In the midst of a solemn struggle of soul, an impression was made upon my mind, as though a voice said to me: "Thy sins are all forgiven thee."

★ ★ Patriot's Prayer ★ ★

Heavenly Father, please forgive my sins. I thank You for that forgiveness, and I accept Your forgiveness. I put my sins behind me and look forward to sweet fellowship with You.

★ ★ Patriot's Promise ★ ★

The author of Hebrews rhetorically asked, "How much more shall the blood of Christ, who through the eternal Spirit offered Himself without spot to God, cleanse your conscience from dead works to serve the living God?" (9:14). God clearly promises that He will thoroughly cleanse us from sin which we confess and repent of.

March 31

April

All liars shall have their part in the lake which burns with fire and brimstone.

REVELATION 21:8

Untruth and Consequences

Founding Father and the third president of the United States (1801–1809), Thomas Jefferson wrote the following:

> He who permits himself to tell a lie once, finds it much easier to do it a second and third time, till at length it becomes habitual; he tells lies without attending to it, and truths without the world's believing him. This falsehood of the tongue leads to that of the heart, and in time depraves all its good dispositions.

★ ★ Patriot's Prayer ★ ★

What a precious blessing, dear God, to be worthy of people's trust. Help me be trustworthy and honest. Keep my words pure with the nectar of truth. Give me strength to address difficult situations with truth. May I never choose lying as an easy out.

★ ★ Patriot's Promise ★ ★

Psalm 63:11 promises that "the mouth of those who speak lies shall be stopped." If we lie, God will stop us. If we lie, we cannot receive His blessing.

April 1

Praying for the Legislature

Warren Earl Burger, chief justice of the US Supreme Court from 1969 to 1986, delivered the court's opinion in the 1982 case of *Marsh v. Chambers*, regarding chaplains opening legislative sessions with prayer:

> The men who wrote the First Amendment religion clause did not view paid legislative chaplains and opening prayers as a violation of that amendment . . .
>
> It can hardly be thought that in the same week the members of the first Congress voted to appoint and pay a chaplain for each House and also voted to approve the draft of the First Amendment . . . [that] they intended to forbid what they had just declared acceptable. . . .
>
> The legislature by majority vote invites a clergyman to give a prayer, neither the inviting nor the giving nor the hearing of the prayer is making a law. On this basis alone . . . the sayings of prayers, per se, in the legislative halls at the opening session is not prohibited by the First and Fourteenth Amendments.

★ ★ Patriot's Prayer ★ ★

Father, I pray that we, as a nation, become people of prayer, both acknowledging that our blessings come only from You and praying for Your will to be done in our country.

★ ★ Patriot's Promise ★ ★

Hear the hope of 2 Chronicles 7:14—"If My people who are called by My name will humble themselves, and pray and seek My face, and turn from their wicked ways, then I will hear from heaven, and will forgive their sin and heal their land."

Be strong and of good courage;
do not be afraid.

JOSHUA 1:9

Shield of Strength

Captain Russell Rippetoe was serving in Operation Iraqi Freedom in March 2003. Previously, while serving in Afghanistan, Rippetoe saw—for the first time in his life—men die, and that experience brought a renewal to his Christian faith and a new passion for the Bible. On the chain around his neck, he wore a "Shield of Strength," a 1-by-2-inch emblem displaying a US flag on one side and words from Joshua 1:9 on the other.

On April 3, 2003, Rippetoe's company was manning a nighttime checkpoint near the Hadithah Dam in western Iraq when a vehicle approached. Suddenly, a woman jumped out and cried, "I'm hungry. I need food and water!" Protecting his men, Rippetoe gave the order to hold back as he moved toward the woman to see how he could help. When she hesitated, the driver detonated a car bomb that killed Captain Rippetoe, Sergeant Nino Livaudais, and Specialist Ryan Long and wounded several others.

Rippetoe believed the ancient words of Joshua 1:9: "The LORD your God is with you wherever you go." Rippetoe, who died trying to help someone, was the first casualty of the Iraq conflict to be buried at Arlington National Cemetery, the hallowed ground that honors more than 250,000 American soldiers spanning back to the Revolutionary War.

★ ★ Patriot's Prayer ★ ★

Heavenly Father, help me live in such as way that others see You through me. Enable me to help others no matter the cost.

★ ★ Patriot's Promise ★ ★

Psalm 30:5 says, "For His anger is but for a moment, His favor is for life; weeping may endure for a night, but joy comes in the morning." We may not always know the reason for our pain and suffering, but we can know that it is not without purpose and meaning and that joy will come soon.

* For more information about Shield
of Strength, see ad on page 380.

Following Christ's Example

Behold what manner of love the
Father has bestowed on us!

1 JOHN 3:1

Benjamin Franklin Butler (1795–1858), US Attorney General under President Andrew Jackson (1833–1838), knew the value of God's Word:

He is truly happy, whatever may be his temporal condition, who can call God his Father in the full assurance of faith and hope. And amid all his trials, conflicts, and doubts, the feeblest Christian is still comparatively happy; because cheered by the hope . . . that the hour is coming when he shall be delivered from "this body of sin and death" and in the vision of his Redeemer . . . approximate to the . . . felicity of angels.

Not only does the Bible inculcate, with sanctions of the highest import, a system of the purest morality, but in the person and character of our Blessed Savior it exhibits a tangible illustration of that system.

In Him we have set before us . . . a model of feeling and action, adapted to all times, places, and circumstances; and combining so much of wisdom, benevolence, and holiness, that none can fathom its sublimity; and yet, presented in a form so simple, that even a child may be made to understand and taught to love it.

★ ★ Patriot's Prayer ★ ★

Heavenly Father, Your Word offers hope, truth, and Christ's example of a moral life. I thank You for Scripture's sublime and simple picture of my Savior.

★ ★ Patriot's Promise ★ ★

Psalm 33:18 proclaims: "The eye of the LORD is on those who fear Him, on those who hope in His mercy."

Come and let us build.

NEHEMIAH 2:17

Building Character and Lives

Adviser to Presidents Theodore Roosevelt and William Howard Taft, educator Booker T. Washington (April 5, 1856–November 14, 1915) founded Tuskegee Institute, a vocational school for African-Americans in Tuskegee, Alabama. Its graduates became leaders and educators across the nation.

Born a slave, Washington worked in Virginia coal mines and salt furnaces starting at age nine. Determined to get an education, at age sixteen he went to Hampton Institute, an industrial school for African-Americans in Hampton, Virginia. Graduating with honors in just three years (1875), he joined the faculty and was soon asked to lead a new school in Tuskegee. Starting with an old abandoned church, he built Tuskegee Institute into a school of 107 buildings on 2,000 acres with over 1,500 students and more than 200 teachers and professors—all by 1915.

Wanting to produce small businessmen, farmers, and teachers, Washington offered traditional academic courses; industry and trade skills like bricklaying, forestry, sewing, cooking, and agriculture (every student was obligated to master at least two trades); and the training of "head, hand, and heart," an emphasis on high moral character shaped by the Christian faith Washington had learned as a child in Sunday school. Morning devotions and evening prayers were held at Tuskegee. Washington wrote that "the Christ-like work which the Church of all denominations in America has done" would have convinced him of the value of the Christian life if he weren't already a believer.

★ ★ Patriot's Prayer ★ ★

Dear Lord, shape me—"head, hand, and heart"—so that I may honor You in all I do.

★ ★ Patriot's Promise ★ ★

"He who follows righteousness and mercy finds life, righteousness, and honor" (Proverbs 21:21).

99

A Godly Legacy

[Abraham] was strengthened in
faith, giving glory to God.

ROMANS 4:20

At age six, Henry John Heinz (1844–1919) helped his mother tend a small family garden. At twelve, he was working more than three acres and using a horse and cart to make deliveries to Pittsburgh grocery stores. He went on to found a company that he named 57 Varieties. Today the H. J. Heinz Company, incorporated in 1905, sells more than 1,300 products, ranging from ketchup to baby food, worldwide.

Heinz's company pioneered safe and sanitary food preparation and was ahead of its time in employee relations, providing free medical benefits and swimming and gymnasium facilities. Women held supervisory and other positions of responsibility. Henry Heinz was also very involved in promoting Sunday school in Pittsburgh and around the world.

In his will, Heinz said, "I desire to set forth at the very beginning of this will, as the most important item in it, a confession of my faith in Jesus Christ as my Savior. I also desire to bear witness to the fact that throughout my life, in which there were unusual joys and sorrows, I have been wonderfully sustained by my faith in God through Jesus Christ. This legacy was left me by my consecrated mother, a woman of strong faith, and to it I attribute any success I have attained."

★ ★ Patriot's Prayer ★ ★

Thank You for Your sustaining presence in my life and the many blessings that proceed from it.

★ ★ Patriot's Promise ★ ★

"Fear not, for I am with you . . . I will strengthen you . . . help you, I will uphold you with My righteous right hand"—so proclaims the Lord in Isaiah 41:10.

Here is the king whom you have chosen
and whom you have desired.

1 SAMUEL 12:13

A Privilege
and Responsibility

Voting is the most basic way citizens participate in a democracy. By voting, we help determine who will make the laws and protect our liberties. Unfortunately, people of faith often vote at an alarmingly low rate. When believers fail to vote, is it any wonder that policies contrary to our core values are enacted? America's leaders have always understood the importance of voting:

If America is to survive, we must elect . . . individuals who will seek Divine guidance in the affairs of state.

—BILLY GRAHAM, EVANGELIST

God cannot sustain this free and blessed country . . . unless the Church will take right ground.

—CHARLES FINNEY, LEADER IN AMERICA'S SECOND GREAT AWAKENING

The people are responsible for the character of their Congress. If that body be ignorant, reckless, and corrupt, it is because the people tolerate ignorance, recklessness, and corruption.

—PRESIDENT JAMES A. GARFIELD

God commands you to choose for rulers, just men who will rule in the fear of God. The preservation of a republican government depends on the faithful discharge of this duty; if the citizens neglect their duty and place unprincipled men in office, the government will soon be corrupted.

—NOAH WEBSTER, THE "FATHER OF AMERICAN SCHOLARSHIP AND EDUCATION"

★ ★ Patriot's Prayer ★ ★

Everlasting God, You know the hearts of all those involved in politics. Compel them to seek wisdom from You and from Your people.

★ ★ Patriot's Promise ★ ★

"Let us be strong for our people and for the cities of our God. And may the LORD do what is good in His sight" (2 Samuel 10:12).

101

Obeying God

> We ought to obey God rather than men.
>
> ACTS 5:29

Perhaps surprisingly, New England ministers played a key role in rallying popular support for war against England. They pressed their congregations to overthrow King George because they believed that rebellion to tyrants was obedience to God. From many pulpits, ministers recruited troops and strengthened them for battle.

These church leaders knew that the Bible places great emphasis on due submission to civil authorities (Romans 13), but they noted that many passages approve resistance to ungodly authority (see Acts 5:29 above).

It is, therefore, no coincidence that one of watchwords of the American Revolution was "No King But King Jesus." Most of the patriots found in their faith and in God's Word the courage to risk their lives and properties in order to break the tyranny of an unjust human authority. According to their Christian worldview, obedience to God took precedence over loyalty to country or government: their primary allegiance was to the Lord Jesus Christ.

★ ★ Patriot's Prayer ★ ★

May seeking You, O God, be my top priority and the top priority of this nation. Following Christ's teachings means everything to me. Where I have failed, forgive me. When I falter, give me a nudge. If I grow weary, encourage me. Let me keep the ears of my heart open so I can hear You speak to me. And I pray these things for my beloved country.

★ ★ Patriot's Promise ★ ★

"If you earnestly obey My commandments . . . then I will give you the rain for your land in its season" (Deuteronomy 11:13–14).

April 8

102

My servant Moses . . . is faithful in all My house.

Principles of Patriotism

Stephen Grover Cleveland served as both the twenty-second and twenty-fourth president of the United States, and he brought to that office a respect for Jesus' teachings:

> All must admit that the reception of the teachings of Christ results in the purest patriotism, in the most scrupulous fidelity to public trust, and in the best type of citizenship.
>
> Those who manage the affairs of government are by this means reminded that the law of God demands that they should be courageously true to the interests of the people, and that the Ruler of the universe will require of them a strict account of their stewardship.
>
> The teachings of both human and Divine law thus merging into one word, *duty*, form the only union of church and state that a civil and religious government can recognize.

★ ★ Patriot's Prayer ★ ★

Father, help me recognize that I have a duty to You, my God, and to my family, my community, and my country. I pray that I courageously fulfill these duties and, as I do so, honor and glorify You.

★ ★ Patriot's Promise ★ ★

"If you will indeed obey My voice and keep My covenant, then you shall be a special treasure to Me above all people" is God's promise in Exodus 19:5. God calls us to obey His covenant. If we do, then we—as the people of a nation that recognizes the "Ruler of the universe"—will be a special treasure to God.

The Goal from the Start

Go therefore and make disciples of all nations.

MATTHEW 28:19

The first permanent settlement in the New World was the English colony established in 1607 at Jamestown, Virginia. Similar to the other colonial charters, the First Charter of Virginia emphasized the Christian character of the colonists' purpose:

> We, greatly commending, and graciously accepting of, their desires for the furtherance of so noble a work, which may, by the providence of Almighty God, hereafter tend to the glory of His Divine Majesty, in propagating of Christian religion to such people, as yet live in darkness and miserable ignorance of the true knowledge and worship of God.

Similarly, in 1620, the Pilgrims established a colony at Plymouth, Massachusetts. Their purpose was to establish a political commonwealth governed by biblical standards. The Mayflower Compact, their initial governing document, clearly stated that what they had undertaken was for "the glory of God and the advancement of the Christian faith." William Bradford, the second governor of Plymouth, said, "[The colonists] cherished a great hope and inward zeal of laying good foundations . . . for the propagations and advance of the Gospel of the kingdom of Christ in the remote parts of the world."

★ ★ Patriot's Prayer ★ ★

Dear God, those first settlers came to America with the purpose of sharing the good news of Your Son Jesus Christ with those who had not yet heard. May I follow their example and be ready to share the gospel with those whom I meet along life's way.

★ ★ Patriot's Promise ★ ★

"I am not ashamed of the gospel of Christ, for it is the power of God to salvation for everyone who believes" (Romans 1:16).

Contend earnestly for the faith which was
once for all delivered to the saints.

JUDE 3

A Call to Battle

While several New Testament books confront the problem of false teachers,
the short book of Jude goes beyond all other New Testament epistles in its
passionate denunciation of the apostate teachers who have crept into the church.
Combining the theme of 2 Peter with the style of James, Jude's letter is potent in
spite of its brevity. Jude challenged believers—then and now—to contend for the
faith and to expose anyone who was turning God's grace into unbounded license
to do as they please. The danger was and is very real and not to be minimized.

Such vigilance is equally important when it comes to guarding our freedoms as
Americans, and General Douglas MacArthur understood that. MacArthur officially accepted the Japanese surrender at the end of World War II and, when he over-
saw the Occupation of Japan from 1945 to 1951, was credited with implementing
far-ranging democratic changes in that country. Well aware of the constant threats
to freedom in this world, he stated: "No man is entitled to the blessings of freedom unless he be vigilant in its preservation."

★ ★ Patriot's Prayer ★ ★
Dear Lord, thank You for the faithful men and women who have contended
for Your gospel so that others may know the truth about Jesus Christ. May I, if
needed, also "contend for the faith" which is so precious a gift from You.

★ ★ Patriot's Promise ★ ★
God provides what we need to contend for His gospel truth: "Put on the whole
armor of God, that you may be able to stand against the wiles of the devil" (Ephesians 6:11).

April 11

Words That Bless

Write the things which you have seen, and the things which are, and the things which will take place after this.

REVELATION 1:19

The book of Revelation unveils our Lord Jesus Christ at His Second Coming, the future times, and the world to come. Penned by the apostle John during his exile on the island of Patmos, Revelation centers around visions and symbols of the resurrected Christ, who alone has the authority to judge the earth, remake it, and rule it in righteousness. Revelation shows the divine plan of redemption being brought to fruition.

In the final chapter, Jesus Christ says to the apostle John, "I am the Alpha and the Omega, the Beginning and the End, the First and the Last" (22:13). There is no doubt that the risen Christ is indeed worthy to be praised and worshiped throughout eternity. It is interesting that in our nation's Capitol, the first and last rays of sunlight fall every day upon its tallest building—the 555-foot Washington Monument. And there on its top, inscribed on the four-sided aluminum capstone are the Latin words *Laus Deo*, which means "Praise be to God." This simple expression of praise reflects America's abiding belief that God has blessed our country with liberty and divine favor.

★ ★ Patriot's Prayer ★ ★

Heavenly Father, thank You for revealing Jesus to me. How awesome to one day be with Him who is King of kings and Lord of lords (Revelation 19:16)!

★ ★ Patriot's Promise ★ ★

"Blessed is he who reads and those who hear the words of this prophecy, and keep those things that are written in it; for the time is near" (Revelation 1:3).

He has shown you, O man, what is good.

Micah 6:8

A Frugal Government

In his 1801 inaugural address, President Thomas Jefferson (April 13, 1743–July 4, 1826) said the following:

> Enlightened by a benign religion, professed, indeed, and practiced in various forms, yet all of them inculcating honesty, truth, temperance, gratitude, and the love of man; acknowledging and adoring an overruling Providence, which by all its dispensations proves that it delights in the happiness of man here and his greater happiness hereafter. With all these blessings, what more is necessary to make us a happy and prosperous people? Still one thing more, fellow citizens—a wise and frugal government, which shall restrain men from injuring one another, shall leave them otherwise free to regulate their own pursuits of industry and improvement, and shall not take from the mouth of labor the bread it has earned. . . .
>
> You should understand what I deem the essential principles of our government. . . . Equal and exact justice to all men, of whatever state or persuasion, religious or political . . . the arraignment of all abuses at the bar of the public reason; freedom of religion; freedom of the press, and freedom of person under the protection of the habeas corpus and trial by jury impartially selected.

★ ★ Patriot's Prayer ★ ★

Dear heavenly Father, teach me to be an effective and generous steward of the money You entrust to my care.

★ ★ Patriot's Promise ★ ★

"The love of money is a root of all kinds of evil. Some people, eager for money, have wandered from the faith and pierced themselves with many griefs" (1 Timothy 6:10 NIV).

Glorious and Pure Morality

All Scripture is given . . . that the man of God may be complete, thoroughly equipped for every good work.

2 TIMOTHY 3:16–17

In the 1844 *Vidal v. Girard's Executors*, Justice Joseph Story upheld the use of the Bible and the teaching of Christian moral principles in a city-run school.

In this case, Girard's will permitted the teaching of the Christian religion, just not by members of the clergy. Story's opinion that Girard's will was not derogatory to the Christian religion rested on two determinations. First, a layman was capable of teaching the general principles of Christianity: "Why may not laymen instruct in the general principles of Christianity as well as ecclesiastics?"

Second, Girard's will actually permitted the teaching of the Bible in the school:

> Why may not the Bible, and especially the New Testament, without note or comment be read and taught as a divine revelation . . . its general precepts expounded, its evidences explained, and its glorious principles of morality inculcated? . . . Where can the purest principles of morality be learned so clearly or so perfectly as from the New Testament? Where are benevolence, the love of truth, sobriety, and industry, so powerfully and irresistibly inculcated as in the sacred volume?

The Court's decision held that Girard's will did not attack or revile Christianity: it simply permitted the teaching of Christian values and moral principles in a nonsectarian way.

★ ★ Patriot's Prayer ★ ★
Lord God, I pray that You will use Your people to return to our schools the privilege of Bible reading.

★ ★ Patriot's Promise ★ ★
"The commandment of the LORD is pure, enlightening the eyes" (Psalm 19:8).

Render to Caesar the things that are Caesar's.

MARK 12:17

Choosing Christ or Chaos?

Peter Marshall, the chaplain of the US Senate (1947–1949), issued a call for Americans to honor God:

> The choice before us is plain: Christ or chaos, conviction or compromise, discipline or disintegration. I am rather tired of hearing about our rights and privileges as American citizens. The time is come—it is now—when we ought to hear about the duties and responsibilities of our citizenship. America's future depends upon her accepting and demonstrating God's government.

★ ★ Patriot's Prayer ★ ★

Father, enable me to know and then to do my civic duty. I pray that, first, I will make my home a sanctuary for my family members. Help me to also make my neighborhood a better place for those who are hurting, lonely, and needing help. Use my efforts, Lord, to help improve my city and my state.

★ ★ Patriot's Promise ★ ★

Read the amazing promise of Deuteronomy 28:1–2: "Now it shall come to pass, if you diligently obey the voice of the LORD your God, to observe carefully all His commandments which I command you today, that the LORD your God will set you high above all nations of the earth. And all these blessings shall come upon you and overtake you, because you obey the voice of the LORD your God." God promises that if we make the right choices, if we live according to His Word, we will know blessing, not chaos.

April 15

When Prosperity Devours Religion

You say, "I am rich."

REVELATION 3:17

Cotton Mather (1663–1728), an American colonial clergyman and educator, wrote the most detailed history of the first fifty years of New England, *The Great Achievement of Christ in America*. Noting the rising trend toward materialism in the colonies, he wrote this:

Religion begat prosperity, and the daughter devoured the mother.

★ ★ Patriot's Prayer ★ ★

Whatever You resolve to give me, Father, I know is for the best. Help me handle with wisdom the blessings You give me. Please let nothing that I have stand in the way of my serving You.

★ ★ Patriot's Promise ★ ★

"If they obey and serve Him, they shall spend their days in prosperity, and their years in pleasures" (Job 36:11). This verse assures that the only way to true prosperity is through obedience and service to God.

After my skin is destroyed . . . I shall see God.

JOB 19:26

A Resurrection Body

When he was in his early twenties, Benjamin Franklin (January 17, 1706–April 17, 1790) wrote this verse, reminiscent of Job's words, to serve as his epitaph:

<blockquote>
The Body of
Franklin, Printer,
Like the cover of an old book,
Its contents torn out
And stripted of its lettering and gilding,
Lies here, food for worms.
But the work shall not be lost;
For it will, as he believ'd, appear once more
In a new and more elegant edition,
Revised and Corrected
By the Author.
</blockquote>

★ ★ Patriot's Prayer ★ ★

I thank You, Lord, that this life is just the beginning of what You have for me. I thank You that one day, "revised and corrected," I will be in heaven with You.

★ ★ Patriot's Promise ★ ★

Jesus commanded His people to "let your light so shine before men, that they may see your good works and glorify your Father in heaven" (Matthew 5:16). God promised that those good works would glorify Him.

No Ordinary Claims

No one comes to the Father except through Me.

JESUS IN JOHN 14:6

Simon Greenleaf (1783–1853) was the Royall Professor of Law at Harvard and considered one of the greatest legal minds in Western history. One of the principal founders of Harvard Law School, Greenleaf examined the evidence for the Resurrection, came to the conclusion that it happened, and became a believer. In his *Testimony of the Evangelists*, Greenleaf wrote this:

> The religion of Jesus Christ aims at nothing less than the utter overthrow of all other systems of religion in the world; denouncing them as inadequate to the wants of man, false in their foundations, and dangerous in their tendency.
>
> These are no ordinary claims; and it seems hardly possible for a rational being to regard them with even a subdued interest; much less to treat them with mere indifference and contempt. If not true, they are little else than the pretensions of a bold imposture, which, not satisfied with having already enslaved millions of the human race, seeks to continue its encroachments upon human liberty, until all nations shall be subjugated under its iron rule.
>
> But if they are well-founded and just, they can be no less than the high requirements of heaven, addressed by the voice of God to the reason and understanding of man, concerning things deeply affecting his relations to his sovereign, and essential to the formation of his character and of course to his destiny, both for this life and for the life to come.

★ ★ Patriot's Prayer ★ ★

Merciful God, thank You for enabling me to recognize the truth about Jesus and Your Word.

★ ★ Patriot's Promise ★ ★

"Do what is good, and you will have praise from [government rulers]" (Romans 13:3).

April 18

Blessed is the nation whose God is the LORD.

PSALM 33:12

Hear these thoughts from Charles Malik (1906–1987), Lebanon's ambassador to the United Nations and president of the thirteenth session of the UN General Assembly in 1959:

> The good [in the United States] would never have come into being without the blessing and power of Jesus Christ....Whoever tries to conceive the American word without taking full account of the suffering and love and salvation of Christ is only dreaming. I know how embarrassing this matter is to politicians, bureaucrats, businessmen, and cynics; but, whatever these honored men think, the irrefutable truth is that the soul of America is, at its best and highest, Christian.

★ ★ Patriot's Prayer ★ ★

Thank You, O God, for Calvary. Thank You that Jesus shed His blood for me that I might receive eternal life. Thank You for the resurrection power that came on that first Easter morning. Thank You for the blessings that You bestow upon my family and me every day.

★ ★ Patriot's Promise ★ ★

Romans 1:16 says, "I am not ashamed of the gospel of Christ, for it is the power of God to salvation for everyone who believes." God assures the salvation of anyone who believes the gospel of Jesus Christ.

Spiritual Warfare

The weapons of our warfare are not carnal but mighty in God for pulling down strongholds.

2 Corinthians 10:4

After receiving Paul's first letter, the Corinthian church was swayed by false teachers who accused Paul of being proud, unimpressive, and unqualified to be an apostle of Jesus Christ. Recognizing this as spiritual war, Paul sent Titus to Corinth to address this issue.

Every believer needs to know that the opposition that comes their way has its source in evil forces that oppose God and His truth. As Paul himself wrote, "We do not wrestle against flesh and blood, but against principalities, against powers, against the rulers of the darkness of this age, against spiritual hosts of wickedness in the heavenly places" (Ephesians 6:12).

Whether they face immorality or false teaching, church leaders must take action to remedy the problem. The same is true of government. President Thomas Jefferson stated, "When once a republic is corrupted, there is no possibility of remedying any of the growing evils but by removing the corruption and restoring its lost principles; every other correction is either useless or a new evil."

★ ★ Patriot's Prayer ★ ★

What, O Lord, is Satan using to undermine my relationship with You? May Your Holy Spirit reveal to me any stronghold and then empower me to pull it down so that I might enjoy fellowship with You.

★ ★ Patriot's Promise ★ ★

Before He died, Jesus promised that "the Helper, the Holy Spirit . . . will teach you all things, and bring to your remembrance all things that I said to you" (John 14:26).

April 20

The Son of Man did not come to be served, but to serve, and to give His life a ransom for many.

JESUS IN MARK 10:45

Jesus the Christ

The shortest of the four gospels, the book of Mark gives a crisp, fast-moving look at Christ's service and His sacrifice. In His teaching, preaching, and healing and even as He hangs on the cross, Jesus ministers to the needs of others. Mark traces the steady building of hostility and opposition to Jesus as He resolutely moves toward the fulfillment of His earthy ministry—to give His life as a ransom for many.

The pivotal event of the book is Peter's confession, "You are the Christ" (8:29). And so begins a new phase in Jesus' ministry: He starts to strengthen and prepare His disciples for His upcoming death.

When Benjamin Franklin was confronted by a disgruntled American, complaining that his country had failed to provide him with the happiness it had promised, Franklin is said to have smiled and calmly replied, "The Constitution only gives people the right to pursue happiness. You have to catch it yourself." Similarly, Jesus gave His life to ransom ours, but we must join Peter in confessing that Jesus is the Christ, and accepting Him as our Savior, if we are to receive the eternal life He has for us.

★ ★ Patriot's Prayer ★ ★

Lord Jesus, thank You for giving Your life to pay the debt for my sins. Today give me an opportunity to tell someone about the gifts of forgiveness and eternal life that You have given me.

★ ★ Patriot's Promise ★ ★

"Whoever calls on the name of the LORD shall be saved" (Romans 10:13).

"The Infallible Word of God"

> My beloved is . . . chief among ten thousand.
>
> SONG OF SOLOMON 5:10

William Strong served as an associate justice of the US Supreme Court from 1870–1880. Hear this educated man's conclusion about Jesus and Scripture:

> You ask me what I think of Christ? He is the chiefest among ten thousand, and altogether lovely—my Lord, my Savior, and my God.
>
> What do I think of the Bible? It is the infallible Word of God, a light erected all along the shores of time to warn against the rocks and breakers, and to show the only way to the harbor of eternal rest.

★ ★ Patriot's Prayer ★ ★

Father God, Your Word is a light to me. I want to know Your Word and You better! Help me be firm in my commitment to meet with You regularly. May nothing interfere with my time with You.

★ ★ Patriot's Promise ★ ★

Isaiah 40:5 tells us that "the glory of the LORD shall be revealed." What a promise!

Simon Peter answered and said, "You are the Christ, the Son of the living God."

Matthew 16:16

Jesus, Messiah and King

The Old Testament prophets predicted and longed for the coming of the Messiah, the One who would enter history to bring redemption and deliverance to God's chosen people. Through a carefully selected series of Old Testament quotations, the New Testament book of Matthew documents and verifies Jesus Christ's claim to be the King of the Jews. In Matthew's gospel, Jesus' genealogy, baptism, messages, and miracles all clearly point to the same inescapable conclusion: Jesus is King, the long-awaited Messiah.

President Thomas Jefferson believed that the teachings of Jesus embody the "most sublime system of morals" in the whole world. He stated, "We all agree in the obligation of the moral precepts of Jesus, and nowhere will they be found delivered in greater purity than in His discourses."

Early in Jesus' public life, the apostle Peter recognized who this Carpenter was. In his gospel, Matthew confirmed that Jesus is the Messiah. And in his politics, Thomas Jefferson embraced His teachings. Who do you need to talk to about Jesus?

★ ★ Patriot's Prayer ★ ★

Lord Jesus, I come to worship You this day. Your life is my example, Your cross is my hope, and Your resurrection is my salvation—show me whom I need to share this truth with.

★ ★ Patriot's Promise ★ ★

In John 10:10, Jesus promised, "I have come that [My followers] may have life, and that they may have it more abundantly."

117

Bible or Bayonet?

Whoever hears these sayings of Mine, and does them . . . [is building] his house on the rock.

JESUS IN MATTHEW 7:24

Consider the boldness of Robert Winthrop, lawyer, philanthropist, and speaker of the US House of Representatives (1847–1849):

Men may as well build their houses upon the sand and expect to see them stand, when the rains fall, and the winds blow, and the floods come, as to found free institutions upon any other basis than that of morality and virtue, of which the Word of God is the only authoritative rule, and the only adequate sanction.

All societies of men must be governed in some way or other. The less they have of stringent state government, the more they must have of individual self-government. The less they rely on public law or physical force, the more they must rely on private moral restraint.

Men, in a word, must necessarily be controlled either by a power within them or a power without them; either by the Word of God or by the strong arm of man; either by the Bible or by the bayonet.

It may do for other countries and other governments to talk about the state supporting religion. Here, under our own free institutions, it is religion which must support the state.

★ ★ Patriot's Prayer ★ ★

Lord, enable Your people to build this nation on the rock of Your truth.

★ ★ Patriot's Promise ★ ★

Too many choose the bayonet over the Bible, but Micah 4:3 promises, "They shall beat their swords into plowshares, and their spears into pruning hooks; nation shall not lift up sword against nation, neither shall they learn war anymore."

To everything there is a season, a time
for every purpose under heaven.

ECCLESIASTES 3:1

In 1775, the Lutheran pastor John Peter Gabriel Muhlenberg concluded a sermon with this declaration: "In the language of the Holy Writ, there is a time for all things. There is a time to preach and a time to fight. And now is the time to fight." He then threw off his clerical robes to reveal the uniform of a Revolutionary Army officer. That afternoon, at the head of three hundred men, he marched off to join General Washington's troops and became colonel of the 8th Virginia Regiment.

Ministers turned the colonial resistance into a righteous cause not only from the pulpit, but also in state legislatures and on the battlefield where they served at every level in the conflict, from military chaplains to taking up arms and leading troops into battle.

Ultimately, the Continental Army captured two key British armies at Saratoga in 1777 and Yorktown in 1781. That is when the prophetic words of Patrick Henry to his fellow Virginians proved true: "Three millions of people, armed with the holy cause of liberty, and in such a country as that which we possess, are invincible by any force which our enemy can send against us."

★ ★ Patriot's Prayer ★ ★
Lord, thank You for pastors who walk their talk, who live what they preach, who model for us godly living. Keep me faithful in praying for my pastors.

★ ★ Patriot's Promise ★ ★
"There is no fear in love; but perfect love casts out fear" (1 John 4:18).

April 25

The Ultimate Tribute

You were faithful in a very little.

LUKE 19:17

Schuyler Colfax (1823–1885) served as vice president of the United States under Ulysses S. Grant, but he knew that he answered ultimately to God:

Man derives his greatest happiness not by that which he does for himself, but by what he accomplishes for others. This is a sad world at best—a world of sorrow, of suffering, of injustice, and falsification; men stab those whom they hate with the stiletto of slander, but it is for the followers of our Lord to improve it, and to make it more as Christ would have it. The most precious crown of fame that a human being can ask is to kneel at the bar of God and hear the beautiful words, "Well done, good and faithful servant."

★ ★ Patriot's Prayer ★ ★

Today, Lord, may I be a good and faithful servant to You and to my fellowman. By Your grace, my greatest earthly achievements will be those investments I make in other people and in Your name.

★ ★ Patriot's Promise ★ ★

In Matthew 22:34–40, when a Pharisee asked Jesus which commandment was the greatest, He answered with two: love God and love others. These commands are intertwined: if we show our love for others, we are living out our love for God.

I will make you a great nation; I will bless you and make your name great; and you shall be a blessing. I will bless those who bless you, and I will curse him who curses you; and in you all the families of the earth shall be blessed.

GOD TO ABRAHAM IN GENESIS 12:2–3

America's Bedrock

Foundations are crucial to the success of any venture, whether it is building a house or building a nation. When the Founding Fathers set about to establish the bedrock that would define America's greatness, they went right to the source, declaring that all human beings are "endowed by their Creator with certain unalienable Rights."

The Bible contains the foundational truth that God is the Source of all life, sovereign over history, and our only hope for the peace, happiness, and true liberty we all crave. In Genesis, the "book of beginnings," we witness God's creation of heaven and earth by His powerful word, the beginnings of man's rebellion and sin, and God's calling of a covenant people through which He would bring salvation to all the peoples of the earth through His one and only Son.

★ ★ Patriot's Prayer ★ ★

Heavenly Father, thank You that, through the godly men You called to found our country, You have blessed this nation with moral foundations that have held strong for more than two hundred years. Call us as a people back to faithfulness to Your Word so that our country may stay strong.

★ ★ Patriot's Promise ★ ★

"Blessed is the nation whose God is the LORD, the people He has chosen as His own inheritance" (Psalm 33:12).

Spreading the Gospel

You shall receive power when the Holy Spirit has come upon you; and you shall be witnesses to Me.

JESUS IN ACTS 1:8

The founding of our beloved nation and the growth of Christ's glorious church share some inspiring parallels. Consider that America's Founders gathered at Independence Hall on July 4, 1776, to establish a nation that would be a beacon of hope and freedom to countless millions throughout the generations, Similarly, Christ's disciples gathered in Jerusalem to establish a church destined to take the hope of the gospel to the ends of the earth. Acts recounts the bold steps of faith the apostles took after they were filled with the power of the Holy Spirit. God used them to establish an ever-growing community of believers that model Christian virtue and faith in this dark, sin-filled world.

Just as America's Founding Fathers did, those early Christians faced many challenges, real dangers, and much opposition. But by God's grace as well as with prayer, hard work, and a steadfast reliance on the Almighty, they took the truth of the gospel to Jerusalem, Judea, Samaria, and to the ends of the earth. Even today the gospel of Jesus is the only hope for peace upon which individuals—or nations—can rely.

★ ★ Patriot's Prayer ★ ★

Dear Lord, I thank You for the power of Your Holy Spirit and His work on earth through Your church. What a privilege to be a part of that blood-washed fellowship, Your church family.

★ ★ Patriot's Promise ★ ★

Jesus promises to fill us with Himself in John 7:37: "If anyone thirsts, let him come to Me and drink."

April 28

For to me, to live is Christ, and to die is gain.

PHILIPPIANS 1:21

Would You Die?

According to a popular legend surrounding the Declaration of Independence, John Hancock signed his name largely and distinctly so King George could read it without his spectacles. While that may not be true, it is true that Mr. Hancock put his life on the line with that signature. If the revolution were lost or he were caught, he would be hanged by the British.

Each of the fifty-six signers knew the risk: "with a firm reliance on the protection of Divine Providence, we mutually pledge to each other our lives, our fortunes, and our sacred honor."

A few months before signing the Declaration, Patrick Henry addressed the Virginia Convention:

> We are not weak if we make a proper use of those means which the God of nature hath placed in our power. . . . Besides, sir, we shall not fight our battles alone. There is a just God who presides over the destinies of nations, and who will raise up friends to fight our battles for us. The battle, sir, is not to the strong alone; it is to the vigilant, the active, the brave.

Yet in the early 1990s the authors of *The Day America Told the Truth* took polls asking people which beliefs they would die for—and 48 percent said "none." Only 30 percent would die for God and their faith under any circumstance, and fewer would die for their country.

Can America recover its courage?

★ ★ Patriot's Prayer ★ ★
Almighty God, thank You for protecting my family and me.

★ ★ Patriot's Promise ★ ★
"Thus says the LORD to you: 'Do not be afraid nor dismayed because of this great multitude, for the battle is not yours, but God's'" (2 Chronicles 20:15).

April 29

Revival in America

For God so loved the world that He gave His only begotten Son, that whosoever believes in Him should not perish but have everlasting life.

JOHN 3:16

When Jonathan Edwards began preaching in Northampton, Massachusetts, in 1734, the moral conditions of that colony and throughout the British settlements were at an extreme low. The New England that was to be a "city on the hill" had become materialistic, the strict Puritan teachings no longer followed.

From the pulpit, Edwards stressed the importance of an immediate, personal spiritual rebirth. He preached the unworthiness of sinful man and the grace of God upon which any of us is totally dependent for salvation—and a revival began in his church, first among the youth and then spreading to the adults.

Edwards wrote that "in the spring and summer following, anno 1735, the town seemed to be so full of the presence of God; it never was so full of love, nor of joy, and yet so full of distress, as it was then." In two years, three hundred converts were added to the church, and news of the revival spread throughout New England.

★ ★ Patriot's Prayer ★ ★

Dear Lord Jesus, send a great revival in our land today—and let it begin in my heart. Renew my passion for You so that my love for You impacts my life, my family, my friends. And do this, I pray, across this great land so that our nation will return to You in a mighty way.

★ ★ Patriot's Promise ★ ★

"The LORD your God is gracious and merciful, and will not turn His face from you if you return to Him" (2 Chronicles 30:9).

May

Meeting Spiritual Needs in Congress

Moses prayed for the people.

NUMBERS 21:7

Throughout our history our political leaders have turned to spiritual leaders for guidance and prayer. Here are some examples:

- On May 1, 1789, the United States Congress elected the Reverend William Linn, a Dutch Reformed minister from New York City, to be the first chaplain of the US House of Representatives, appropriating $500 dollars from the federal treasury to pay his annual salary.
- During the period when Congress first met in Washington, D.C., the House and Senate chaplains regularly led Christian services every Sunday in the House Chamber.
- In 1860, Rabbi Morris Jacob Raphall was the first Jewish clergyman invited to open a House session with prayer.
- Both the House and the Senate have continued to regularly open every session with prayer.

★ ★ Patriot's Prayer ★ ★

Thank You, Lord, for those times when our nation has recognized her need for Your guidance. May our leaders today understand that our greatness comes only because of Your mercy and grace.

★ ★ Patriot's Promise ★ ★

Matthew 21:22 says that "whatever things you ask in prayer, believing, you will receive." If we, as a nation, continue to humbly come to God in prayer asking for His blessing and protection, then He has promised to hear us and answer our prayers.

Love never fails.

1 CORINTHIANS 13:8

A War Hero without a Gun

Medic Desmond Doss entered the US Army in April 1942 as a conscientious objector because of his religious beliefs. From the beginning, men in his company harassed Doss for his faith. . . .

On Okinawa, in late spring of 1945, his battalion assaulted a jagged escarpment 400 feet high—only to be met with artillery, mortar, and machine-gun fire that inflicted approximately seventy-five casualties. Refusing to seek cover, Doss remained with the many stricken, carrying them one by one to the edge of the cliff and lowering them down its face. Each time he prayed, "Dear God, let me get just one more man."

In three more battles in May, Doss unhesitatingly braved enemy artillery, mortar shells, and grenades to dress his fellow soldiers' wounds and evacuate them to safety. On May 21, he was seriously wounded when a grenade exploded. He waited five hours before litter bearers reached him. As they carried him to cover, Doss insisted they use his stretcher for a badly injured GI. Awaiting the litter bearers' return, he was struck by a bullet that broke one arm. Doss splinted his shattered arm and then crawled 300 yards to the aid station.

Discovering he had lost his Bible, Doss asked the men to watch for it. An entire battalion combed the battlefield, found the Bible, and mailed it to Doss.

Private First Class Doss became the first conscientious objector to receive the Medal of Honor for bravery far above and beyond the call of duty.

★ ★ Patriot's Prayer ★ ★

Lord, I want to be a witness for You who goes above and beyond the call of duty.

★ ★ Patriot's Promise ★ ★

"Our sufficiency is from God" (2 Corinthians 3:5).

127

A Passionate Love

To you who fear My name the Sun of Righteousness shall arise with healing in His wings.

MALACHI 4:2

The prophet Malachi directed his God-given message to a people plagued by corrupt priests and wickedness. He confronted the children of Israel for their hypocrisy, infidelity, divorce, pride, greed, and arrogance. The nation was so complacent about their sin that God's Word no longer had any impact on them. Nevertheless, Malachi challenged them to nurture a relationship with God characterized by faith, obedience, and worship. God loves us passionately and wants us to return that kind of love to Him.

In May 1775, Harvard College President Samuel Langdon delivered a message to the Provincial Congress of Massachusetts that is reminiscent of Malachi's prophecy—and which echoes eloquently through history to today's America:

> We have rebelled against God. We have lost the true spirit of Christianity, though we retain the outward profession and form of it.... My brethren, let us repent and implore the divine mercy.... May the Lord hear us in this day of trouble.... We will rejoice in His salvation, and in the name of our God, we will set up our banners!

★ ★ Patriot's Prayer ★ ★

O Lord my God, I pray today that I will never lose my love for Your Holy Word and that I will never grow complacent or lukewarm in my relationship with You. Keep me always wanting to know You better.

★ ★ Patriot's Promise ★ ★

"We have become partakers of Christ if we hold the beginning of our confidence steadfast to the end" (Hebrews 3:14).

May 3

The Son of Man has come to seek and
to save that which was lost.

LUKE 19:10

Son of Man and Son of God

D r. Luke penned the gospel that bears his name with the compassion of a family physician, carefully documenting the perfect humanity of Jesus Christ.
Luke built this gospel narrative on the foundation of historical reliability, emphasizing Jesus' ancestry, birth, and early life before moving chronologically through
His earthly ministry. Growing belief and growing opposition develop side by side,
with the opposition finally sending the Son of Man to His death on the cross. But
Jesus' resurrection ensured that His purpose of saving the lost was fulfilled.

Christianity welcomes close examination, that the inquirer might "know the
certainty" of its truths (Luke 1:4). Alexander Hamilton, a signer of the Constitution and one of America's first constitutional lawyers, made such an investigation.
This is his conclusion: "I have carefully examined the evidences of the Christian
religion, and if I was sitting as a juror upon its authenticity, I would unhesitatingly
give my verdict in its favor. I can prove its truth as clearly as any proposition ever
submitted to the mind of man."

★ ★ Patriot's Prayer ★ ★
Dear Lord Jesus, I do not question what Your Word proclaims about You, yet I am
glad that even secular history reports Your birth, life, death, and resurrection.

★ ★ Patriot's Promise ★ ★
Jesus' stories of the Lost Sheep, the Lost Coin, and the Lost Son found in Luke 15
vividly teach the gospel message: God through Christ has come to seek people lost
in their sins and save them.

Serving in the Church

I write so that you may know how you ought to conduct yourself in the house of God, which is the church of the living God, the pillar and ground of the truth.

1 TIMOTHY 3:15

Paul, the aged and experienced apostle, wrote to the young pastor Timothy, who was facing a heavy burden of responsibility in the church at Ephesus. False teachings needed to be corrected; public worship, safeguarded; and mature leadership, developed. Paul spoke pointedly about a minister's proper conduct and counseled Timothy on the qualities that make for a godly leader. A Christ-follower must be careful to avoid false teachers and greedy motives, pursuing instead righteousness, godliness, faith, love, perseverance, and the gentleness that befit a servant of God.

As he took over responsibility for the church Paul founded at Ephesus, Timothy could not be a second Paul, but he would need to use all his God-given strengths to lead the church. Likewise, American writer and humorist Charles F. Browne said, "We can't all be Washingtons, but we can all be patriots." We will never be the father of our country, but we can serve our country to the best of our abilities.

★ ★ Patriot's Prayer ★ ★

Lord, according to Your Word, each believer has an important role in Your kingdom. Make clear the path of service You have for me that I might walk in it and use the talents and abilities You have given me for Your kingdom and Your glory.

★ ★ Patriot's Promise ★ ★

"Your ears shall hear a word behind you saying, 'This is the way, walk in it'" (Isaiah 30:21).

If My people . . . will humble themselves, and pray . . . then I will . . . forgive their sin and heal their land.

2 CHRONICLES 7:14

National Day of Prayer

On January 25, 1988, the United States Congress declared the first Thursday of each May to be recognized as a National Day of Prayer.
Be it enacted by the Senate and House of Representatives of the United States of America in Congress assembled, That the joint resolution entitled "Joint Resolution to provide for setting aside an appropriate day as a National Day of Prayer," approved April 17, 1952 (Public Law 82–324; 66 Stat. 64), is amended by striking "a suitable day each year, other than a Sunday," and inserting in lieu thereof "the first Thursday in May in each year."

★ ★ Patriot's Prayer ★ ★
Sovereign God, thank You for this great country where we can set aside a day for the express purpose of praying for our nation. Raise up people to do just that, not only on an official day, but every day.

★ ★ Patriot's Promise ★ ★
God rewards those who pray to Him—those individuals and those nations: "He shall pray to God, and He will delight in him, He shall see His face with joy, for He restores to man His righteousness" (Job 33:26).

South Carolina's Swamp Fox

"The LORD is with you, you mighty man of valor!"

JUDGES 6:12

Considered one of the fathers of modern guerrilla warfare, Francis Marion (1732–1795) was the brigadier general serving in the South Carolina Militia during the Revolutionary War and known as the "Swamp Fox." His volunteer force "Marion's Brigade" could assemble at a moment's notice, hit British and Loyalist garrisons, and then disappear into the swamps, their base of operations.

Hear General Nathanael Greene's praise: "Surrounded on every side with a superior force, hunted from every quarter with veteran troops, you have found means to elude their attempts and keep alive the expiring hopes of an oppressed militia."

After the war, Marion served in the South Carolina Senate for several terms. Listen to this soldier's profound insight:

> Who can doubt that God created us to be happy, and thereto made us to love one another? It is plainly written as the Gospel. The heart is sometimes so embittered that nothing but Divine love can sweeten it, so enraged that devotion can only becalm it, and so broken down that it takes all the forces of heavenly hope to raise it. In short, the religion of Jesus Christ is the only sure and controlling power over sin.

★ ★ Patriot's Prayer ★ ★

Dear Lord, give me a heart free of bitterness and full of love. And continue, Lord Jesus, to rein in the sin that can be so appealing.

★ ★ Patriot's Promise ★ ★

Psalm 136:12 (NIV) praises God for His "mighty hand and outstretched arm; His love endures forever." With this mighty hand, God redeems His people and delivers those who serve Him.

My word . . . shall not return to Me void.

ISAIAH 55:11

The Bible's Influence

In 1984, University of Houston political scientists Donald Lutz and Charles Hyneman wrote about the sources that most influenced the development of American political thought during our nation's Founding Era, 1760–1805. Their research paper "The Relative Influence of European Writers on Late Eighteenth-Century American Political Thought" was published in *The American Political Science Review*, 78 (1984).

After analyzing some fifteen thousand items published during that forty-five-year period, Lutz and Hyneman isolated 3,154 direct quotes cited by the Founders, identified the source of these quotes, and discovered that 34 percent came directly out of the Bible. French legal philosopher Baron Charles de Montesquieu was quoted 8.3 percent of the time. Sir William Blackstone, a renowned English jurist whose *Commentaries on the Laws of England* were highly accepted in America, was next at 7.9 percent, and English philosopher John Locke was fourth with 2.9 percent.

Three-fourths of the biblical citations in the 1760 to 1805 sample came from reprinted sermons (one of the most popular types of political writing during these years), and only 9 percent came from secular literature. These statistics clearly reflect the Bible's impact on the Founding Fathers.

★ ★ Patriot's Prayer ★ ★
Lord, make me such a student of Your Word that it informs my thinking—as it did the Founding Fathers'—and my words and actions as well.

★ ★ Patriot's Promise ★ ★
God's Word "shall accomplish what I please, and it shall prosper in the thing for which I sent it" (Isaiah 55:11).

May 8

The Bible of the Early Colonists

The sword of the Spirit . . . is the word of God.

EPHESIANS 6:17

Early colonists brought the Geneva Bible to America's shores. With more than 140 editions printed from 1560 to 1644, this was the most widely read and influential English Bible of the sixteenth and seventeenth centuries. Despite its size of nearly 6 inches by 8 inches, it was called a "pocket" Bible. (After all, earlier editions of the Bible were huge and unwieldy.) Now, with the Geneva Bible, an individual could own and read God's Word without having to rely on a king or church official to interpret what the Bible said.

The most unique feature of the Geneva Bible was its extensive margin notes, included to explain and interpret the Scriptures for the common people. These notes—totaling approximately 300,000 words, or one-third the length of the Bible text itself—were largely the work of reformers who had been driven from Great Britain during the reigns of Bloody Mary (1553) and James I (1603), two advocates of the Divine Right of Kings and of the authority of the State over the Church. The commentaries in the Geneva Bible reflected reformation thought and took an anti-autocratic tone toward both church leaders and state leaders.

★ ★ Patriot's Prayer ★ ★

Lord, may I never take for granted Your written Word. Open my mind and heart to its truth and its power so that I may live according to Your ways and glorify You in my everyday life.

★ ★ Patriot's Promise ★ ★

"The commandment of the LORD is pure, enlightening the eyes; . . . the judgments of the LORD are true and righteous altogether" (Psalm 19:8–9).

May 9

★ 134 ★

Let deacons be the husbands of one wife, ruling their children and their own houses well.

1 Timothy 3:12

Ronald Reagan, the fortieth president of the United States (1981–1989), wrote the following:

> The family has always been the cornerstone of American society. Our families nurture, preserve, and pass on to each succeeding generation the values we share and cherish, values that are the foundation for our freedoms. In the family, we learn our first lessons of God and man, love and discipline, rights and responsibilities, human dignity and human frailty.
>
> Our families give us daily examples of these lessons being put into practice. In raising and instructing our children, in providing personal and compassionate care for the elderly, in maintaining the spiritual strength of religious commitment among our people—in these and other ways, America's families make immeasurable contributions to America's well-being.
>
> Today more than ever, it is essential that these contributions not be taken for granted and that each of us remember that the strength of our families is vital to the strength of our nation.

★ ★ Patriot's Prayer ★ ★

Thank You, Lord, for my mother and father. Show me specific ways to honor them in obedience to Your Word.

★ ★ Patriot's Promise ★ ★

Exodus 20:12 is the only one of the Ten Commandments that comes with a promise: "Honor your father and your mother, that your days may be long upon the land which the LORD your God is giving you."

May 10

The Power of God

As the president of Yale College (1778–1795), Ezra Stiles spoke before the governor and the General Assembly of Connecticut in May 1783:

In our lowest and most dangerous state, in 1776 and 1777, we sustained ourselves against the British Army of sixty thousand troops, commanded by . . . the ablest generals Britain could procure throughout Europe, with a naval force of twenty-two thousand seamen in above eighty men-of-war.

Who but a Washington, inspired by Heaven, could have conceived the surprise move upon the enemy at Princeton—that Christmas eve when Washington and his army crossed the Delaware?

Who but the Ruler of the winds could have delayed the British reinforcements by three months of contrary ocean winds at a critical point of the war?

Or what but "a providential miracle" at the last minute detected the treacherous scheme of traitor Benedict Arnold, which would have delivered the American army, including George Washington himself, into the hands of the enemy?

On the French role in the Revolution, it is God who so ordered the balancing interests of nations as to produce an irresistible motive in the European maritime powers to take our part. . . .

The United States are under peculiar obligations to become a holy people unto the Lord our God.

★ ★ Patriot's Prayer ★ ★

Lord, great is Your faithfulness. Transform us into holier people, able to live lives of gratitude and service to You.

★ ★ Patriot's Promise ★ ★

Isaiah 60:1 celebrates: "Arise, shine; for your light has come! And the glory of the LORD is risen upon you."

May 11

How the mighty have fallen in the
midst of the battle!

2 SAMUEL 1:25

"Duty, Honor, Country"

I n his May 12, 1962 farewell speech to the Corps of Cadets at West Point,
General Douglas MacArthur gave a moving tribute to the American soldier. The
following paragraph is from that stirring speech:

> Duty, Honor, Country....
>
> The code which those words perpetuate embraces the highest
> moral laws and will stand the test of any ethics or philosophies ever
> promulgated for the uplift of mankind. Its requirements are for the
> things that are right, and its restraints are from the things that are
> wrong. The soldier, above all other men, is required to practice the
> greatest act of religious training—sacrifice. In battle and in the face
> of danger and death, he discloses those divine attributes which his
> Maker gave when He created man in His own image. No physical
> courage and no brute instinct can take the place of the Divine help
> which alone can sustain [the soldier]. However horrible the incidents
> of war may be, the soldier who is called upon to offer and to give his
> life for his country is the noblest development of mankind.

★ ★ Patriot's Prayer ★ ★

Gracious heavenly Father, I pray for the safety of soldiers—from America and
other countries—who are standing against evil in this world. Strengthen and encourage them, protect and sustain them, as they face danger and death.

★ ★ Patriot's Promise ★ ★

Hear what God promises to be for His people: "The LORD is my rock and my fortress and my deliverer; my God, my strength, in whom I will trust; my shield and
the horn of my salvation, my stronghold" (Psalm 18:2).

137

The Right to Dissent

Considered by historians as one of journalism's greatest figures, Edward R. Murrow (1908–1965) made this observation:

> If we confuse dissent with disloyalty—if we deny the right of the individual to be wrong, unpopular, eccentric, or unorthodox—if we deny the essence of racial equality, then hundreds of millions in Asia and Africa who are shopping about for a new allegiance will conclude that we are concerned to defend a myth and our present privileged status. Every act that denies or limits the freedom of the individual in this country costs us the . . . confidence of men and women who aspire to that freedom and independence of which we speak and for which our ancestors fought.

★ ★ Patriot's Prayer ★ ★

My loyalty lies with You first, O God. May I obey the laws of this land to the fullest while always having You as my top priority. Let nothing ever divert me from loving You. Please help me keep my eyes focused on You, that I may praise You, God, as long as I live.

★ ★ Patriot's Promise ★ ★

"He does not delight in the strength of the horse; He takes no pleasure in the legs of a man. The LORD takes pleasure in those who fear Him" (Psalm 147:10–11). In this passage, *fear* doesn't mean shaking in your boots or being scared. This fear is standing in awe of who God is, knowing His power and respecting it to the point of total obedience to Him. God promises us that if we fear Him, He will be pleased with us.

If I forget you, O Jerusalem, let my
right hand forget its skill!

PSALM 137:5

The Jewish State, 1948

According to Margaret Truman, the most difficult decision Harry S. Truman faced as president was whether to support the creation of a Jewish homeland in Palestine after World War II. "What I am trying to do is make the whole world safe for Jews," he wrote. In November 1947, he lobbied for the United Nations' resolution that divided Palestine into Jewish and Arab states.

Great Britain announced it would transfer its authority over Palestine to the United Nations by May 14, 1948. On the eve of British withdrawal, most American experts strongly opposed the creation of a Jewish state, warning Truman that Arab countries would cut off oil and unite to destroy the Jews. But Truman weighed the multifaceted concerns and held firm.

On May 14, Israeli statesman and that nation's first prime minister David Ben-Gurion read a declaration of Jewish independence: "The name of our state shall be Israel." At midnight, British rule over Palestine lapsed; eleven minutes later, White House spokesman Charlie Ross announced US recognition. The American statement recognizing the new State of Israel bears President Truman's last-minute handwritten changes.

"With Truman's decision, the hopes of the Jewish people were realized, but so too were Marshall's fears. Arab opponents of the new nation immediately declared war, prompting a bloody struggle over Israel's existence that continues today.

★ ★ Patriot's Prayer ★ ★
Lord, I pray for the peace of Jerusalem. Bring calm and quiet into its gates and silence her enemies. And draw the inhabitants to the Risen and Coming Again Messiah!

★ ★ Patriot's Promise ★ ★
"Pray for the peace of Jerusalem: 'May they prosper who love you'" (Psalm 122:6).

The Power of Prayer

In everything by prayer and supplication,
with thanksgiving, let your requests
be made known to God.

PHILIPPIANS 4:6

General Robert E. Lee (1807–1870) commanded the Confederate Army of Northern Virginia. In 1860, the great general called the nation to prayer with these words:

> Knowing that intercessory prayer is our mightiest weapon and supreme call for Christians today, I pleadingly urge our people everywhere to pray.... Let there be prayer at sunup, at noonday, at sundown, at midnight, all through the day. Let us all pray for our children, our youth, our aged, our pastors, our homes. Let us pray for our churches.
>
> Let us pray for ourselves, that we may not lose concern for those who have never known Jesus Christ and redeeming love, for moral forces everywhere, for our national leaders. Let prayer be our passion. Let prayer be our practice.

★ ★ Patriot's Prayer ★ ★

I want to pray for those today, Lord, who have lost their jobs. Give them courage to face each new day with hope, rooted in Your great faithfulness, that this will be the day they find employment. Be with my loved ones: enable them find peace and joy. Bless my church, dear God, that we may be a light on a hill that cannot be hidden. Anoint my pastor as You never have before.

★ ★ Patriot's Promise ★ ★

The apostle James assures us that "the effective, fervent prayer of a righteous man avails much" (James 5:16). If we pray passionately, our prayers will not float out in space, but they will be significant and meaningful. This is a great promise to keep in mind when praying for yourself as well as for others.

May 15

★ ★
★ 140 ★
★ ★

A tree is known by its fruit.

Genuinely Good Works

Founding Father Benjamin Franklin wrote the following:

I can only show my gratitude for these mercies from God, by a readiness to help His other children and my brethren. For I do not think that thanks and compliments, though repeated weekly, can discharge our real obligations to each other, and much less those to our Creator.

You will see in this my notion of good works, that I am far from expecting to merit heaven by them. By heaven we understand a state of happiness, infinite in degree, and eternal in duration. I can do nothing to deserve such rewards. . . .

The faith you mention has certainly its use in the world. . . . But I wish it were more productive of good works than I have generally seen it; I mean real good works; works of kindness, charity, mercy, and public spirit; not holiday keeping, sermon reading or hearing; performing church ceremonies, or making long prayers, filled with flatteries and compliments. . . .

The worship of God is a duty; the hearing and reading of sermons may be useful; but, if men rest in hearing and praying, as too many do, it is as if a tree should value itself on being watered and putting forth leaves, though it never produce any fruit.

★ ★ Patriot's Prayer ★ ★

Gracious Father, show me what acts of kindness, love, and mercy You would have me do today.

★ ★ Patriot's Promise ★ ★

"If anyone cleanses himself from [dishonor], he will be . . . sanctified and useful for the Master, prepared for every good work" (2 Timothy 2:21).

May 16

Christianity in America

You will keep him in perfect peace,
whose mind is stayed on You.

ISAIAH 26:3

Samuel Chase signed the Declaration of Independence and later served as a justice on the United States Supreme Court. The following is an excerpt from the Court's opinion he wrote for the 1799 case of *Runkel v. Winemiller*:

> Religion is of general and public concern, and on its support depend, in great measure, the peace and good order of government, the safety and happiness of the people. By our form of government, the Christian religion is the established religion; and all sects and denominations of Christians are placed upon the same equal footing, and are equally entitled to protection in their religious liberty.

★ ★ Patriot's Prayer ★ ★

Lord, I praise You for the liberty I enjoy in this country. Thank You especially for freedom to worship You. Protect that freedom, Lord, so that we who are Your people may continue to serve You openly and freely.

★ ★ Patriot's Promise ★ ★

Second Corinthians 3:17 gives us this wonderful assurance: "Where the Spirit of the Lord is, there is liberty."

Righteousness exalts a nation.

PROVERBS 14:34

A Nation Exalted

Patrick Henry was the American Revolutionary leader who pushed through the Stamp Act Resolves in May 1765, the most anti-British political action up to that point. He wrote the following about the Stamp Act:

> Whether this will prove a blessing or a curse will depend upon the use our people make of the blessings, which a gracious God hath bestowed on us. If they are wise, they will be great and happy. If they are of a contrary character, they will be miserable.
>
> Righteousness alone can exalt them as a nation. Reader! Whoever thou art, remember this, and in thy sphere practice virtue thyself, and encourage it in others.

★ ★ Patriot's Prayer ★ ★

Gracious and merciful God, You are with me all the time. So I ask You to give me wisdom to know how to hear Your voice and follow Your direction. Let me never do good works for my own benefit, but for Your glory, Lord.

★ ★ Patriot's Promise ★ ★

First Samuel 26:23 tells us that the Lord will repay every single one of us for our righteousness and faithfulness. If we live according to God's principles and are faithful to Him, He will reward us.

May 18

Choose Life

> I have set before you life and death, blessing and cursing; therefore choose life . . . that you may love the LORD your God, that you may obey His voice, and that you may cling to Him.
>
> MOSES IN DEUTERONOMY 30:19–20

As God's people prepared to enter the land of Canaan after their nearly forty-year sojourn in the desert, Moses took the opportunity to remind the Israelites of both God's faithfulness to them and their obligation to live as His holy, righteous, and chosen people.

The word *deuteronomy* means "a repeating of the law," and this repetition underscores how crucial it is for God's people to keep His Word always on their hearts, minds, and lips. Only then will they be in position for God's blessing in all their endeavors.

As "one nation under God," America has traditionally placed a high priority on remaining faithful to God's Word. Each generation has made it a priority to pass on to the next a commitment to knowing and living by Scripture. Just as He did with the people of Israel, God has set before us life and death, so let us choose life, that our children and children's children may live unto the Lord and under His blessing.

★ ★ Patriot's Prayer ★ ★

Dear Lord, let Your Word be within my heart and upon my lips today so that I might not sin against You (see Psalm 119:11). After all, You are my life and my hope for tomorrow. Teach me to cling to You.

★ ★ Patriot's Promise ★ ★

"The Lord will greatly bless you in the land which the LORD your God is giving you to possess as an inheritance—only if you carefully obey the voice of the LORD your God, to observe with care all these commandments which I command you today" (Deuteronomy 15:4–5).

Seek first the kingdom of God… and all these things shall be added to you.

MATTHEW 6:33

God's Bigger Shovel

Frustrated at his first job—moving dirt in Stockton, California—R. G. Le-Tourneau (1888–1969) was committed to finding a better, more efficient way to get the work done. As the father of the modern earthmoving industry, he is credited with nearly 300 inventions, including the bulldozer, scrapers of all sorts, dredgers, portable cranes, rollers, dump wagons, bridge spans, logging equipment, mobile sea platforms for oil exploration, the electric wheel, and many others. During World War II, he produced 70 percent of all the army's earthmoving machinery.

With Matthew 6:33 as his life verse, LeTourneau felt called to be a "business-man for God," saying that God was the Chairman of his board. Reporting that money came in faster than he could give it away, he established the LeTourneau Foundation to channel 90 percent of his multimillion-dollar salary to Christian endeavors. LeTourneau was convinced that he could not out give God: "I shovel it out, and God shovels it back, but God has a bigger shovel."

Although incredibly successful, LeTourneau's business efforts never deterred him from his reason for existence: to glorify God and spread the gospel. He shared his faith with millions during his life, founded missionary efforts in Liberia and Peru, and, with his wife, founded a college in Longview, Texas. LeTourneau University has produced more than 10,000 alumni who are faithfully serving the Lord in all 50 states and in 55 nations.

★ ★ Patriot's Prayer ★ ★
Father, help me give more to Your work so that people can hear about Your saving grace.

★ ★ Patriot's Promise ★ ★
"He who sows bountifully will also reap bountifully" (2 Corinthians 9:6).

May 20

A Frenchman's Perspective

Jesus said to them, "Have you never read in the Scriptures: '*The stone which the builders rejected has become the chief cornerstone. This was the Lord's doing and it is marvelous in our eyes*'?"

MATTHEW 21:42

In 1835, French historian Alexis de Tocqueville traveled America as it was coming into its own as a nation. He wrote down his observations in *Democracy in America*. This classic book provides unique insights into what made America such a success so quickly. He clearly believed the primary reason to be Christianity.

Here is his description of what he saw happen as American settlers spread across the continent:

> I have known of societies formed by the Americans to send out ministers of the Gospel into the new Western States to found schools and churches there, lest religion should be suffered to die away in those remote settlements, and the rising States be less fitted to enjoy free institutions than the people from which they emanated. I met with wealthy New Englanders who abandoned the country in which they were born in order to lay the foundations of Christianity and of freedom on the banks of the Missouri or in the prairies of Illinois.

★ ★ Patriot's Prayer ★ ★

Lord, thank You for Your sovereign hand in this country's development and growth. Please don't remove that hand of grace and provision. Draw us close to You that we may once again be building our land on the cornerstone of Your truth, which will never pass away.

★ ★ Patriot's Promise ★ ★

"Heaven and earth will pass away, but My words will by no means pass away" (Mark 13:31).

May 21

The light shines in the darkness.

JOHN 1:5

Lighting the World

A philanthropist later in life, Samuel Colgate (1822–1897) was the American manufacturer whose industriousness resulted in the Colgate-Palmolive Company. Clearly, he recognized Jesus as God's Son and the value of the written Word:

The only spiritual light in the world comes through Jesus Christ and the inspired Book; redemption and forgiveness of sin alone through Christ. Without His presence and the teachings of the Bible, we would be enshrouded in moral darkness and despair.

The condition of those nations without a Christ, contrasted with those where Christ is accepted, reveals so marked a difference that no arguments are needed. It is an object lesson so plain that it can be seen and understood by all. May "the earth be full of the knowledge of the Lord, as the waters cover the sea."

★ ★ Patriot's Prayer ★ ★

Lord, shine Your light into this dark world. Convict the dark world of its sin and bring each one of us to a full knowledge of You. Let us see Your glory, dear God, and then live in a way that truly honors You. May we be citizens of a nation that truly honors You.

★ ★ Patriot's Promise ★ ★

The promise of Habakkuk 2:14 has yet to be fulfilled—"The earth will be filled with the knowledge of the glory of the LORD, as the waters cover the sea." What a glorious day that will be!

147

May 22

Samuel Morse

Samuel Morse (1791–1872) was captivated with the notion that electricity could be used to transmit messages instantly. He worked for years before inventing a single-wire telegraph system in 1937 and, with Alfred Vail in the 1840s, the Morse Code.

Although Morse had a patent on his telegraph, it took him years of failures and poverty before he was able to secure the financial backing necessary to implement his project. About those years, he said, "The only gleam of hope . . . is from confidence in God. When I look upward it calms any apprehension for the future, and I seem to hear a voice saying: 'If I clothe the lilies of the field, shall I not also clothe you?' Here is my strong confidence, and I will wait patiently for the direction of Providence."

In 1843, Congress finally awarded Morse $30,000 to construct a telegraph line between Baltimore and Washington. By May 24, 1844, the lines were ready, and the words of the first official message were sent: "What hath God wrought!" in recognition that God had inspired, empowered, and sustained Samuel Morse in this revolutionary effort.

★ ★ Patriot's Prayer ★ ★

Thank You, dear Lord, for being my Strength and Sustainer in seasons of labor, waiting, and frustration. In those times, keep me mindful that You, who clothe the lilies of the field, can and will provide for my every need.

★ ★ Patriot's Promise ★ ★

Jesus said, "Do not worry about your life, what you will eat; nor about the body, what you will put on. Life is more than food, and the body is more than clothing" (Luke 12:22–23). God provides for the lilies of the field and the birds of the air. Certainly He will provide for you, His beloved child.

Turn to Me with all your heart, with fasting, with weeping, and with mourning.

Joel 2:12

A Day of Fasting

After the Boston Tea Party, the British navy retaliated by blockading the port of Boston. The colonies surrounding Massachusetts responded with sympathy and action. On May 24, 1773, the House of Burgesses in Virginia proposed and approved a Day of Fasting, Humiliation, and Prayer:

> This House, being deeply impressed with apprehension of the great dangers to be derived to British America from the hostile invasion of the city of Boston in our Sister Colony of Massachusetts Bay, whose commerce and harbor are, on the first day of June next, to be stopped by an armed force, deem it highly necessary that the said first day of June be set apart, by the members of this House, as a Day of Fasting, Humiliation, and Prayer, devoutly to implore the Divine interposition, for averting the heavy calamity which threatens destruction to our civil rights and the evils of civil war; to give us one heart and mind firmly opposed, by all just and proper means, [to] every injury to American rights; and that the minds of his Majesty and his Parliament, may be inspired from above with wisdom, moderation, and justice, to remove from the loyal people of America all cause of danger from a continued pursuit of measures pregnant with their ruin.

★ ★ Patriot's Prayer ★ ★
Teach me to fast, Lord, so that the discipline is all about You and only for Your glory.

★ ★ Patriot's Promise ★ ★
"Do not appear to men to be fasting . . . your Father who sees in secret will reward you openly" (Matthew 6:18).

Make Your Way Prosperous

This Book of the Law shall not depart from your mouth, but you shall meditate in it day and night, that you may observe to do according to all that is written in it. For then you will make your way prosperous, and then you will have good success.

JOSHUA IN JOSHUA 1:8

Horace Greeley, one of America's leading nineteenth-century newspaper editors, reminded his fellow citizens of what many of the Founding Fathers of the previous generation had emphasized: "Liberty cannot be established without morality, nor morality without faith."

Similarly, as Joshua prepared the children of Israel to begin their conquest of Canaan, he reminded them that their success depended upon keeping God's Word in their hearts and minds and on their lips. He went on to challenge the people of Israel—and the challenge applies to us today, to us as individuals, as families, as a nation—to make an important choice: "Choose for yourselves this day whom you will serve. . . . But as for me and my house, we will serve the LORD" (Joshua 24:15). This choice is foundational to the moral and spiritual resolve that will give us success in all we set out to accomplish as individuals and as a nation.

★ ★ Patriot's Prayer ★ ★

Father in heaven, today I choose to follow You. I will listen for Your voice and seek Your will in all I say and do.

★ ★ Patriot's Promise ★ ★

"Blessed are those who keep my ways. Hear instruction and be wise, and do not disdain it" (Proverbs 8:32–33).

By this we know love, because He laid down His life for us. And we also ought to lay down our lives for the brethren.

1 JOHN 3:16

Freedom for All

Colin Powell, the US Secretary of State (2001–2005) serving under President George W. Bush, stated this truth:

> Over the years, the United States has sent many of its fine young men and women into great peril to fight for freedom beyond our borders. The only amount of land we have ever asked for in return is enough to bury those who did not return.

★ ★ Patriot's Prayer ★ ★

I pray today, Father, for the men and women of our armed forces on foreign and domestic soil. Be with each one of them and protect them as they protect us. Give them strength and courage and show them that You are with them.

★ ★ Patriot's Promise ★ ★

John 3:16 tells us how gracious and generous God was to give His only Son to save us from our sin. First Chronicles 29:17 shows us how we can be an example to others by reflecting God's generosity with our own: "I know also, my God, that You test the heart and have pleasure in uprightness. As for me, in the uprightness of my heart I have willingly offered all these things; and now with joy I have seen Your people, who are present here to offer willingly to You." God's offering of Jesus as our Savior is an example to us. He showed us how to give by the ultimate sacrifice of His Son so that we may know how to give.

May 26

God's Laws for God's Creatures

As Americans know, the Declaration of Independence declared not only the colonies' independence from Britain, but also a dependence on "the Laws of Nature and of Nature's God." These had been defined by historic legal writers, such as Sir William Blackstone, as the laws that God had established for the governance of people, nations, and nature. Blackstone's *Commentaries on the Law*, the primary law book of the Founding Fathers, defined "the laws of nature" as the will of God for man. Blackstone explained:

> Man, considered as a creature, must necessarily be subject to the laws of his Creator, for he is entirely a dependent being.... And consequently ... it is necessary that he should in all points conform to his Maker's will. This will of his Maker is called the law of nature.... It is binding over all the globe, in all countries, and at all times; no human laws are of any validity, if contrary to this....
>
> But every man now finds ... that his reason is corrupt, and his understanding full of ignorance and error. This has given manifold occasion for the benign interposition of Divine Providence.... The doctrines thus delivered we call the revealed or divine law, and they are to be found only in the Holy Scriptures....
>
> Upon these two foundations, the law of nature and the law of revelation, depend all human laws ... no human laws should be suffered to contradict these.

★ ★ Patriot's Prayer ★ ★

Almighty God, lead those who govern as they make decisions that will affect us through the course of our history.

★ ★ Patriot's Promise ★ ★

"The testimony of the LORD is sure, making wise the simple" (Psalm 19:7).

You shall teach [the people] the statutes and the laws, and show them the way in which they must walk and the work they must do.

EXODUS 18:20

Sunday School

Noticing the migration west from the Appalachian cabins to settlements along the Oregon Trail, the American Sunday School Union (ASSU) set as a goal for itself the establishment of a Sunday school in every new community on the western frontier and sent out a large number of Sunday school missionaries to make that happen. These Sunday schools eventually gave rise to thousands of churches across America.

One example of the tremendous influence the Sunday school movement had in American frontier life was the Mississippi Valley Enterprise (MVE), the effort of the ASSU to "establish a Sunday school in every destitute place where it is practicable throughout the Valley of the Mississippi." In fifty years there, the MVE established over 61,000 Sunday schools and enrolled 2,650,000 pupils. Remarkably, during his twenty years of service with the mission, missionary Stephen Paxson, who was born with a speech impediment that later earned him the nickname "Stuttering Stephen," started 1,314 Sunday schools that taught 83,000 students about Jesus' love for them.

★ ★ Patriot's Prayer ★ ★
Lord God, when I speak for Jesus, may I trust that You have gone before me, that You will provide me with words people need to hear, and that Your truth will accomplish what You please in each person's life and my own.

★ ★ Patriot's Promise ★ ★
"Incline your ear, and come to Me. Hear, and your soul shall live" (Isaiah 55:3).

153

Wisdom and Instruction for Life

> Trust in the LORD with all your heart,
> and lean not on your own understanding;
> in all your ways acknowledge Him,
> and He shall direct your paths.
>
> PROVERBS 3:5–6

There is no better source of practical wisdom and instruction for how to live an upright and righteous life than the book of Proverbs. Its counsel, however, is not just relevant to individuals, but to nations as well. Proverbs 14:34, for instance, is a truth that godly leaders have cited for generations: "Righteousness exalts a nation, but sin is a reproach to any people."

Patrick Henry, one of early America's most outspoken Revolutionary leaders, predicted that whether or not the newly formed United States would prove "a blessing or a curse will depend upon the use our people make of the blessings which a gracious God hath bestowed on us. If they are wise, they will be great and happy. If they are of a contrary character, they will be miserable. Righteousness alone can exalt them as a nation."

The state of our nation today suggests we have strayed from God's wisdom. We—as individuals and corporately as a nation—must seek God and His righteousness if we are to continue in His grace.

★ ★ Patriot's Prayer ★ ★

Father in heaven, grant me this day wisdom that I might please You, that I might walk in purity and confidence among those who look to me for leadership and trust my judgment.

★ ★ Patriot's Promise ★ ★

"If any of you lacks wisdom, let him ask of God, who gives to all liberally and without reproach, and it will be given to him" (James 1:5).

[Jerusalem] did not consider her destiny; therefore her collapse was awesome.

LAMENTATIONS 1:9

God's Providence

On Memorial Day in 1923, Calvin Coolidge, the thirtieth president of the United States (1923–1929), spoke about the Puritan forefathers in "The Destiny of America":

> If there be a destiny, it is of no avail to us unless we work with it. The ways of Providence will be of no advantage to us unless we proceed in the same direction. If we perceive a destiny in America, if we believe that Providence has been our guide, our own success, our own salvation requires that we should act and serve in harmony and obedience....
>
> Settlers came here from mixed motives, some for pillage and adventure, some for trade and refuge, but those who have set their imperishable mark upon our institutions came from far higher motives....They were intent upon establishing a Christian commonwealth in accordance to the principle of self-government.
>
> They were an inspired body of men....They had a genius for organized society on the foundations of piety, righteousness, liberty, and obedience of the law. They brought with them the accumulated wisdom and experience of the ages....Who can fail to see ...the hand of destiny? Who can doubt that it has been guided by a Divine Providence?

★ ★ Patriot's Prayer ★ ★

O Lord, thank You for Your hand on this nation. As unworthy as we are, may You never remove it.

★ ★ Patriot's Promise ★ ★

"Be careful to observe [God's laws]; for this is your wisdom and your understanding" (Deuteronomy 4:6).

May 30

Circuit Riders and Farmer-Preachers

Go into all the world and preach the gospel to every creature.

MARK 16:15

As Americans moved out West in the late 1700s, preachers braved the cold weather, the lack of roads, and the threat of Indian attacks to take the gospel to the pioneers.

Led by the colossal efforts of Francis Asbury, who traveled nearly 300,000 miles on horseback and preached more than 16,000 sermons between 1771 and 1816, an army of Methodist circuit riders was inspired to go wherever the pioneers went. In that span of time, the denomination grew in number from only 300 members with four ministers to over 200,000 with 2,000 ministers, many of whom had little formal education but who spoke the language of the frontier folk. The Methodists also gave unprecedented freedom to both women and African-Americans to participate in God's church.

Similarly, the Baptists sent out "farmer-preachers." Most of them had little education and were poorly paid, but they were in touch with the pioneers' lives. With an emphasis on the need for a personal conversion and salvation from sin through faith in Jesus Christ, these ministers spread the gospel far and wide. Just as the Methodists had, the Baptists made it easy for committed laypeople to be involved in God's kingdom work.

★ ★ Patriot's Prayer ★ ★

Lord, may I—like the Methodists and Baptists during the western expansion—see where You're working and get involved. And, Almighty God, empower my efforts to build Your kingdom.

★ ★ Patriot's Promise ★ ★

"He put all things under His feet, and gave Him to be head over all things to the church, which is His body, the fullness of Him who fills all in all" (Ephesians 1:22–23).

June

Words for a College Graduate

William Samuel Johnson (1727–1819), president of Columbia University (King's College before 1784), spoke to the first graduating class after the Revolutionary War:

> You have ... received a public education, the purpose whereof hath been to qualify you the better to serve your Creator and your country....Your first great duties ... are those you owe to Heaven, to your Creator and Redeemer. Let these be ever present to your minds and exemplified in your lives and conduct.
>
> Imprint deep upon your minds the principles of piety toward God, and a reverence and fear of His holy name. The fear of God is the beginning of wisdom, and its consummation is everlasting felicity.... Remember, too, that you are the redeemed of the Lord, that you are bought with a price, even the inestimable price of the precious blood of the Son of God. Adore Jehovah, therefore, as your God and your Judge. Love, fear, and serve Him as your Creator, Redeemer, and Sanctifier. Acquaint yourselves with Him in His Word and holy ordinances.
>
> Make Him your friend and protector and your felicity is secured both here and hereafter. And with respect to particular duties to Him, it is your happiness that you are well assured that he best serves his Maker, who does most good to his country and to mankind.

★ ★ Patriot's Prayer ★ ★

Lord, please give me a humble, teachable spirit now . . . and always.

★ ★ Patriot's Promise ★ ★

Hear the promise Jesus makes: "Take My yoke upon you and learn from Me . . . and you will find rest for your souls" (Matthew 11:29).

June 1

[King Hezekiah] trusted in the
LORD God of Israel.

2 KINGS 18:5

The Key to Survival

On June 2, 1995, US Air Force Captain Scott O'Grady was patrolling the United Nations designated no-fly zone over war-torn Bosnia when, at 27,000 feet, his F-16 fighter was struck by a surface-to-air missile. He desperately pulled his ejection lever and was catapulted into the sky at 350 miles per hour. Remarkably, he managed to land unscathed—but in enemy territory.

For six incredible days and nights, O'Grady eluded capture by the Bosnian Serbs who relentlessly pursued him. Relying in part on his military survival training, O'Grady said his faith in God also sustained him. During his third day on the ground, he experienced the love of God to such a degree that it took away his fear of death. On the sixth day, in a daring daylight rescue, an elite team of Marines moved in with a chopper, dodged enemy fire, and pulled the young American to safety.

At a national press conference following his triumphant return to the US, O'Grady said, "If it weren't for my love for God and God's love for me, I wouldn't be here right now."

★ ★ Patriot's Prayer ★ ★

Thank You, Lord, for the truths, illustrated by Scott O'Grady's experience, that You are with us always and that Your love can and does sustain Your people even in the darkest night.

★ ★ Patriot's Promise ★ ★

Psalm 56:3 says, "Whenever I am afraid, I will trust in You." We do not have to live in fear because God is worthy of our trust, and He will answer when we call upon Him.

God's Light

In June 1630, John Winthrop landed in Massachusetts Bay with 700 people in eleven ships, thus beginning the Great Migration. During this sixteen-year period, more than 20,000 Puritans sailed for New England. The Puritans so believed that this New World would be free of the corruptions in their own church-state homeland, they called their colony a "Zion in wilderness" and "a city upon a hill." In the New England Confederation, Winthrop stated that the aim of the colonists was "to advance the kingdom of our Lord Jesus Christ, and to enjoy the liberties of the gospel thereof in purities and peace."

In 1638, the Reverend John Davenport and Theophilus Eaton established a colony in New Haven, Connecticut. A year later, the Fundamental Orders of Connecticut was adopted. It reads in part:

> "For as much as it hath pleased Almighty God by the wise disposition of His Divine Providence so to order and dispose of things that we the inhabitants and residents . . . ; and well knowing where a people are gathered together the Word of God requires that to maintain the peace and union of such a people there should be an orderly and decent government established according to God, to order and dispose of the affairs of the people at all seasons as occasion shall require."

★ ★ Patriot's Prayer ★ ★

Lord, let my life be a light to people lost in the darkness of sin. If they never read a Bible, Lord, help them to read Jesus in me.

★ ★ Patriot's Promise ★ ★

"If we walk in the light as He is in the light, we have fellowship with one another" (1 John 1:7).

Zion shall be redeemed with justice, and her penitents with righteousness.

ISAIAH 1:27

Criminal Punishment

Consider this bit of history, shared by Charles Colson, special counsel to President Richard Nixon and founder of Prison Fellowship:

> Imprisonment as a primary means of criminal punishment is a relatively modern concept. It was turned to as a humane alternative to the older patterns of harsh physical penalties for nearly all crimes. Quakers introduced the concept in Pennsylvania.
>
> The first American prison was established in Philadelphia when the Walnut Street Jail was converted into a series of solitary cells where offenders were kept in solitary confinement. The theory was that they would become "penitents," confessing their crimes before God and thereby gaining a spiritual rehabilitation. Hence, the name "penitentiary"—a place for penitents.

★ ★ Patriot's Prayer ★ ★

Lord, I pray for those in prison today. Every man and every woman is free to accept Your forgiveness if they repent of their sins, no matter how heinous those sins might be. I pray that, despite and within the prison walls, they will find freedom from sin through the blood of Jesus Christ.

★ ★ Patriot's Promise ★ ★

The apostle John boldly and confidently stated this promise: "If we confess our sins, He is faithful and just to forgive us our sins and to cleanse us from all unrighteousness" (1 John 1:9). That promise applies to all people, no matter their circumstances.

Fulfilling Our Responsibilities

In those days there was no king in Israel; everyone did what was right in his own eyes.

JUDGES 21:25

US Supreme Court Justice Clarence Thomas recalls that when he was growing up, his grandfather taught him some important foundational lessons about the connection between personal responsibility and liberty: "What my grandfather believed was that people have their responsibilities and that if they are left alone to fulfill their responsibilities, that is freedom . . . Honesty and responsibility, those are the things [my grandfather] taught."

Justice Thomas added that in today's society, there is not enough emphasis on the responsibilities of all Americans to live in such a way that will maintain and protect the foundations of freedom. "Too many conversations today have to do with rights and wants," he noted. "There is not enough talk about responsibilities and duties."

The book of Judges offers a graphic demonstration of the consequences of such self-seeking behavior among the citizens of a nation—and of the need for personal and collective humility, repentance, and steadfast faith in God if a nation is to turn back to righteousness.

★ ★ Patriot's Prayer ★ ★

Lord God, I pray that America, the land that I do love, will turn once again toward You. Help us see the need for repentance and restoration to righteousness, and begin this work today in my own heart.

★ ★ Patriot's Promise ★ ★

"If My people who are called by My name will humble themselves, and pray and seek My face, and turn from their wicked ways, then I will hear from heaven, and will forgive their sin and heal their land" (2 Chronicles 7:14).

I set my face toward the Lord God
to make request by prayer.

Daniel 9:3

A D-Day Prayer

President Franklin D. Roosevelt read this prayer, originally entitled "Let Our Hearts Be Stout," over radio to an anxious nation as Allied troops were invading Nazi-occupied Europe on D-Day, June 6, 1944:

> Almighty God, our sons, pride of our nation, this day have set upon a mighty endeavor, a struggle to preserve our Republic, our religion, and our civilization, and to set free a suffering humanity. Lead them straight and true; give strength to their arms, stoutness to their hearts, steadfastness in their faith.

> They will need Thy blessings. Their road will be long and hard. For the enemy is strong.... Success may not come with rushing speed, but ... we know that by Thy grace, and by the righteousness of our cause, our sons will triumph....

> [Our men] fight to liberate. They fight to let justice arise and tolerance and goodwill among all Thy people. They yearn but for the end of battle, for their return to the haven of home. Some will never return. Embrace these, Father, and receive them, Thy heroic servants, into Thy kingdom.

> With Thy blessing, we shall prevail over the unholy forces of our enemy.... Lead us to the saving of our country, and with our sister nations into a world unity that will spell a sure peace....

> Thy will be done, Almighty God. Amen.

★ ★ Patriot's Prayer ★ ★

Lord, I pray for the men and women—and their families—who are making sacrifices to protect my freedom. Thank You for their willingness to stand against evil in this world.

★ ★ Patriot's Promise ★ ★

"The face of the Lord is against those who do evil" (Psalm 34:16).

★ 163 ★

Thomas Paine's
Common Sense

The LORD reigns; let the peoples tremble!

PSALM 99:1

In early 1776, Americans still hoped for reconciliation with Britain, and the British were preparing to take advantage of that sentiment with a generous offer of peace that many Americans would have welcomed. But then Thomas Paine anonymously published the political pamphlet *Common Sense* in January 1776. In it he presented the American colonists with a convincing argument for independence from British rule, an argument that resonated with the colonists. In the first year alone, over five hundred thousand copies were sold, and the passion for independence caught fire.

To make his case to the people, Paine structured *Common Sense* like a sermon and relied on biblical references and allusions, such as, "But where, says some, is the king of America? I'll tell you, friend, He reigns above." Paine's vision stirred the colonists to strengthen their resolve. By spring 1776, there was significant support for American independence, and the Virginia Convention voted to instruct their delegates to Congress to propose that the colonies formally declare their independence. On June 7, Richard Henry Lee moved that Congress declare the United Colonies to be free and independent.

★ ★ Patriot's Prayer ★ ★

May You, O Lord, be lifted up, You who are the true and only King, the King of kings, who reigns from above.

★ ★ Patriot's Promise ★ ★

When Jesus said, "'If I am lifted up from the earth, [I] will draw all peoples to Myself,'" He revealed—with a promise—how He would die (John 12:32). When we lift up Christ with our words and actions, He promises to influence the hearts of others to name Him as their Savior and Lord.

June 7

Where then is my hope?

The Second Fatherland

Richard Wurmbrand (1909–2001), a Romanian evangelical Christian minister and author who spent a total of fourteen years imprisoned in Romania for his faith, founded the Voice of the Martyrs, an interdenominational organization working with and for persecuted Christians around the world. In 1967, he shared his view of America:

> Every freedom-loving man has two fatherlands; his own and America. Today, America is the hope of every enslaved man, because it is the last bastion of freedom in the world. Only America has the power and spiritual resources to stand as a barrier between militant communism and the people of the world.
>
> It is the last dike holding back the rampaging floodwaters of militant communism. If it crumples, there is no other dike, no other dam; no other line of defense to fall back upon.
>
> America is the last hope of millions of enslaved peoples. They look to it as their second fatherland. In it lie their hopes and prayers.
>
> I have seen fellow-prisoners in communist prisons beaten, tortured, with fifty pounds of chains on their legs—praying for America . . . that the dike will not crumple; that it will remain free.

★ ★ Patriot's Prayer ★ ★

Lord, I place my hope in You who are totally trustworthy. I entrust to You my future, all that I have, and all I will ever be.

★ ★ Patriot's Promise ★ ★

Psalm 130:7 calls us to "hope in the Lord; for with the Lord there is mercy, and with Him is abundant redemption."

The Great Awakening

Will You not revive us again, that Your people may rejoice in You?

PSALM 85:6

British preacher George Whitefield made seven trips to America and spent nine years preaching throughout the colonies. God used his messages to prompt the Great Awakening: between 1740 and 1742, an estimated 25,000 to 50,000 people were added to the New England church.

The revival spread first into the Middle Colonies, beginning in New Jersey largely among the Presbyterians trained under William Tennent, and then it reached the South as Samuel Davies preached among the Presbyterians of Virginia (1748–1759) and the Baptists in North Carolina (1760s). There was also a rapid spread of Methodism shortly before the American Revolution.

The Great Awakening served to build up interests that were intercolonial in character, and it increased opposition to the Anglican Church and the royal officials who supported it. Both these results, many historians say, sparked a democratic spirit that fueled America's quest for political freedom. The Great Awakening is also credited with an outburst of missionary activity among Native Americans by such men as David Brainerd; the first significant movement against slavery; and the founding of several colleges, notably Princeton, Brown, Rutgers, and Dartmouth.

★ ★ Patriot's Prayer ★ ★

Refresh my personal faith, dear Lord. Awaken my soul to a new and brighter knowledge of You and of Your will for my life. Guide me, Father, so I will live according to Your Word and after the example of Christ so that others see Jesus in me.

★ ★ Patriot's Promise ★ ★

"Ask for the old paths, where the good way is, and walk in it; then you will find rest for your souls" (Jeremiah 6:16).

> I have blotted out, like a thick cloud, your transgressions, and like a cloud, your sins. Return to Me, for I have redeemed you.

ISAIAH 44:22

B y the year 1800, nearly a million people had made their way west, settling west of the Blue Ridge in Virginia, Kentucky, Tennessee, the Northwest, and the Indian Territory. Most of these hardy souls did not have access to a church, but a second great spiritual revival began and continued into the 1830s.

Many historians consider Logan County in Kentucky its starting point. There, in 1799, several Methodist and Presbyterian ministers joined efforts. An 1801 gathering held at Cane Ridge, Kentucky, drew perhaps as many as 15,000 to 20,000 people. More than 10,000 people joined Kentucky churches between 1800 and 1803. This great revival quickly spread throughout Kentucky, as well as into Tennessee and southern Ohio.

Contributing to this spread of the gospel was the Methodist Church's efficient organization of "districts," each of which was served by preachers who traveled from church to church. These circuit riders came from among the common people, enabling them to establish a rapport with the frontier families they hoped to bring to faith. These itinerant preachers also promoted "Sunday schools" where children learned reading, writing, and arithmetic. They laid the ground for the Holy Spirit to do His work of revival.

★ ★ Patriot's Prayer ★ ★

Thank You, Lord, for Your forgiveness—the key to personal as well as national revival. Enable me to extend that same grace of forgiveness to those who hurt and offend me.

★ ★ Patriot's Promise ★ ★

"If you forgive men their trespasses, your heavenly Father will also forgive you" (Matthew 6:14).

June 10

Spiritual Revival = Social Change

What then shall I do with Jesus who is called Christ?

PILATE IN MATTHEW 27:22

The Second Great Awakening focused primarily on personal salvation, but it had a huge impact on American society as well. Through a multitude of channels, this revival encouraged Christians to become involved in social causes like prison reform, temperance, women's suffrage, and the crusade to abolish slavery.

Consider Charles Finney, one of the greatest American preachers in the 1800s and president of Ohio's Oberlin College. He strongly supported giving freedom to the slaves, so the college was a busy station for the Underground Railroad, secretly guiding slaves to freedom. Oberlin was also among the first American colleges to educate blacks and women alongside white men. Finney also helped form a network of volunteer societies to address social problems. By 1834, their combined budget was nearly as large as the federal budget of that time.

During Boston revivals, fifty thousand people put their faith in Christ in a single week. Finney always demanded an answer to this question: "What will you do with Jesus Christ?" Across America during the Second Great Awakening, hundreds of thousands responded by putting their faith in Christ and then, as salt and light, making a difference in the social fabric of the day.

★ ★ Patriot's Prayer ★ ★

Lord God, heal my blindness to Your presence and my insensitivity to Your leading. I do once again commit my way to you, Lord. I trust You; help my lack of trust.

★ ★ Patriot's Promise ★ ★

"Commit your way to the LORD, trust also in Him, and He shall bring it to pass" (Psalm 37:5).

The word of God is . . . a discerner of the thoughts and intents of the heart.

HEBREWS 4:12

In the first half of the twentieth century, Dr. Howard A. Kelly was a pioneer in the field of gynecology and radium therapy, a professor at Johns Hopkins University, a surgeon at John Hopkins Hospital, and the author of twenty books and five hundred articles.

When asked, Dr. Kelly shared the secret of his greatness:

> I rise regularly at six, and after dressing, give all of my time until our eight o'clock breakfast to the study of God's Word. I find time for brief studies during the day and again in the evening. I make it a general rule to touch nothing but the Bible after the evening meal.

What difference did the Bible make in Dr. Kelly's life?

> The Bible . . . reveals to me, as does no other book in the world, that which appeals to a physician—a clear diagnosis of my spiritual condition, showing me clearly what I am by nature, one lost in sin and alienated from life that is in God. I find it to be a consistent and wonderful revelation, from Genesis to Revelation, of the character of God. . . . It also reveals a tenderness and nearness of God in Christ that satisfies the heart's yearnings and presents the infinite God, Creator of the world, as taking our very nature upon Him in infinite love to become one of His people in order to redeem them.

★ ★ Patriot's Prayer ★ ★

Lord, may I follow Dr. Kelly's example and become a serious student of Your Word.

★ ★ Patriot's Promise ★ ★

"Your word is a lamp to my feet and a light to my path" (Psalm 119:105).

An Earnest Prayer

Elijah was a man with a nature like ours, and he prayed earnestly.

JAMES 5:17

The prayer below was written by George Washington at Newburgh, New York, at the close of the Revolutionary War on June 14, 1783. He sent it to the thirteen governors of the newly freed states in a "Circular Letter Addressed to the Governors of all the States on the Disbanding of the Army":

> I now make it my earnest prayer that God would have you, and the State over which you preside, in His holy protection; that He would incline the hearts of the citizens to cultivate a spirit of subordination and obedience to government, to entertain a brotherly affection and love for one another, for their fellow-citizens of the United States at large, and particularly for brethren who have served in the field; and finally that He would most graciously be pleased to dispose us all to do justice, to love mercy, and to demean ourselves with that charity, humility, and pacific temper of mind, which were the characteristics of the Divine Author of our blessed religion, and without an humble imitation of whose example in these things, we can never hope to be a happy nation.

★ ★ Patriot's Prayer ★ ★

God, I am well aware of how often my prayers are far from earnest. Forgive me, Lord, and kindle within me a fire for prayer, that I may partner with You in Your kingdom work in my family, my community, and this land.

★ ★ Patriot's Promise ★ ★

Proverbs 14:21 assures us that "he who has mercy on the poor, happy is he."

The glory has departed from Israel!

1 Samuel 4:21

"A Nation's Flag"

Henry Ward Beecher, a prominent nineteenth-century Congregationalist clergyman and social reformer, stated this:

A thoughtful mind, when it sees a nation's flag, sees not the flag only, but the nation itself; and whatever may be its symbols, its insignia, he reads chiefly in the flag the government, the principles, the truths, the history which belongs to the nation that sets it forth.

★ ★ Patriot's Prayer ★ ★

Dear God, I know that, as a Christian, I may be the only Bible that some people ever read. I want to always be aware of that. Help me to act and react in a way that shows Jesus to those around me. May those with whom I come in contact today see the love of Jesus as a banner in my life.

★ ★ Patriot's Promise ★ ★

"And in that day there shall be a Root of Jesse, who shall stand as a banner to the people; for the Gentiles shall seek Him, and His resting place shall be glorious" (Isaiah 11:10). God promised us Jesus as our banner, and that will be glory to us. Jesus is our banner.

A New Start

Set magistrates and judges who may judge all the people . . . all such as know the laws of your God.

EZRA 7:25

It wasn't long after the colonists defeated the Red Coats that the state governments that had been controlled by the British had to be established with new state constitutions. It is interesting to read what many of the men who signed the founding documents placed in their original new state constitutions. Delaware provides one example, but other states were similar:

> Every person appointed to public office shall say, "I do profess faith in God the Father, and in Jesus Christ His only Son, and in the Holy Ghost, one God, blessed for evermore; and I do acknowledge the Holy Scriptures of the Old and New Testament to be given by divine inspiration."

★ ★ Patriot's Prayer ★ ★

Through all I say and do this day may I profess my faith in You. May Your Name be lifted high in my life today, Lord God, so that You will be glorified, as You deserve!

★ ★ Patriot's Promise ★ ★

What the Delaware constitution mandated, Jesus promises to reward: "Whoever confesses Me before men, him I will also confess before My Father who is in heaven" (Matthew 10:32).

> The LORD rewarded me according to my righteousness; according to the cleanness of my hands He has recompensed me. For I have kept the ways of the LORD, and have not wickedly departed from my God.
>
> 2 SAMUEL 22:21–22

A Reward for the Righteous

As he sought God's will from the throne, King David's choices dramatically impacted the plight of his people. Likewise, choices made by our nation's leaders can and do determine whether we will suffer or be blessed as a nation. America's Founding Fathers took very seriously this truth about their responsibility as leaders.

John Adams, the second president of the United States, wrote that America's tradition of liberty "is productive of everything which is great and excellent among men. But its principles are as easily destroyed as human nature is corrupted." Noting that effective government can only be built upon a solidly moral foundation, he concluded, "Private and public virtue is the only foundation of Republics."

Choices—by nations as well as by individuals—have consequences for good or for bad.

★ ★ Patriot's Prayer ★ ★

Lord, help me this day to make the right choices—choices that honor You. When I cannot easily decide the path to take, take me by the hand and lead me in the way that You would have me to go.

★ ★ Patriot's Promise ★ ★

God has promised to speak a word to His children whenever we face a decision: "The LORD will guide you continually . . ." (Isaiah 58:11). That is a reward of the righteous.

June 16

The Qualified One

[These redeemed are the ones] who follow the Lamb wherever He goes.

REVELATION 14:4

Benjamin Rush, a signer of the Declaration of Independence who worked with the Rev. Richard Allen to found the AME church, served in the administrations of three different presidents, each of whom was from a different political party. Once when he was asked about his own party affiliation, he said this:

> I have been alternately called an Aristocrat and a Democrat. I am now neither. I am a Christ-ocrat. I believe all power . . . will always fail of producing order and happiness in the hands of man. He alone who created and redeemed man is qualified to govern him.

★ ★ Patriot's Prayer ★ ★

Lord God, I promise my loyalty to You above all parties or politics. I believe that You are the only One who is qualified, by Your Word, to govern men and women. It is on Your Word that I will stand.

★ ★ Patriot's Promise ★ ★

In John 14:21 Jesus says, "He who has My commandments and keeps them, it is he who loves Me. And he who loves Me will be loved by My Father, and I will love him and manifest Myself to him."

> Behold, how good and how pleasant it is for brethren to dwell together in unity!
>
> PSALM 133:1

A Nation Divided

America's Civil War was hardly a one-issue conflict. Political disagreements between the North and South began soon after the American Revolution ended in 1782, and those arguments escalated between 1800 and 1860. Quarrels over unfair taxes paid on foreign goods brought into the South as well as perceived shifts of political power in the federal government to favor the Northern and Midwestern states fueled the South's call for less federal authority in Washington and a restoration of states' rights.

The 1860 election of Abraham Lincoln as president was the last straw for the South. A Republican, Lincoln was considered friendly to abolitionists and northern businessmen. Seven states seceded from the United States. They formed the "Confederate States of America" and elected as their first president Jefferson Davis, a Democratic senator and champion of states' rights from Mississippi. Soon the Civil War raged.

Expected to be over in three months, the war lasted four horrible years (1861–1865), and the cost was more American lives than in all other American wars combined: over 360,000 Union and approximately 260,000 Confederate soldiers died. It remains the greatest, and the most tragic, event in American history, where an incalculable sacrifice of "brothers' blood" was spilled to restore to one a nation bitterly torn in two.

★ ★ Patriot's Prayer ★ ★

Lord God, help this country avoid war—and protect our men and women who are already serving on the frontlines around the world.

★ ★ Patriot's Promise ★ ★

"Walk worthy of the calling with which you were called, with all lowliness and gentleness, with longsuffering, bearing with one another in love, endeavoring to keep the unity of the Spirit in the bond of peace" (Ephesians 4:1–3).

175

Character: The Bottom Line

You shall select from all the people able men, such as fear God.

EXODUS 18:21

Noah Webster (1758–1843) was known as the "Father of American Scholarship and Education" and author of the famous Webster's dictionary. He also had opinions about government leaders:

> In selecting men for office, let principle be your guide. Regard not the particular sect [party] of the candidate—look to his character.... It is alleged by men of loose principles or defective views of the subject that religion and morality are not necessary or important qualifications for political stations. But the Scriptures teach a different doctrine. They direct that rulers should be men "who rule in the fear of God, able men, such as fear God, men of truth, hating covetousness."

★ ★ Patriot's Prayer ★ ★

Lord God, when I go to the polls, guide my thoughts. May my vote be Your vote, a person of character and a person who is in office to serve You.

★ ★ Patriot's Promise ★ ★

When David was a puzzling choice for king, God explained, "The LORD does not see as man sees; for man looks at the outward appearance, but the LORD looks at the heart" (1 Samuel 16:7). This truth about God's perspective sets forth our priorities. The Lord promises to look at your heart. What will be your response to that truth?

Seek righteousness, seek humility.

ZEPHANIAH 2:3

One Great Political Idea

Frederick Douglass was one of the most influential civil rights leaders of the nineteenth century. A former slave who taught himself to read, Douglass gained his freedom and became a prolific writer and counselor to President Lincoln. Hear Douglass's ideas about politics:

> I have one great political idea. . . . That idea is an old one. It is widely and generally assented to; nevertheless, it is very generally trampled upon and disregarded. The best expression of it, I have found in the Bible. It is in substance: "Righteousness exalteth a nation; sin is a reproach to any people." This constitutes my politics—the negative and positive of my politics, and the whole of my politics. . . . I feel it my duty to do all in my power to infuse this idea into the public mind, that it may speedily be recognized and practiced upon by our people.

★ ★ Patriot's Prayer ★ ★

I pray, Lord, that I would seek righteousness today. I also ask You to help me be a positive influence, an example of what is good and right, to those around me.

★ ★ Patriot's Promise ★ ★

Hear the promise of Job: "He does not withdraw His eyes from the righteous; but they are on the throne with kings, for He has seated them forever, and they are exalted" (Job 36:7). God tells us that if we are righteous, He will seat us in places of influence.

Virtue's Role

Be an example to the believers in word, in conduct, in love, in spirit, in faith, in purity.

1 TIMOTHY 4:12

On June 21, 1776, John Adams, the man who would one day be the second president of the United States, wrote this:

Statesmen . . . may plan and speculate for liberty, but it is religion and morality alone which can establish the principles upon which freedom can securely stand.

The only foundation of a free constitution is pure virtue, and if this cannot be inspired into our people in a greater measure, than they have it now, they may change their rulers and the forms of government, but they will not obtain a lasting liberty.

★ ★ Patriot's Prayer ★ ★

Father, may we, in this country, understand the importance of virtue to the sustaining of our nation and our way of life. Help me be virtuous in my thoughts, my words, and my actions today.

★ ★ Patriot's Promise ★ ★

Philippians 4:8–9 is a promise of peace: "Finally, brethren, whatever things are true, whatever things are noble, whatever things are just, whatever things are pure, whatever things are lovely, whatever things are of good report, if there is any virtue and if there is anything praiseworthy—meditate on these things. The things which you learned and received and heard and saw in me, these do, and the God of peace will be with you."

Faith comes by hearing, and hearing
by the word of God.

Romans 10:17

Freedom to Teach

In the July 1993 case of *Crowley, Gaines, and Ries v. Tilton*, the Oklahoma State Court, Tulsa County, granted the defendants summary judgment. Here is part of the argument:

> Initially Christianity was taught by Christ. He then taught disciples who went out over the world to teach others. This process has spread to a major world body of believers. Religion should be permitted to use contemporary means to communicate religious messages in the form of TV appeal to mass audiences, follow-up communication by computerized mailing designed to convert, and symbolic tokens to cause response to the messages.
>
> The context of the message is belief, and the freedom for belief is absolute. When a minister or a church urges one to take certain actions based upon a representation that God will act toward that person in positive and rewarding ways, they are entitled to absolute protection as a belief.

★ ★ Patriot's Prayer ★ ★

Father, send into the world people to preach Your Gospel. Give them words to say that will—by Your Spirit—compel men and women, boys and girls, to accept Jesus Christ as their Savior and Lord.

★ ★ Patriot's Promise ★ ★

In 2 Timothy 4:2, Paul charged Timothy, "Preach the word," and that is God's charge to us believers today. It is our duty to spread the gospel and share the promise of salvation with all who will hear.

When Kings Un-King Themselves

> Now your kingdom shall not continue.
>
> 1 Samuel 13:14

In the lines below, Jonathan Mayhew (1720–1766), a Congregational minister and distinguished Dudlein Lecturer at Harvard in 1765, reflected the colonists' feelings toward King George III's hated Stamp Act:

> The king is as much bound by his oath not to infringe the legal rights of the people, as the people are bound to yield subjection to him. From whence it follows that as soon as the prince sets himself above the law, he loses the king in the tyrant. He does, to all intents and purposes, un-king himself.

★ ★ Patriot's Prayer ★ ★

God, You are my only King. I thank You that I do not live under the rule of a mere man, but of You who are wise and just.

★ ★ Patriot's Promise ★ ★

Exodus 19:5 gives us a very great incentive to keep God alone as our King: "Now therefore, if you will indeed obey My voice and keep My covenant, then you shall be a special treasure to Me above all people; for all the earth is Mine." All believers are God's special treasure when we keep His commands.

I exhort . . . that supplications, prayers, intercessions, and giving of thanks be made for . . . all who are in authority.

1 TIMOTHY 2:1–2

Pray for America

It is our responsibility as believers to pray for America. The Supreme Court, Congress, and the president are not our hope. Only God Himself can sustain this nation.

We must humble ourselves and confess the sins of our nation as well as our own lives. God has said, "If My people who are called by My name will humble themselves, and pray and seek My face, and turn from their wicked ways, then I will hear . . . forgive their sin and heal their land" (2 Chronicles 7:14).

We must pray for our leaders. Ask the Lord to give godly wisdom, protection, and direction to the president, Congress, state and local officials, judges, and anyone else God has raised up to lead. Our mandate is to intercede for those in authority—nonbelievers and believers alike—and trust the Lord to restore godliness to our nation and communities.

We must ask the Lord to work in the hearts of believers and people from all walks of life. Only He has the power to free people from the sins that destroy both their lives and this nation.

We must pray for families, school systems, the military, the economy, and the media. We need to be aware of what is going on—and pray.

★ ★ Patriot's Prayer ★ ★
Father, give our leaders wisdom, forgive our nation from its sins, and grant Your people courage and wisdom as we stand for Your principles.

★ ★ Patriot's Promise ★ ★
"The effective, fervent prayer of a righteous man avails much" (James 5:16).

181

The Lord's Side

Moses stood in the entrance of the camp, and said, "Whoever is on the LORD's side—come to me!"

EXODUS 32:26

As the Civil War escalated, most people in the South believed that, with the North threatening their way of life, it was their sovereign right to secede from the Union. The North believed the South was in rebellion and, if allowed to secede, would destroy the republic.

In a letter to Horace Greeley, whose strong antislavery newspaper editorials helped stir the North to oppose slavery, Abraham Lincoln said that his first priority was saving the Union, not destroying slavery. But to save the Union meant solving the problem of slavery: a constitutional government founded on the principle of equality for all had come to a breaking point.

Ironically, each side believed unequivocally that God was on its side. From early colonial days, New England political and religious leaders had considered themselves God's "chosen people." With the start of the Civil War, Southerners invoked "the favor and guidance of Almighty God" in their constitution, proclaiming themselves a Christian nation. People of all walks of life—ministers, generals, political leaders, and newspaper editors—claimed that God had ordained the war and was sovereign to determine all its outcomes.

The real issue, though, was who was on the Lord's side.

★ ★ Patriot's Prayer ★ ★

Lord, show me today where I am more concerned about Your being on my side rather than my being on Your side. And help me make that paradigm shift: I want to be on Your side.

★ ★ Patriot's Promise ★ ★

"If you are Christ's, then you are Abraham's seed, and heirs according to the promise" (Galatians 3:29).

> Stand fast therefore in the liberty by which Christ has made us free, and do not be entangled again with a yoke of bondage.

GALATIANS 5:1

The History of Liberty

The twenty-eighth president of the United States (1913–1921), Woodrow Wilson was also a distinguished historian and a well-read student of government. He had much to say about the history of liberty and what we can learn from that history today:

> The history of liberty is the history of resistance. The history of liberty is a history of the limitation of governmental power, not the increase of it. When we resist the concentration of power, we are resisting the powers of death. Concentration of power precedes the destruction of human liberties.

★ ★ Patriot's Prayer ★ ★

My prayer today, Father, is that we Americans will always be aware that You are the source of our liberty and that if we, as a nation, turn our liberty over to men, then we will lose this precious gift You have entrusted to us.

★ ★ Patriot's Promise ★ ★

Jesus said in Matthew 28:20, "I am with you always, even to the end of the age." Rest in the assurance that, regardless of your circumstances, the Lord will always be with you.

June 26

God's Place

The LORD God . . . sent warnings
to them by His messengers.

2 CHRONICLES 36:15

On June 27, 1962, two days after the Supreme Court declared prayer in schools unconstitutional, Democratic Senator Robert Byrd warned Congress about such disastrous decisions:

> Inasmuch as our greatest leaders have shown no doubt about God's proper place in the American birthright, can we, in our day, dare do less? . . . In no other place in the United States are there so many, and such varied official evidences of deep and abiding faith in God on the part of government as there are in Washington. . . .
>
> Every session of the House and the Senate begins with prayer. Each house has its own chaplain.
>
> A small room in the Capitol, just off the rotunda, [is] for the private prayer and meditation of members of Congress. . . . The room's focal point is a stained glass window showing George Washington kneeling in prayer . . . [and] these words from Psalm 16:1: "Preserve me, O God, for in Thee do I put my trust." . . .
>
> "In God We Trust" appears opposite the vice-president of the United States. The same phrase . . . backdrops the Speaker of the House of Representatives.
>
> Above the head of the Chief Justice of the Supreme Court are the Ten Commandments, with the great American eagle protecting them. Moses is included among the great lawgivers in Herman A. MacNeil's marble sculpture group on the east front. . . .
>
> To remove God from this country will destroy it.

★ ★ **Patriot's Prayer** ★ ★

God, watch over and reawaken this nation to Your power and glory.

★ ★ **Patriot's Promise** ★ ★

"Blessed is the nation whose God is the LORD" (Psalm 33:12).

Heaven and earth will pass away, but My words will by no means pass away.

JESUS IN LUKE 21:33

The General Principles of Liberty

In a letter to Thomas Jefferson on June 28, 1813, John Adams wrote this:

The general principles, on which the Fathers achieved independence, were the only principles in which that beautiful assembly of young gentlemen could unite....And what were these general principles? I answer, the general principles of Christianity, in which all these sects were united: And the general principles of English and American liberty, in which all those young men united, and which had united all parties in America, in majorities sufficient to assert and maintain her independence.

Now I will avow, that I then believed, and now believe, that those general principles of Christianity, are as eternal and immutable, as the existence and attributes of God; and that those principles of liberty, are as unalterable as human nature and our terrestrial, mundane system.

★ ★ Patriot's Prayer ★ ★

Gracious heavenly Father, I acknowledge the value of the principles of Christianity: they are the cornerstone of this great nation. That being the case, ground us once again in those truths. Make us a nation that truly shines Your light in this darkened world.

★ ★ Patriot's Promise ★ ★

Psalm 119:160 says, "The entirety of Your word is truth, and every one of Your righteous judgments endures forever." The Word of God is therefore a place of refuge, a source of strength, and the rock upon which we can build our lives.

June 28

"America the Beautiful"

I will meditate on the glorious splendor of Your majesty.

PSALM 145:5

America the Beautiful" was written by professor, poet, and writer Katharine Lee Bates (1859–1929) after an inspiring trip to the top of Pikes Peak, Colorado, in 1893. She said, "All the wonder of America seemed displayed there, with the sea-like expanse." Such was the inspiration for this hymn:

O beautiful for spacious skies,
For amber waves of grain,
For purple mountain majesties
Above the fruited plain!
America! America!
God shed His grace on thee,
And crown thy good with brotherhood
From sea to shining sea!

O beautiful for pilgrim feet
Whose stern impassion'd stress
A thoroughfare for freedom beat
Across the wilderness.
America! America!
God mend thine ev'ry flaw,
Confirm thy soul in self-control,
Thy liberty in law.

O beautiful for heroes prov'd
In liberating strife,
Who more than self their country loved,
And mercy more than life.
America! America!
May God thy gold refine
Till all success be nobleness,
And ev'ry gain divine.

O beautiful for patriot dream
That sees beyond the years
Thine alabaster cities gleam
Undimmed by human tears.
America! America!
God shed His grace on thee,
And crown thy good with brotherhood
From sea to shining sea.

★ ★ Patriot's Prayer ★ ★

Thank You, Father, for the beauty of this land You have blessed us with. May we do all we can to protect the beauty of America as well as the freedom we enjoy.

★ ★ Patriot's Promise ★ ★

"A faithful man will abound with blessings" (Proverbs 28:20).

June 29

Give thanks to the LORD, for he is
good; his love endures forever.

PSALM 118:1 NIV

In 1564, René de Laudonniere led a group of Huguenots (Protestants from France) to colonize and build Fort Caroline near present-day Jacksonville, Florida. Here is his journal entry for June 30, 1564: "We sang a psalm of thanksgiving unto God, beseeching Him that it would please Him to continue His accustomed goodness toward us."

Many times we find ourselves complacent about the goodness that God so consistently and generously showers us with. We must be careful to always give thanks for the goodness and love that He shows us each and every day. The consequences of forgetting the goodness of God are tragic. Eternally so.

★ ★ **Patriot's Prayer** ★ ★

My gracious heavenly Father, thank You for Your goodness and love that will sustain me, my family, and this nation forever. I sing songs of praise and thanksgiving to You today!

★ ★ **Patriot's Promise** ★ ★

Jeremiah 30:19 tells what God will do for those who give Him thanks: "I will multiply them, and they shall not diminish; I will also glorify them, and they shall not be small."

July

The law of the Spirit of life in Christ
Jesus has made me free.

ROMANS 8:2

Adopted on July 4, 1776, the Declaration of Independence stated that the thirteen American colonies were "Free and Independent States" and that "all political connection between them and the State of Great Britain, is and ought to be totally dissolved." Our Founding Fathers acknowledged God as the source of our rights:

> We hold these truths to be self-evident, that all men are created equal, that they are endowed by their Creator with certain unalienable Rights, that among these are Life, Liberty and the pursuit of Happiness—That to secure these rights, Governments are instituted among Men, deriving their just Powers from the consent of the governed—That whenever any Form of Government becomes destructive of these ends, it is the Right of the People to alter or to abolish it, and to institute new Government, laying its foundation on such principles and organizing its powers in such form, as to them shall seem most likely to effect their Safety and Happiness....
>
> For the support of this Declaration, with a firm reliance on the protection of Divine Providence, we mutually pledge to each other our Lives, our Fortunes and our sacred Honor.

As Founding Father Benjamin Rush said:

> "Without [religion] there can be no virtue, and without virtue there can be no liberty, and liberty is the object and life of all republican governments."

★ ★ Patriot's Prayer ★ ★

Lord, You gave us our basic rights. May we therefore live as You would have us live.

★ ★ Patriot's Promise ★ ★

"The LORD gives freedom" (Psalm 146:7).

Sharing America's Song

For I know the thoughts that I think toward you, says the LORD, thoughts . . . to give you a future and a hope.

JEREMIAH 29:11

Few US presidents have had Ronald Reagan's ability to ignite hope in people's hearts. Hear these words from his second inaugural address in 1985:

> History is a journey. And as we continue our journey, we think of those who traveled before us. . . . A general falls to his knees in the hard snow of Valley Forge; a lonely president paces the darkened halls and ponders his struggle to preserve the Union; the men of the Alamo call out encouragement to each other; a settler pushes west and sings a song, and the song echoes out forever. . . .

> It is the American sound. It is hopeful, big-hearted, idealistic, daring, decent, and fair. That's our heritage; that is our song. We sing it still. For all our problems, our differences, we are together as of old, as we raise our voices to the God who is the Author of this most tender music. And may He continue to hold us close as we fill the world with our sound—sound in unity, affection, and love—one people under God, dedicated to the dream of freedom that He has placed in the human heart, called upon now to pass that dream on to a waiting and hopeful world.

★ ★ Patriot's Prayer ★ ★

Almighty God, may this nation always shine the light of freedom to the rest of the world and share with them our song of hope in unity, affection, and love.

★ ★ Patriot's Promise ★ ★

Psalm 133:1 says, "Behold, how good and how pleasant it is for brethren to dwell together in unity!" God will bless our efforts to build unity in our homes, churches, communities, and nation.

And there was very great gladness.

NEHEMIAH 8:17

Erma Bombeck, one of America's most popular humorists in the second half of the twentieth century, wrote these words:

> You have to love a nation that celebrates its independence every July 4, not with a parade of guns, tanks, and soldiers who file by the White House in a show of strength and muscle, but with family picnics where kids throw Frisbees, the potato salad gets "iffy," and the flies die from happiness. You may think you have overeaten, but it is patriotism.

★ ★ Patriot's Prayer ★ ★

Dear God, please put the love of God and country in my heart like never before. Make my heart overflow with concern for the well-being of my fellow citizens. May I make a difference in my circle of influence as I pledge my allegiance to this great land.

★ ★ Patriot's Promise ★ ★

Psalm 85:9 (KJV) says this: "Surely his salvation is nigh them that fear him; that glory may dwell in our land." God promises that if we hold Him high in awe, He will dwell with us. When you think about it, *glory* means magnificence, beauty, grandeur, and splendor. Doesn't that sound like fireworks, celebration, and joy? God has blessed this nation beyond comprehension. Come on, let's celebrate her birth!

The Fourth of July Celebration

Remember His marvelous works which He has done.

PSALM 105:5

O n July 3, 1776, following the signing of the Declaration of Independence, John Adams reflected on that important day:

> The second day of July 1776 will be the most memorable epoch in the history of America. I am apt to believe that it will be celebrated by succeeding generations as the great anniversary festival. It ought to be commemorated as the day of deliverance, by solemn acts of devotion to God Almighty. It ought to be solemnized with pomp and parade, with shows, games, sports, guns, bells, bonfires, and illuminations, from one end of this continent to the other, from this time forward forever.
>
> You will think me transported with enthusiasm, but I am not. I am well aware of the toil and blood and treasure that it will cost to maintain this Declaration and support and defend these States. Yet through all the gloom I can see the rays of ravishing light and glory. I can see that the end is worth more than all the means; that posterity will triumph in that day's transaction, even though we [may regret] it, which I trust in God we shall not.

★ ★ Patriot's Prayer ★ ★

Thank You, Lord, for the men and women who gave their lives for the freedom of the republic in which we live today. Help me to be as bold and brave as they were when it is my turn to protect this land.

★ ★ Patriot's Promise ★ ★

"The righteous cry out, and the LORD hears, and delivers them out of all their troubles" (Psalm 34:17).

July 4

So this day shall be to you a memorial.

EXODUS 12:14

"What We Can Do for Our Country"

In honor of the veterans of the Civil War, Supreme Court Justice Oliver Wendell Holmes Jr., who had been wounded three times during that war, said the following in a Memorial Day Address in 1884:

> It is now the moment when by common consent we pause to become conscious of our national life and to rejoice in it, to recall what our country has done for each of us, and to ask ourselves what we can do for our country in return.

★ ★ Patriot's Prayer ★ ★

The greatest thing I can do for my country, Lord, is to honor You. If I hold You in the highest regard, I will do my civic duty with pleasure. Let me do service to my country and to others with a genuine willingness. Guide me to do those things that will make a difference for You.

★ ★ Patriot's Promise ★ ★

In 1 Samuel 24:6, David had a perfect opportunity to kill King Saul—who was, after all, out to kill David. But David acknowledged to his men that the king had been anointed by God and that no one should stretch out his hand against him. Also, in 1 Chronicles 16:22, David credited God with commanding, "Do not touch My anointed ones." We must hold our leaders in high regard and pray for them every day. Because David honored and respected King Saul, God honored David, and He will keep that promise to us as well.

The "God-Made Rights of God-Made Man"

God sent me before you to preserve life.

JOSEPH IN GENESIS 45:5

Clarence Manion, dean of the Notre Dame College of Law (1941–1952), said this about the Declaration of Independence:

> Look closely at these self-evident truths, these imperishable articles of American faith upon which all our government is firmly based. First and foremost is the existence of God. Next comes the truth that all men are equal in the sight of God. Third is the fact of God's great gift of unalienable rights to every person on earth. Then follows the true and single purpose of all American government, namely, to preserve and protect these God-made rights of God-made man.

★ ★ Patriot's Prayer ★ ★

You were there in the beginning, Creator God. You are the First and the Last. You are the Beginning and the End, the Alpha and the Omega, the King of kings and Lord of lords. I sing Your praises and thank You, O God, for calling me to know Jesus as my Savior and Lord.

★ ★ Patriot's Promise ★ ★

Read the Psalm 91:4 promise that God "shall cover you with His feathers, and under His wings you shall take refuge; His truth shall be your shield and buckler." Indeed, the God of all truth will be the Shield and Protector of every believer.

He has sent Me . . . to proclaim
liberty to the captives.

Isaiah 61:1

The Key to Liberty

Thomas Jefferson authored the Declaration of Independence and served as the third president of the United States. Consider this observation about Christianity:

> The Christian religion, when divested of the rags in which [the clergy] have enveloped it, and brought to the original purity and simplicity of its benevolent Institutor, is a religion of all others most friendly to liberty, science, and the freest expansion of the human mind.

★ ★ Patriot's Prayer ★ ★

Dear God, I pray today for revival in our nation, for a reawakening to You as Sovereign Lord. I pray that the Holy Spirit will move upon hearts across this land and that souls will turn to You.

★ ★ Patriot's Promise ★ ★

The promise of 2 Chronicles 20:20: "Believe in the LORD your God, and you shall be established; believe His prophets, and you shall prosper."

The Liberty Bell

You shall . . . proclaim liberty
throughout all the land.

LEVITICUS 25:10

In 1751, the Pennsylvania Assembly ordered a bell to commemorate the golden anniversary of William Penn's 1701 Charter of Privileges, Pennsylvania's original constitution, which speaks of the rights and freedoms valued by people the world over. The biblical quotation "Proclaim liberty throughout all the land unto all the inhabitants thereof" was particularly apt, for the words immediately preceding "proclaim liberty" are "And ye shall hallow the fiftieth year." What better way to pay homage to Penn and hallow the fiftieth year than with a bell that would proclaim liberty?

Tradition says that on July 8, 1776, the Liberty Bell rang out from the tower of Independence Hall, summoning the citizens of Philadelphia to hear the first public reading of the Declaration of Independence. The truth is that the steeple was already in bad condition, and historians today highly doubt this account. However, the Liberty Bell's association with the Declaration of Independence became fixed in America's collective mind.

In 1837, the Liberty Bell gained iconic importance when abolitionists, in their efforts to put an end to slavery throughout America, adopted it as a symbol of emancipation and liberty. And so it is today.

★ ★ Patriot's Prayer ★ ★

Lord, You have graciously bestowed spiritual and political liberty upon us American Christians. Please guard—and use me to guard—this liberty for my children and my children's children.

★ ★ Patriot's Promise ★ ★

The promise of a life in Christ is freedom. Galatians 5:1 teaches that it is for freedom's sake that Christ saved us. We never again have to live in the bondage of slavery to sin.

As for me, I would seek God, and to God I
would commit my cause.

Job 5:8

The Pledge of Allegiance

Every school morning across the United States, over 60 million teachers and
students recite the Pledge of Allegiance. Written in 1892, the pledge was a
celebratory remark used throughout public schools to mark the 400th anniversary
of Columbus discovering the New World. Since then, it has become a national
oath of loyalty to the country, a statement of unity, and a defense of the American
way of life.

The Pledge of Allegiance gained popularity among adults during the patriotic
fervor created by World War II. It was an unofficial pledge until June 22, 1942,
when Congress included the pledge in the United States Flag Code (Title 36).
This was the first official sanction given to the words that schoolchildren had been
saying for almost fifty years. (One year later the US Supreme Court ruled that
schoolchildren could not be forced to recite the Pledge as part of their daily rou-
tine.) In 1945, the pledge received its official title: The Pledge of Allegiance.

In 1954, President Dwight D. Eisenhower approved the addition of *under God*
in order to differentiate the United States from the officially atheist Soviet Union:
"In this way we are reaffirming the transcendence of religious faith in America's
heritage and future; in this way we shall constantly strengthen those spiritual
weapons which forever will be our country's most powerful resource in peace and
war."

★ ★ **Patriot's Prayer** ★ ★
Help us, Lord, to always live as a nation under Your authority.

★ ★ **Patriot's Promise** ★ ★
"There is no authority except from God, and the authorities that exist are appointed by God. Therefore whoever resists the authority resists the ordinance of God,
and those who resist will bring judgment on themselves" (Romans 13:1–2).

Correcting Abuses

In the place of righteousness, iniquity was there.

ECCLESIASTES 3:16

On July 10, 1832, President Andrew Jackson vetoed the Bank Renewal Bill, preventing the rechartering of the Bank of the United States. Believing the bank was unauthorized by the Constitution and concentrated too much economic power in the hands of a small moneyed elite, he presented the following arguments:

In the full enjoyment of the gifts of Heaven and the fruits of superior industry, economy, and virtue, every man is equally entitled to protection by law; but when the laws undertake to add to these natural and just advantages artificial distinctions, to grant titles, gratuities, and exclusive privileges, to make the rich richer and the potent more powerful, the humble members of society—the farmers, mechanics, and laborers ... have a right to complain of the injustice of their Government.

There are no necessary evils in government. Its evils exist only in its abuses. If it would confine itself to equal protection, and, as Heaven does its rains, shower its favors alike on the high and the low, the rich and the poor, it would be an unqualified blessing....

Let us firmly rely on that kind Providence which I am sure watches with peculiar care over the destinies of our Republic, and on the intelligence and wisdom of our countrymen. Through His abundant goodness and their patriotic devotion our liberty and Union will be preserved.

★ ★ Patriot's Prayer ★ ★

Lord God, help me to stand for what is right, against any abuse of power and authority in this nation and this world.

★ ★ Patriot's Promise ★ ★

God has provided for us "an inheritance that can never perish, spoil or fade—kept in heaven" (1 Peter 1:4 NIV).

July 10

The Spirit of the LORD is upon Me . . . to set at liberty those who are oppressed.

LUKE 4:18

The Statue of Liberty

The Statue of Liberty was presented to the United States by the people of France in 1886. Located in New York Harbor, it stands on Liberty Island as a symbol of freedom and a welcome to all visitors, immigrants, and returning Americans. Engraved on a bronze plaque and mounted inside the Statue of Liberty is this famous sonnet by Emma Lazarus:

The New Colossus

Not like the brazen giant of Greek fame,
With conquering limbs astride from land to land;
Here at our sea-washed, sunset gates shall stand
A mighty woman with a torch, whose flame
Is the imprisoned lightning, and her name
Mother of Exiles. From her beacon-hand
Glows worldwide welcome; her mild eyes command
The air-bridged harbor that twin cities frame.
"Keep, ancient lands, your storied pomp!" cries she
With silent lips. "Give me your tired, your poor,
Your huddled masses yearning to breathe free,
The wretched refuse of your teeming shore.
Send these, the homeless, tempest-tost to me,
I lift my lamp beside the golden door!"

★ ★ Patriot's Prayer ★ ★

Sovereign and gracious Lord, thank You for this country and its doors that open wide to welcome those who yearn to be free.

★ ★ Patriot's Promise ★ ★

"Having been set free from sin, you became slaves of righteousness" (Romans 6:18). And that is the promise of eternal liberty.

Taking Liberty for Granted

> And [his brothers] sold [Joseph] to the Ishmaelites for twenty shekels of silver.
>
> GENESIS 37:28

Dick Cheney, the 46th vice president of the United States, made the following statement:

> It is easy to take liberty for granted when you have never had it taken from you.

★ ★ Patriot's Prayer ★ ★

For a long time, Lord, I have relied on You. I desperately want to put You first in my life and keep You there. And just as I don't want to take for granted the freedoms I enjoy as an American, let me also never take You for granted. Keep me mindful that You are with me all the time. I give You praise and admiration today. Fill my heart with anticipation for tomorrow.

★ ★ Patriot's Promise ★ ★

Joseph lost his freedom when his brothers sold him into slavery. We can only imagine what Joseph must have felt as he was bound and forced to join that caravan of Ishmaelites. Just days before, Joseph had been wandering around freely, attempting to locate his brothers, and now he was being taking off into slavery. He had no idea what was going to happen to him. Suddenly his freedom—his liberty—was snatched from him. If you know the story of Joseph, you will recall that this was only the beginning of his struggle for freedom. But God was with Joseph and blessed him beyond what he could have ever thought or imagined. He trusted God even though his situation was impossible. That's the key: "Trust and obey, for there's no other way."

You shall teach [My commandments] diligently to your children.

DEUTERONOMY 6:7

On July 13, 1787, the Continental Congress passed the Northwest Ordinance, declaring that the United States intended to settle the region north of the Ohio River and east of the Mississippi River. It also set up the method by which new states would be admitted to the Union, giving them the same rights and powers that established states enjoyed, including the freedom of religion. Interestingly, the ordinance also stated the importance that Congress attached to religion: "Religion, morality, and knowledge being necessary to good government and the happiness of mankind, schools and the means of education shall forever be encouraged."

The exact meaning of this sentence is still hotly debated. James Wilson, one of only six Founders to have signed both the Declaration of Independence and the Constitution, said this in his law lectures at the University of Pennsylvania: "Far from being rivals or enemies, religion and law are twin sisters, friends, and mutual assistants." Not surprisingly, throughout American history up until the middle of the twentieth century, government looked positively on both religion and morality. Religious freedom was respected and religion was regarded as a "seedbed of virtue" strengthening American society.

★ ★ Patriot's Prayer ★ ★

May we always, Lord, remember that goodness, morality, and virtue only come from You. I pray that America will be a nation that upholds these principles and will once again fully protect the religious freedom of all citizens.

★ ★ Patriot's Promise ★ ★

The promise of our good Shepherd in Psalm 23:6 is "Surely goodness and mercy shall follow me all the days of my life."

America on Its Knees

Incline your ear, O LORD, and hear; open
Your eyes, O LORD, and see.

ISAIAH 37:17

Founder of the Hilton Hotel chain, Conrad Hilton (1887–1979) published this prayer on full-page ads in major magazines on July 4, 1952:

Our Father in heaven.

We pray that You save us from ourselves.

The world that You have made for us, to live in peace, we have made into an armed camp. We live in fear of war to come. We are afraid of "the terror that flies by night, and the arrow that flies by day, the pestilence that walks in darkness and the destruction that wastes at noon-day."

We have turned from You to go our selfish way. We have broken Your commandments and denied Your truth. We have left Your altars to serve the false gods of money and pleasure and power.

Forgive us and help us.

Now, darkness gathers around us, and we are confused in all our counsels. Losing faith in You, we lose faith in ourselves.

Inspire us with wisdom, all of us of every color, race, and creed, to use our wealth, our strength to help our brother, instead of destroying him. Help us to do Your will as it is done in heaven and to be worthy of Your promise of peace on earth. Fill us with new faith, new strength and new courage, that we may win the Battle for Peace.

Be swift to save us, dear God, before the darkness falls.

★ ★ Patriot's Prayer ★ ★

Father, fill me with Your Holy Spirit so that I will be a positive influence to all I see today.

★ ★ Patriot's Promise ★ ★

"Let us hold fast the confession of our hope without wavering, for He who promised is faithful" (Hebrews 10:23).

For who has despised the day of small things?

ZECHARIAH 4:10

True Christian, True Citizen

Consider the following observations by Theodore Roosevelt, the twenty-sixth president of the United States (1901–1909) and the youngest man to hold that office:

> The true Christian is the true citizen, lofty of purpose, resolute in endeavor, ready for a hero's deeds, but never looking down on his task because it is cast in the day of small things; scornful of baseness, awake to his own duties as well as to his rights, following the higher law with reverence, and in this world doing all that in his power lies, so that when death comes he may feel that mankind is in some degree better because he lived.
>
> Every thinking man, when he thinks, realizes that the teachings of the Bible are so interwoven and entwined with our whole civic and social life that it would be literally impossible for us to figure ourselves what that life would be if these standards were removed. We would lose almost all the standards by which we now judge both public and private morals; all the standards toward which we, with more or less resolution, strive to raise ourselves.

★ ★ Patriot's Prayer ★ ★

Lord God, make me a truer Christian that I may be a truer citizen of this land You allow me to call home. What a privilege to live in this country! What a privilege to be Your child!

★ ★ Patriot's Promise ★ ★

Proverbs 14:35 reads, "The king's favor is toward a wise servant, but his wrath is against him who causes shame."

July 15

Defending the Unborn

> Let the little children come to Me, and do not forbid them; for of such is the kingdom of heaven.
>
> MATTHEW 19:14

During his thirty-two years of service in the House of Representatives, Henry Hyde came to be known as a passionate and eloquent defender of the unborn. On July 16, 1993, he made this statement:

"That all men are created equal and are endowed by their Creator"—human beings upon creation, not upon birth. That is where our human dignity comes from. It comes from the Creator. It is an endowment, not an achievement.

By membership in the human family, we are endowed by our Creator with "inalienable rights." They can't be voted away by a jury or a court.

"Among which are life"—the first inalienable right, the first endowment from the Creator. That is mainstream America, the predicate for our Constitution, our country's birth certificate. To respect the right to life as an endowment from the Creator...

It is the unborn who are the least of God's creatures. We have been told that whatsoever we do for the least of these we do unto Jesus.

★ ★ Patriot's Prayer ★ ★

My heart is broken for those who do not understand when human life begins or recognize from whom it comes. Show me, Lord, what You would have me do to be a defender of the unborn, an ally of those who do not have their own voice.

★ ★ Patriot's Promise ★ ★

Notice the love promised and inherent in this truth: "You created my inmost being; you knit me together in my mother's womb . . . I am fearfully and wonderfully made" (Psalm 139:13–14 NIV).

Thus says the LORD of hosts:
"Execute true justice."

ZECHARIAH 7:9

"Saving Principles"

Frederick Douglass (1818–1895) was an abolitionist, orator, author, statesman, and one of the most prominent figures in African-American and American history, who stated the following:

> The Declaration of Independence is the ringbolt to the chain of your nation's destiny; so, indeed, I regard it. The principles contained in that instrument are saving principles. Stand by those principles, be true to them on all occasions, in all places, against all foes, and at whatever cost.

God gives us rules, not merely suggestions, to live by. They are called the Ten Commandments, and if we obey them, our Creator God assures us that we will be able to live more fully in the peace and harmony He intended. So it is with the Declaration of Independence. If we Americans follow its principles, we will be more able to live in the peace and harmony our Founding Fathers envisioned.

★ ★ Patriot's Prayer ★ ★

God, I want to stand fast by Your principles and precepts. Ingrain Your Word in my heart so that I can recall the way You would want me to handle any situation in life. When I am under pressure, let me think of Your Word and Your promises to me. Help me to persevere.

★ ★ Patriot's Promise ★ ★

"If you want to enter into life, keep the commandments (Matthew 19:17).

July 17

Sage Advice

Unless the LORD builds the house, they labor in vain who build it.

PSALM 127:1

In the summer of 1787, tempers flared among the delegates of the thirteen colonies meeting to draft the Constitution. With the convention in danger of breaking down, an eighty-one-year-old statesman spoke words of profound wisdom. Not especially religious, Benjamin Franklin nonetheless appealed to Psalm 127:1 and counseled delegates to seek the aid of Almighty God:

> The longer I live, the more convincing proofs I see of this truth, that God governs in the affairs of men. And if a sparrow cannot fall to the ground without His notice, is it probable that an empire can rise without His aid? We have been assured, sir, in the Sacred Writings, that "except the Lord builds the house, they labor in vain that build it." I firmly believe this; and I also believe that without His concurring aid we shall succeed in this political building no better than the builders of Babel: We shall be divided . . . our projects will be confounded. And what is worse, mankind may hereafter . . . despair of establishing Governments by Human Wisdom and leave it to chance, war, and conquest.
>
> I therefore . . . move that henceforth prayers imploring the assistance of Heaven . . . be held in this assembly every morning before we proceed to business.

God answered the prayers: on September 17, 1787, the draft was completed, supporting Franklin's assertion: that they should fail in this "grand experiment" of liberty unless they sought the "assistance of Heaven."

★ ★ Patriot's Prayer ★ ★

Lord, may our country—and may I—seek Your wisdom in everything we do.

★ ★ Patriot's Promise ★ ★

"I will pray . . . and He shall hear my voice" (Psalm 55:17).

Behold the proud, his soul is not upright in him;
but the just shall live by his faith.

HABAKKUK 2:4

Living by Faith

As America suffered defeat after defeat in the War of 1812, President James Madison proclaimed a national day of prayer. In his July 1813 message, he emphasized the importance of a nation humbling itself before Almighty God and pleading for His help against injustice:

> "Whereas in times of public calamity, such as that of the war brought on the United States by the injustice of a foreign government, it is especially becoming that the hearts of all should be touched with the same and the eyes of all be turned to that Almighty Power in whose hands are the welfare and the destiny of nations."

The Old Testament prophet Habakkuk struggled personally with God on the issues of injustice and evil. Habakkuk anguished over the sins of the Hebrew people and wondered why this evil as well as the evil of the conquering Babylonians went unpunished. God assured Habakkuk that His justice will always prevail, prompting Habakkuk to turn from despondency to powerful praise and a declaration that, no matter the circumstances, "Yet I will rejoice in the LORD, I will joy in the God of my salvation" (3:18).

★ ★ Patriot's Prayer ★ ★

Heavenly Father, I may not understand the why behind many of life's difficulties, but I do know that I can trust in Your care. Justified by Jesus' death on the cross, I will choose to live by faith in that truth.

★ ★ Patriot's Promise ★ ★

"The Almighty . . . is excellent in power, in judgment and abundant justice; He does not oppress" (Job 37:23).

Communion on the Moon

I am the vine.

JESUS IN JOHN 15:5

The first lunar landing occurred on July 20, 1969, and Buzz Aldrin was the lunar module pilot on the Apollo 11 space mission. He was also the second person to set foot on the moon, descending the module after Neil Armstrong.

Aldrin had taken with him a tiny Communion kit, given him by his church. So, that morning, he radioed, "Houston, this is Eagle. . . . I would like to request a few moments of silence. I would like to invite each person listening . . . to contemplate for a moment the events of the last few hours, and to give thanks in his own individual way."

During the radio blackout, Aldrin took the Communion elements and read John 15:5: "I am the vine, you are the branches. He who abides in Me, and I in him, bears much fruit." Aldrin had been asked to not read the verse publicly because of the legal challenge against NASA already brought by famed atheist Madalyn Murray O'Hair after the Genesis account of creation was read during the Apollo 8 mission.

Incredible! The first thing this American patriot did when he arrived on the moon was worship God!

★ ★ Patriot's Prayer ★ ★

Holy God, as I look to the heavens today I acknowledge that You are the Creator of heaven and earth, and for this, I give You thanks. May I—like Buzz Aldrin—be quick to recognize opportunities to remember and to acknowledge You and Your greatness.

★ ★ Patriot's Promise ★ ★

"Take, eat; this is My body which is broken for you" (1 Corinthians 11:24)—these were Jesus' instructions at the Last Supper, and Buzz Aldrin took Him literally—and to the moon! Jesus' body broken for us! The promises implicit in such love are indescribable!

I am not ashamed of the gospel of Christ, for it is the power of God to salvation for everyone who believes. . . . For in it the righteousness of God is revealed from faith to faith; as it is written, *"The just shall live by faith."*

ROMANS 1:16–17

God's Saving Power

In the New Testament, the four Gospels present the words and works of Jesus Christ. Then Paul's letter to the Romans sets forth the significance of Jesus' sacrificial death on the cross. Using a question-and-answer format, Paul crafted the most systematic presentation of Christian doctrine in the Bible, and he balanced it with practical exhortation. The Good News at work in the life of a believer results in a life of righteousness that reflects God's grace and love.

In his famous address "The Bible and Progress," delivered in Denver, Colorado, in 1911, President Woodrow Wilson told his audience this: "America was born a Christian nation. America was born to exemplify that devotion to the elements of righteousness which are derived from the revelations of Holy Scripture." Based on the foundation established by the Declaration of Independence and the Constitution, people of America are free to live righteous and godly lives.

★ ★ Patriot's Prayer ★ ★

Heavenly Father, may I never be ashamed of the gospel of Jesus Christ, Your Son and my Savior. By Your grace, help Me live fully surrendered to You and clearly reflecting Your love and grace.

★ ★ Patriot's Promise ★ ★

Romans 6–8 contain foundational teachings on the spiritual life. These chapters answer questions about God's grace and love, deliverance from sin, and living in the power of the Holy Spirit.

Worthy of the Name

Francis Scott Key (1779–1843) was the American lawyer and poet who wrote "The Star-Spangled Banner." He also wrote the following:

The patriot who feels himself in the service of God, who acknowledges Him in all his ways, has the promise of Almighty direction, and will find His Word in his greatest darkness, "a lantern to his feet and a lamp unto his paths.". . . He will therefore seek to establish for his country in the eyes of the world, such a character as shall make her not unworthy of the name of a Christian nation.

★ ★ Patriot's Prayer ★ ★

Precious Father, let Your Spirit fill me today, anoint my character, and make me a testimony for Jesus in all that I say and do. I also pray for my country, that she may be reawakened to You, Lord.

★ ★ Patriot's Promise ★ ★

God describes the character of a Christian: "The fruit of the Spirit is love, joy, peace, longsuffering, kindness, goodness, faithfulness, gentleness, self-control" (Galatians 5:22–23). God promises that if we walk in the Spirit, these qualities—evidence of the Spirit's presence in us—will shine in us, and we will live worthy of His Name.

You have forgotten the law of your God.

Human Law, Divine Law

Justice James Wilson was one of the Supreme Court's original members and a signer of both the Declaration of Independence and the Constitution. A major voice in the drafting of the Constitution, he also wrote several legal works, including a 1792 *Commentary on the Constitution of the United States of America* and a three-volume set of lectures delivered to law students. Wilson played a significant role in laying the early foundation of an American system of jurisprudence. Notice what he taught his students:

> It should always be remembered that this law ... made for men or for nations, flows from the same Divine source: it is the law of God. ... What we do, indeed, must be founded on what He has done; and the deficiencies of our laws must be supplied by the perfections of His. Human law must rest its authority, ultimately, upon the authority of that law which is Divine. ... We now see the deep and the solid foundations of human law. ... From this short, but plain and, I hope, just statement of things, we perceive a principle of connection between all the learned professions; but especially between the two last mentioned [the profession of Divinity and the profession of law]. Far from being rivals or enemies, religion and law are twin sisters, friends, and mutual assistants. Indeed, these two sciences run into each other.

★ ★ Patriot's Prayer ★ ★

Lord, teach me to live according to Your law, that I may experience the freedom it is designed to give.

★ ★ Patriot's Promise ★ ★

"By [Your laws] Your servant is warned, and in keeping them there is great reward" (Psalm 19:11).

July 23

"Sink or Swim Together"

William Prescott (1726–1795) commanded the colonial militia at the Battle of Bunker Hill and was also an instrumental part of the battles of Long Island and Saratoga during the Revolutionary War. In 1774, when the British blockaded the Boston harbor, he wrote to the city's inhabitants:

> We heartily sympathize with you, and are always ready to do all in our power for your support, comfort, and relief, knowing that Providence has placed you where you must stand the first shock. We consider that we are all embarked in [the same boat] and must sink or swim together.... Let us all be of one heart, and stand fast in the liberty wherewith Christ has made us free. And may He, of His infinite mercy, grant us deliverance of all our troubles.

★ ★ Patriot's Prayer ★ ★

Gracious God, I know that a house divided against itself cannot stand. So please give unity of heart to my family, my friends, my co-workers, and my church family. When conflict arises, give me wisdom to know what to do and what to say. Teach me how to live in harmony with others.

★ ★ Patriot's Promise ★ ★

"Behold, how good and how pleasant it is for brethren to dwell together in unity!" is what Psalm 133:1 tells us. If we live together in harmony, the psalm goes on to promise, we will find refreshment like nothing on earth offers.

Live a life of love, just as Christ loved us and gave himself up for us as a fragrant offering and sacrifice to God.

EPHESIANS 5:1–2 NIV

In 1774, the Massachusetts Provincial Congress reorganized the state's militia. They wanted one-fourth of the army to be "Minutemen"—patriots who vowed to be ready to fight at a minute's notice. This was the charge Congress issued that elite group:

> You . . . are placed by Providence in the post of honor, because it is the post of danger. . . . The eyes not only of North America and the whole British Empire, but of all Europe, are upon you. Let us be, therefore, altogether solicitous that no disorderly behavior, nothing unbecoming our characters as Americans, as citizens and Christians, be justly chargeable to us.

★ ★ Patriot's Prayer ★ ★

Providential God, may there by "nothing unbecoming" in my behavior as a Christian. I pray that my words and actions will be guided by the mind of Christ within me.

★ ★ Patriot's Promise ★ ★

First Corinthians 2:16 asks a question and answers it: "'Who has known the mind of the LORD that he may instruct Him?' But we have the mind of Christ." If we focus our minds on the Lord, He will guide us in all we do.

Established by God

Now if you walk before Me as your father David walked, in integrity of heart and in uprightness, to do according to all that I have commanded you, and if you keep My statutes and My judgments, then I will establish the throne of your kingdom over Israel forever.

1 KINGS 9:4–5

First Kings records the reign of Israel's King Solomon, considered the wisest man who ever lived. When Solomon heeded God's Word and followed the directives handed down through his father, King David, Israel enjoyed unprecedented peace, prosperity, and blessings, all from the hand of God. But when, toward the end of his life, Solomon took his eyes off the Lord and turned from the God-inspired vision for Israel his father had shared with him, the nation began its slow decline toward a divided kingdom.

Similarly, the godly leadership of America's forefathers did not prevent our nation from splintering into civil war. Self-centered ideologies and a militant spirit threatened to destroy this nation. Through those dark days and since, only God's mercy, righteous leadership, and the prayers of individuals who love God and their country have helped keep America unified. That which is established by the mercies and grace of God can only be preserved by the people of God.

★ ★ Patriot's Prayer ★ ★

God of heaven, let me live this day focused on You. Enable me to make choices that keep me living with integrity of heart and uprightness, and to remain fully established in Your mercy and grace.

★ ★ Patriot's Promise ★ ★

Hear the prophet Isaiah's confidence in God: "You will keep him in perfect peace, whose mind is stayed on You, because he trusts in You" (26:3).

The LORD said, "I will also remove Judah from My sight, as I have removed Israel, and will cast off this city Jerusalem which I have chosen, and the house of which I said, 'My name shall be there.'"

2 KINGS 23:27

Second Kings is an account of the downward spiral of Israel and Judah as, by and large, the divided nations walk a path of disobedience and rebellion against God. During this time, prophets like Elijah and Elisha warned the people of sin, idolatry, and consequent judgment. They explained the need to turn from evil and follow God's commands. For the most part, the people refused to believe these warnings and paid a heavy toll.

Just as God used prophets in Israel and Judah to encourage righteousness and warn against idolatry and evil, so He has raised up men and women to speak in defense of liberty, justice, morality, and righteousness.

Jonathan Edwards, Charles Finney, Frederick Douglass, Harriet Beecher Stowe, D. L. Moody, Peter Marshall, Billy Graham, and many others have reminded this nation, from its beginnings to the present, that God will bless us only as we seek His lordship. May America heed the warnings found in God's Word and seek His gracious forgiveness and restoration.

★ ★ Patriot's Prayer ★ ★

Almighty God, forgive our sins. Hear our cries for mercy. Strengthen those who lead us toward that which is right; remove from leadership those who would keep us from following You.

★ ★ Patriot's Promise ★ ★

The warnings of God, our loving heavenly Father, are blessings to all who will hear and heed them: "The LORD God of their fathers sent warnings to them by His messengers . . . because He had compassion on His people and on His dwelling place" (2 Chronicles 36:15).

215

Covenant Faithfulness

Yours, O LORD, is the greatness, the power
and the glory, the victory and the majesty;
for all that is in heaven and in earth is
Yours; Yours is the kingdom, O LORD,
and You are exalted as head over all.

1 CHRONICLES 29:11

While 1 and 2 Chronicles might seem to repeat the narratives of 1 and 2 Samuel and 1 and 2 Kings, they were actually penned for those Israelites returning after years of bondage in Babylon. The writer wanted to remind them of God's unchanging covenant with His people. After initially listing the generations of God's chosen family, 1 Chronicles recounts the reign of King David and reiterates God's promise to establish his throne forever. Such a promise offered great comfort to the returning exiles.

Heritage and history are important reference points for any nation, offering lessons from successes as well as failures and examples of both righteousness and shortcomings, all of which can serve as signposts for future generations. Our forefathers fought for liberty in the Revolutionary War, battled one another in our nation's great Civil War, and, during the middle part of the twentieth century, granted civil rights to all Americans. These and countless other incidents from history offer a rich source of wisdom from which every citizen can draw in the ongoing effort to maintain our liberties.

★ ★ Patriot's Prayer ★ ★

O Lord, thank You for Your covenant promises. May I be faithful in loving and serving You just as You faithfully keep Your promises to Your people.

★ ★ Patriot's Promise ★ ★

"'If a man is just and does what is lawful and right . . . if he has walked in My statutes and kept My judgments faithfully—He is just; He shall surely live!' says the Lord GOD" (Ezekiel 18:5, 9).

[The feasts and sacrifices] shall be a memorial for you before your God: I am the LORD your God.

NUMBERS 10:10

Christian religious symbols and biblical references adorn buildings in Washington, D.C., a testimony to the place God has in our nation's history.

The Washington Monument

Engraved on the aluminum capstone is *Laus Deo*, "Praise be to God." Lining the walls of the stairwell are blocks carved with phrases like "Holiness to the Lord"; "Search the Scriptures"; and "Train up a child in the way he should go."

The Jefferson Memorial

A quote around the interior dome says, "I have sworn upon the altar of God, eternal hostility against every form of tyranny over the minds of man." One panel reads: "God who gave us life gave us liberty. Can the liberties of a nation be secure when we have removed a conviction that these liberties are the gift of God? Indeed I tremble for my country when I reflect that God is just, that His justice cannot sleep forever."

The Lincoln Memorial

To the right of the magnificent statue of Abraham Lincoln is his second inaugural address, which mentions God fourteen times and quotes the Bible twice. On Mr. Lincoln's left is the Gettysburg Address: "We here highly resolved that these dead shall not have died in vain, that this nation, under God, shall have a new birth of freedom."

★ ★ **Patriot's Prayer** ★ ★

It's awesome, Lord, that memorials in Washington remind us of Your role in our nation's history. May we not only remember, but preserve that divine legacy.

★ ★ **Patriot's Promise** ★ ★

"If you by any means forget the LORD your God, and follow other gods . . . you shall surely perish" (Deuteronomy 8:19).

★ 217 ★

The US Capitol Building

Exalt Him also in the assembly of the people.

Psalm 107:32

The Capitol Building in Washington, D.C., points to the Lord's presence in history, both the past and that which is unfolding today.

In the House chamber is the inscription "In God We Trust." Above the Gallery door stands a marble relief of Moses, surrounded by twenty-two other lawgivers in history. At the east entrance to the Senate chamber are the words *Annuit Coeptis,* Latin for "He has favored our undertakings." The words "In God We Trust" are also written over the southern entrance.

In the Rotunda are the paintings "The Baptism of Pocahontas" and "The Embarkation of the Pilgrims" that shows William Brewster leading the Pilgrims in prayer. Clearly seen in an open Bible are the words "the New Testament according to our Lord and Savior, Jesus Christ." The words "God with Us" are inscribed on the sail of the ship.

In the Capitol's chapel is a stained-glass window showing George Washington in prayer under the inscription "This Nation Under God." Psalm 16:1 is etched in the window: "Preserve me, God, for in Thee do I put my trust."

★ ★ Patriot's Prayer ★ ★

Lord, thank You for the courageous and godly people who come to this land for religious freedom—and thank You for a Capitol building that points to that heritage and Your faithfulness.

★ ★ Patriot's Promise ★ ★

"He has declared to His people the power of His works, in giving them the heritage of the nations" (Psalm 111:6).

Some Gadites joined David . . . mighty men of
valor . . . whose faces were like the faces of lions.

1 CHRONICLES 12:8

Poet Josiah Gilbert Holland (1819–1881), founder and editor of the popular
Scribner's Monthly (later, *Century Magazine*), penned these famous words:

> God, give us men! A time like this demands
>> Strong minds, great hearts, true faith and ready hands;
>> Men whom the lust of office does not kill;
> Men whom the spoils of office can not buy;
>> Men who possess opinions and a will;
> Men who have honor; men who will not lie;
> Men who can stand before a demagogue
>> And damn his treacherous flatteries without winking!
> Tall men, sun-crowned, who live above the fog
>> In public duty, and in private thinking;
> For while the rabble, with their thumb-worn creeds,
> Their large professions and their little deeds,
> Mingle in selfish strife, lo! Freedom weeps,
> Wrong rules the land and waiting Justice sleeps.

★ ★ Patriot's Prayer ★ ★

Lord, help me be true to You and Your principles and live a life of integrity and
honor, free of hypocrisy and untruth. Give me a strong mind, great heart, true
faith, and ready hands to do Your work.

★ ★ Patriot's Promise ★ ★

In Psalm 91:14 the psalmist has God speak: "He has set his love upon Me, therefore I will deliver him; I will set him on high, because he has known My name." If
we love God, He will deliver us.

August

Go into all the world and preach the gospel.

JESUS IN MARK 16:15

The Haystack Prayer Meeting

In August 1806, as five Williams College students met in a field for one of their twice-weekly prayer meetings, a thunderstorm drove them to take refuge in a nearby haystack. Continuing in prayer, Samuel John Mills shared his burden that Christianity be sent abroad, and the group prayed that American missions would spread Christianity through the Far East. Many scholars consider this Haystack Prayer Meeting, held in Williamstown, Massachusetts, the spark that ignited American support for world missions.

Within a few years, the Haystack Prayer group and other Williams students inspired the founding of the American Board of Commissioners for Foreign Missions (ABCFM), sending the first foreign missionaries from America in 1812 and, in its first fifty years, over 1,250 missionaries. Samuel Mills stayed stateside to recruit others. He later helped organize the American Bible Society and the United Foreign Missionary Society.

In 1961, the American Board became a part of the United Church Board for World Missions. During its 150 years, the American Board had sent out nearly five thousand missionaries to thirty-four different fields. And it all began with five young men praying in a haystack.

★ ★ Patriot's Prayer ★ ★

Heavenly Father, help me never forget that You can use just a handful of Your people to make a difference that will last for many generations and even for eternity.

★ ★ Patriot's Promise ★ ★

Psalm 123:1–3 promises that if we, as a generation, look to the Lord, He will pour out His mercy upon us. Just a few committed individuals, blessed by God's grace and power, can change the course of history.

221

Christianity Principles and American Law

Nor thieves, nor covetous, nor drunkards, nor revilers, nor extortioners will inherit the kingdom of God.

1 CORINTHIANS 6:10

At age thirty-two, Joseph Story became the youngest associate justice of the Supreme Court: he served from 1811–1845 and wrote 286 opinions. He was also the Dane Professor of Law at Harvard and, as such, wrote many legal texts now considered classics. His three-volume *Commentaries on the Constitution of the United States* remains the standard treatise on the subject.

At a point in his life when Story doubted the truth of Christianity, he "labored and read with assiduous attention all of the arguments of its proof" and became committed to the principles of Christianity, which he repeatedly expressed throughout his lengthy legal career. It was his conviction that American law and legal practices must never be separated from Christian principles:

> One of the beautiful boasts of our municipal jurisprudence is that Christianity is a part of the Common Law....There never has been a period in which the Common Law did not recognize Christianity as lying at its foundations.... [The law] pronounces illegal every contract offensive to [Christianity's] morals. It recognizes with profound humility [Christianity's] holidays and festivals, and obeys them [even to the point of suspending all government functions on those days]. It still attaches to persons believing in [Christianity's] divine authority the highest degree of competency as witnesses.

★ ★ Patriot's Prayer ★ ★

May my words and actions, Lord, reveal my gratitude and respect for Your law.

★ ★ Patriot's Promise ★ ★

"The solid foundation of God stands, having this seal: 'The Lord knows those who are His'" (2 Timothy 2:19).

Walk before Me . . . in integrity of
heart and in uprightness.

1 KINGS 9:4

The World's Best Currency

William McKinley, the twenty-fifth president of the United States (1897–
1901), said this:

There is no currency in this world that passes at such a premium
anywhere as good Christian character. . . . The time has gone by when
the young man or the young woman in the United States has to
apologize for being a follower of Christ. . . . No cause but one could
have brought together so many people, and that is the cause of our
Master.

★ ★ Patriot's Prayer ★ ★

"May the words of my mouth and the meditation of my heart be pleasing in your
sight, O LORD, my Rock and my Redeemer" (Psalm 19:14 NIV). Make my life a
steadfast witness to others. Allow me to speak out for You in a way that will win
them to Your Kingdom.

★ ★ Patriot's Promise ★ ★

Romans 5:3-4 says, "We also glory in tribulations, knowing that tribulation pro-
duces perseverance; and perseverance, character; and character, hope." Scripture
promises us that enduring difficult times will build our character and, in turn, our
hope in Christ.

August 3

"God of Our Fathers"

God said to Moses, "Thus you shall say to the children of Israel: 'The LORD God of your fathers, the God of Abraham, the God of Isaac, and the God of Jacob, has sent me to you.'"

EXODUS 3:15

Civil War veteran and rector of a small Episcopal parish in Brandon, Vermont, Daniel C. Roberts wanted a new hymn for his congregation to sing in celebration of the American Centennial in 1876. He wrote "God of Our Fathers," and his congregation sang it on July 4. In 1892, this hymn was chosen to be sung at the centennial celebration of the United States Constitution.

God of our fathers, whose almighty hand
Leads forth in beauty all the starry band
Of shining worlds in splendor through the skies
Our grateful songs before Thy throne arise.
Thy love divine hath led us in the past,
In this free land by Thee our lot is cast,
Be Thou our Ruler, Guardian, Guide, and Stay,
Thy Word our law, Thy paths our chosen way.
From war's alarms, from deadly pestilence,
Be Thy strong arm our ever sure defense;
Thy true religion in our hearts increase,
Thy bounteous goodness nourish us in peace.
Refresh Thy people on their toilsome way,
Lead us from night to never ending day;
Fill all our lives with love and grace divine,
And glory, laud, and praise be ever Thine.

★ ★ Patriot's Prayer ★ ★

Lord, I pray that this nation will follow the principles in Your Word. May we rely on Your strength, follow Your guidance, and be faithful to Your path.

★ ★ Patriot's Promise ★ ★

"The rock of my strength, and my refuge, is in God" (Psalm 62:7).

Ezra had prepared his heart to seek the Law of the LORD, and to do it, and to teach statutes and ordinances in Israel.

EZRA 7:10

As God's people returned to Jerusalem after years of exile, Ezra, a humble priest and unassuming leader, was instrumental in reestablishing worship and righteousness among the children of Israel. The book of Ezra demonstrates how ordinary people who submit to God can accomplish extraordinary things.

The history of America is filled with accounts of similarly unassuming individuals who rose to greatness through their humble dedication to God and righteousness. One such example is Harriet Tubman, who, perhaps more than any other American, was responsible for helping slaves escape bondage and reach their promised land of freedom. An escaped slave herself, Tubman recalled that during the years when she was an instrumental figure in the Underground Railroad—which took hundreds of slaves to freedom—she would tell God, "I trust You. I don't know where to go or what to do, but I expect You to lead me."

What a perfect reflection of the kind of humble, yielded spirit through which God is pleased to work His will on the earth!

★ ★ Patriot's Prayer ★ ★

Dear Lord, use me to do Your work this day. I say to You the same words that Harriet Tubman prayed, "God, I trust You. I don't know where to go or what to do, but I expect You to lead me."

★ ★ Patriot's Promise ★ ★

"For whom [God] foreknew, He also predestined to be conformed to the image of His Son" (Romans 8:29).

Women's Rights

There is neither Jew nor Greek, there is neither slave nor free, there is neither male nor female; for you are all one in Christ Jesus.

GALATIANS 3:28

Monumental fights for freedom and justice in the US—the American Revolution, the abolitionist movement, the women's suffrage movement, the civil rights movement—have been led by activists strengthened by their faith in God.

The women's rights movement in America was largely birthed out of the ranks of the movement to end slavery. In 1848, at the Seneca Falls Convention in New York, activists including Elizabeth Cady Stanton and Susan B. Anthony began a seventy-year struggle to secure the right to vote for women. Nearly all of the major leaders of the suffrage movement came from Christian backgrounds. These women believed that God created women equal to men, so they demanded that the same rights guaranteed to men in the Constitution be extended to women.

Most of the activists were mistreated and subject to arrests; many were jailed. However, during the beginning of the twentieth century, women's suffrage gained in popularity as more and more people began to realize that there was no biblical support for inequality between the sexes. Finally, President Woodrow Wilson urged Congress to pass what became, in 1920, the Nineteenth Amendment, which stated, "The right of citizens of the United States to vote shall not be denied or abridged by the United States or by any State on account of sex."

★ ★ Patriot's Prayer ★ ★

I am Your workmanship, Father, created for a purpose. May my faith in You empower me to fulfill that purpose.

★ ★ Patriot's Promise ★ ★

"If you belong to Christ, then you are . . . heirs according to the promise" (Galatians 3:29).

Who knows whether you have come to the kingdom for such a time as this?

Mordecai in Esther 4:14

Taking Risks

Persian King Ahasuerus had decreed the destruction of the Jews living in his realm, but God used Queen Esther to derail the king's deadly plan. Although God's name is not mentioned even once in the book of Esther, His influence and character are evident throughout: By His intervention the orphaned Jewish girl Esther becomes queen of Persia. In spite of great personal risk, Esther and her cousin Mordecai serve as God's agents to bring deliverance to His people. The victory of Esther's fear of God over her fear of man results in freedom for her people.

American journalist Robert Parry has noted, "From the Lexington Green to the Normandy beaches, from the Sons of Liberty to the Freedom Riders, it has been part of the American narrative that risks are taken to expand freedom, not freedoms sacrificed to avoid risk." Over the 200-plus years of the American republic, liberty has been protected only by the sacrifices of men and women who "more than self their country loved," as the patriotic hymn reminds us.

★ ★ Patriot's Prayer ★ ★

Lord God, be at work in my heart so that I will have the courage to take risks for You and Your kingdom work. When I have that opportunity, may my courage be rooted in my knowledge of You and my motivation be my commitment to serve You as Lord.

★ ★ Patriot's Promise ★ ★

"The Lord is on my side; I will not fear. What can man do to me?" (Psalm 118:6).

August 7

The Book of Books

The grass withers, the flower fades, but the word of our God stands forever.

ISAIAH 40:8

The Bible holds a unique place in American history, politics, religion, and popular culture. God's Word continues to transform hearts and lives today.

The secret of my success? It is simple. It is found in the Bible, "In all thy ways acknowledge Him and He shall direct thy paths."

GEORGE WASHINGTON CARVER, INVENTOR AND HORTICULTURALIST

The Word of God tends to make large-minded, noble-hearted men.

HENRY WARD BEECHER, CLERGYMAN

The Bible is worth all the other books which have ever been printed.

PATRICK HENRY, REVOLUTIONARY WAR LEADER AND ORATOR

If we and our posterity neglect [the Bible's] instructions and authority, no man can tell how sudden a catastrophe may overwhelm us and bury all our glory in profound obscurity.

DANIEL WEBSTER, STATESMAN, LAWYER, AND ORATOR

★ ★ Patriot's Prayer ★ ★

Thank You, God, for Your Word and for how important it has been to America's leaders. I praise Your Name for the truth and power of Scripture.

★ ★ Patriot's Promise ★ ★

"Hope does not disappoint, because the love of God has been poured out in our hearts by the Holy Spirit who was given to us" (Romans 5:5).

Fear God and keep His commandments, for this is man's all.

ECCLESIASTES 12:13

Recognizing Life's Meaning

Every human being searches for meaning and purpose in life. In his own pursuit, the writer of Ecclesiastes finds that earthly goals—those that do not lead to God—bring only dissatisfaction, frustration, and uncertainty.

American businessman James Cash (J. C.) Penney came to a similar conclusion. Through hard work and a thrifty lifestyle, J. C. Penney built one of America's most prosperous retail franchises. But during the Great Depression, heavy financial losses caused him enormous stress, which led to hospitalization with a life-threatening illness. Believing he was going to die, Penney wrote farewell letters to his wife and son. When he awoke the next morning, he went for a walk down the hospital hallway and heard singing coming from the chapel. Heavy-hearted, he went in and listened. The song "God Will Take Care of You" spoke to him deeply.

In a life-transforming instant, Penney discovered that God actually was there to help. "From that day to this, my life has been free from worry," he later declared. Like the preacher of Ecclesiastes, J. C. Penney found the answer to all of life—God's love.

★ ★ Patriot's Prayer ★ ★

Who is like You, O Lord? There is none. And because of this truth, following Your will for my life is that which gives it true meaning. May I seek not to follow the ways of men but Your ways this day, O Lord.

★ ★ Patriot's Promise ★ ★

"Seek the LORD your God, and you will find Him if you seek Him with all your heart and with all your soul" (Deuteronomy 4:29).

229

A Covenant Love

I am my beloved's, and his desire is toward me.

SONG OF SOLOMON 7:10

The Song of Solomon is a beautiful love story full of rich metaphors and vivid imagery. While it may be read as a poetic account of intimate love between a man and a woman, its highest value is found allegorically as the description of the deep spiritual passion and intimacy that exist between Christ and His bride, the church.

The great early American preacher Jonathan Edwards was convinced that this unique book "was designed for a divine song and of divine authority, for we read in 1 Kings 4:32 that Solomon's songs were 'a thousand and five.' This he called the 'Song of Songs.'" Edwards noted that such a designation proves that God considers it "a song of the most excellent subject, treating of the love, union, and communion between Christ and His spouse, of which marriage and conjugal love was but a shadow. These are the most excellent lovers and their love the most excellent love."

★ ★ Patriot's Prayer ★ ★

God, let me this day live with a keen awareness of Your great love for me. And let me humbly love You in return in such a way that it is clear that You are my heart's desire.

★ ★ Patriot's Promise ★ ★

When we enter into a covenant relationship with God and fulfill our part in that agreement, He is bound by His word to faithfully fulfill His promises to us. We cannot love God without God loving us in return. "For God so loved the world that He gave His only begotten Son, that whoever believes in Him should not perish but have everlasting life" (John 3:16).

August 10

All we like sheep have gone astray; we have turned, every one, to his own way; and the LORD has laid on Him the iniquity of us all.

ISAIAH 53:6

Our Costly Salvation

The prophet Isaiah's name means "Yahweh is salvation." Even as Isaiah warned of God's impending judgment because of Judah's sin, depravity, and spiritual idolatry, he preached of God's faithfulness to His covenant promise of salvation for His people through the coming Messiah.

Like Isaiah, Jonathan Edwards (1703–1758) emphasized not only the just wrath of God against sin, but also the glory of the Suffering Messiah:

> All the virtues that appeared in Christ shone brightest in the close of His life, under the trials He then met. Eminent virtue always shows brightest in the fire. Pure gold shows its purity chiefly in the furnace. It was chiefly under those trials that Christ endured in the close of His life that His love to God, His honor of God's majesty, His regard to the honor of His law, His spirit of obedience, His humility, contempt of the world, His patience, meekness, and spirit of forgiveness toward men, appeared. Indeed, everything that Christ did to work out redemption for us appears mainly in the close of His life. Here mainly is His satisfaction for sin, and here chiefly is His merit of eternal life for sinners, and here chiefly appears the brightness of His example that He has set us for imitation.

★ ★ Patriot's Prayer ★ ★
Lord Jesus, thank You for suffering and dying that I might be saved. My salvation came at the greatest price imaginable.

★ ★ Patriot's Promise ★ ★
"Whoever calls on the name of the LORD shall be saved" (Romans 10:13).

God's Response to Humility

Has the LORD as great delight in burnt offerings and sacrifices, as in obeying the voice of the LORD? Behold, to obey is better than sacrifice, and to heed than the fat of rams.

1 SAMUEL 15:22

First Samuel offers us a contrast between two very different rulers of Israel: Saul relied on his own abilities and reason to make crucial decisions about leading God's people. David, however, chose a path of humility and faith in God. And as long as King David chose righteousness, God blessed the nation of Judah.

Similarly, as America entered the dark days of the Civil War, President Abraham Lincoln realized that the nation needed to turn its heart to God. On August 12, 1861, after the Union Army's defeat at the Battle of Bull Run, Mr. Lincoln called the American people to a time of repentance, prayer, and fasting, so that "the united prayer of the nation may ascend to the throne of grace and bring down plentiful blessings upon our country."

God greatly delights in such humility.

★ ★ Patriot's Prayer ★ ★

Dear Father in heaven, teach me godly humility in such a way that I will not know that I have it but others will be able to clearly see it demonstrated in my life.

★ ★ Patriot's Promise ★ ★

James 4:6 says, "God resists the proud, but gives grace to the humble."

Christ . . . suffered for us, leaving us an
example, that you should follow His steps.

1 PETER 2:21

The Matchless Life of Jesus

Wesley Merritt, a major general in the Union Army during the Civil War
and the superintendent of the US Military Academy at West Point (1882–
1887), stated:

> The principles of life as taught in the Bible, the inspired Word, and
> exemplified in the matchless life of Him "who spake as never man
> spake," are the rules of moral action which have resulted in civilizing
> the world.
>
> The testimony of great men, like Gladstone and his fellow
> statesmen; like Havelock and his fellow soldiers, who have made the
> teachings of the Scriptures their rule of conduct in life, are wonderful
> helps to men of lesser note and smaller intellectual and moral
> powers. One example, even of the smallest of these, more than
> offsets the efforts of an hundred unbelievers in active opposition.
>
> They are the worthy followers of the religion of the Bible, and in
> their daily lives interpret the inimitable example and Divine precepts
> of the Son of God, our Savior.

★ ★ Patriot's Prayer ★ ★

Father, as I pray and read Your Word today, let me also listen so that I can hear
Your voice speaking to me, guiding me in the path of righteousness that Jesus
modeled.

★ ★ Patriot's Promise ★ ★

Ezekiel 12:25 says, "I am the LORD. I speak, and the word which I speak will come
to pass."

August 13

Without Christ, Without Hope

> You were without Christ . . . having no hope and without God in the world.
>
> EPHESIANS 2:12

In August 1984, Ronald Reagan said this at an ecumenical prayer breakfast in Dallas, Texas:

> We establish no religion in this country, nor will we ever. We command no worship. We mandate no belief. But we poison our society when we remove its theological underpinnings. We court corruption when we leave it bereft of belief. All are free to believe or not believe; all are free to practice a faith or not. But those who believe must be free to speak of and act on their belief, to apply moral teaching to public questions.
>
> I submit to you that the tolerant society is open to and encouraging of all religions. And this does not weaken us; it strengthens us. . . .
>
> Without God, there is no virtue, because there's no prompting of the conscience. Without God, we're mired in the material, that flat world that tells us only what the senses perceive. Without God, there is a coarsening of the society. And without God, democracy will not and cannot long endure. If we ever forget that we're One Nation Under God, then we will be a nation gone under.

★ ★ Patriot's Prayer ★ ★

Father God, You are our Compass, Guide, and Protector. You give meaning to this life, and it is only by Your grace that we, as a nation, endure. May we never forget that we need to live as one nation under God.

★ ★ Patriot's Promise ★ ★

Proverbs 2:6–7 says, "For the LORD gives wisdom; from His mouth come knowledge and understanding; He stores up sound wisdom for the upright; He is a shield to those who walk uprightly." If you look to the Lord, you will never be without His wisdom and protection.

August 14

You formed my inward parts.

PSALM 139:13

O n August 15, 1993, Pope John Paul II addressed more than 375,000 people from seventy different countries in a Mass celebrated at Cherry Creek State Park, Colorado. Below is some of what he said:

> A culture of death seeks to impose itself on our desire to live ... In our own century, as at no other time in history, the culture of death has assumed a social and institutional form of legality to justify the most horrible crimes against humanity: genocide, "final solutions," "ethnic cleansings," and massive taking of lives of human beings even before they are born, or before they reach the natural point of death....
>
> The sacred character of Human Life is denied. Naturally, the weakest members of society are the most at risk. The unborn, children, the sick, the handicapped, the old, the poor and unemployed, the immigrant and refugee....
>
> The church needs your energies, your enthusiasm, your youthful ideas, in order to make the Gospel of Life penetrate the fabric of society, transforming people's hearts and the structures of society in order to create a civilization of true justice and love.

★ ★ Patriot's Prayer ★ ★

Heavenly Father and Author of life, our culture of death must break Your heart. Show me where and how You would have me be involved in defending the life You created.

★ ★ Patriot's Promise ★ ★

"We have known and believed the love that God has for us. God is love, and he who abides in love abides in God, and God in him" (1 John 4:16). What a sweet promise!

When Wisdom Fails

I fell on my knees and spread out my hands to the LORD my God.

EZRA 9:5

After the Union Army's devastating loss at the Second Battle of Bull Run in August 1862, President Abraham Lincoln confessed this:

I have been driven many times upon my knees by the overwhelming conviction that I had nowhere else to go. My own wisdom, and that of all about me, seemed insufficient for that day.

★ ★ Patriot's Prayer ★ ★

Heavenly Father, pour down upon me Your grace and Your wisdom. Give me a double portion that I may be able to do well whatever task comes before me today. Help me live as Jesus did. Let Your light shine through me today.

★ ★ Patriot's Promise ★ ★

"My grace is sufficient for you, for My strength is made perfect in weakness" is the promise of 2 Corinthians 12:9. When we are weak, God is strong.

The LORD is my strength.

EXODUS 15:2

An American Patriot

Born in the eastern Tennessee mountains on August 17, 1786, David Crockett had lived an adventurous life before he was twenty-five, fighting the Creek Indians alongside General Andrew Jackson and hunting bears in the Tennessee mountains with his coonskin cap, his favorite hunting knife, and his beloved musket "Old Betsy." In one week, Davy killed seventeen bears, and his annual total was an amazing 105.

The people of Tennessee elected Davy to represent them in the US Congress. Introducing himself there, he said, "I am the same Davy Crockett, fresh from the backwoods, half horse, half alligator, a little touched with the snapping turtle . . . I can whip my weight in wildcats, and if any gentleman pleases, for a ten dollar bill, he can throw in a panther too."

Although he served well in Congress, Crockett longed for the simpler life in his beloved Tennessee. In 1834 he returned home to his wife and four children.

In February 1836, Davy heard about the Mexican army's imminent attack on the Alamo. Davy and four friends traveled to Texas to fight the Mexicans. Despite the soldiers' courageous stand, the Alamo was overrun by four thousand Mexican soldiers. Davy Crockett and 150 other brave Americans lost their lives. Crockett's unquestioned integrity and courage had already earned him the well-deserved title of "American patriot."

★ ★ Patriot's Prayer ★ ★
Holy Spirit, keep me true to what You have taught me in whatever situation I find myself.

★ ★ Patriot's Promise ★ ★
"[The Holy Spirit] who is in you is greater than he who is in the world" (1 John 4:4).

August 17

The Incomparable Book

> We did not follow cunningly devised fables.
>
> 2 PETER 1:16

Charles Anderson Dana (1819–1897) was editor-in-chief of the *New York Sun*, one of the country's largest newspapers. Consider what this journalist—hailed as the most brilliant American journalist at the time—thought about the Bible:

> I believe in Christianity; that it is the religion taught to men by God Himself in person on earth. I also believe the Bible to be a Divine revelation. . . .
>
> There are some books that are absolutely indispensable to the kind of education that we are contemplating, and to the profession that we are now considering; and of all these, the most indispensable, the most useful, the one whose knowledge is most effective, is the Bible. There is no Book from which more valuable lessons can be learned. I am considering it now as a manual of utility, or professional preparation, and professional use for a journalist.
>
> There is no Book whose style is more suggestive and more instructive, from which you learn more directly that sublime simplicity which never exaggerates, which recounts the greatest event with solemnity, of course, but without sentimentality or affection, none which you open with such confidence and lay down with such reverence; there is no Book like the Bible.

★ ★ Patriot's Prayer ★ ★

Show me, Lord, what I need to do today to serve You. Help me to live in purity as a testimony to my family.

★ ★ Patriot's Promise ★ ★

Proverbs 22:6 contains this promise: "Train up a child in the way he should go, and when he is old he will not depart from it."

The Sun of Righteousness shall arise.

Malachi 4:2

A Guiding Light

Rutgers University was founded in New Jersey in 1766. Inspired by the motto of the University of Utrecht, Netherlands, which was "Sun of Righteousness, Shine Upon Us," Rutgers University chose this as its official motto:

Sun of Righteousness, Shine Upon the West Also

★ ★ Patriot's Prayer ★ ★

Dear Lord Jesus, I pray today as Your servant David did: "My times are in Your hand; deliver me from the hand of my enemies, and from those who persecute me. Make Your face shine upon Your servant; save me for Your mercies' sake. Do not let me be ashamed, O Lord, for I have called upon You" (Psalm 31:15–17).

★ ★ Patriot's Promise ★ ★

Second Samuel 22:4 contains this great promise that if we call upon the Lord, he will save us from our enemies: "I will call upon the Lord, who is worthy to be praised; so shall I be saved from my enemies."

"My Country, 'Tis of Thee"

May the LORD our God be with us, as He was with our fathers.

1 KINGS 8:57

Samuel Francis Smith wrote the words to "My Country, 'Tis of Thee," also known as "America," while studying at Andover Theological Seminary in 1831. The song's inspirational words were matched with a popular international melody used by many nations, including England, where it accompanies "God Save the King/Queen." The song soon became a national favorite, serving as a de facto national anthem of the United States for much of the nineteenth century.

My country, 'tis of thee, sweet land of liberty, of thee I sing:
>> Land where my fathers died, land of the pilgrims' pride,
>> From every mountainside let freedom ring!

My native country, thee, land of the noble free, thy name I love:
>> I love thy rocks and rills, thy woods and templed hills;
>> My heart with rapture thrills, like that above.

Let music swell the breeze, and ring from all the trees sweet freedom's song:
>> Let mortal tongues awake; let all that breathe partake;
>> Let rocks their silence break, the sound prolong.

Our fathers' God, to Thee, author of liberty, to Thee we sing:
>> Long may our land be bright with freedom's holy light.
>> Protect us by Thy might, great God, our King!

★ ★ Patriot's Prayer ★ ★

Father God, protect our nation so that we can be the light of salvation and freedom—political as well as spiritual—in this sin-darkened world.

★ ★ Patriot's Promise ★ ★

"Your word is a lamp to my feet and a light to my path" (Psalm 119:105).

August 20

★ 240 ★

Repentance and Restoration

I commanded them, saying, "Obey My voice, and I will be your God, and you shall be My people. And walk in all the ways that I have commanded you, that it may be well with you." Yet they did not obey or incline their ear, but followed the counsels and the dictates of their evil hearts, and went backward and not forward.

JEREMIAH 7:23–24

The prophet Jeremiah was just a youth when God called him to take a message of repentance to the rebellious nation of Judah. The compassionate Jeremiah agonized over Judah's sin even as he condemned their idolatry, and he proclaimed that God would respond to repentance and bring restoration even as he obediently pronounced God's severe judgment.

American statesman Daniel Webster understood how crucial it is for a nation "under God" to steadfastly guard its foundations of righteousness. In 1852, he warned his beloved America:

"If we and our posterity reject religious instruction and authority, violate the rules of eternal justice, trifle with the injunctions of morality, and recklessly destroy the political constitution which holds us together, no man can tell how sudden a catastrophe may overwhelm us, that shall bury all our glory in profound obscurity."

★ ★ Patriot's Prayer ★ ★

Holy God, convict us of our nation's sins and turn our hearts back to You in repentance. Do this not only for our sake, but for the sake of the generations of Americans who will follow us.

★ ★ Patriot's Promise ★ ★

"I dwell . . . with him who has a contrite and humble spirit, to revive the spirit of the humble, and to revive the heart of the contrite ones" (Isaiah 57:15).

August 21

His Unfailing Compassions

Through the LORD's mercies we are not consumed, because His compassions fail not. They are new every morning; great is Your faithfulness.

LAMENTATIONS 3:22–23

Written soon after the destruction of Jerusalem, the book of Lamentations describes the suffering of a nation as a result of the people's sin and rebellion. But this heartrending account doesn't merely focus on the tragic events that have left the children of God in despair; Lamentations also emphasizes God's unrelenting grace, mercy, and faithfulness.

The United States of America has faced a number of potentially catastrophic periods in its own history, but perhaps nothing threatened its utter destruction more than the issue of slavery. In her classic novel, *Uncle Tom's Cabin*, published in 1852, Harriet Beecher Stowe attacked the cruelty of slavery, making the slavery issue tangible to millions and energizing antislavery forces in the American North. Her book ends with this:

"A day of grace is yet held out to us. Both North and South have been guilty before God; and the Christian church has a heavy account to answer. Not by combining together, to protect injustice and cruelty, and making a common capital of sin, is this Union to be saved, but by repentance, justice, and mercy."

★ ★ **Patriot's Prayer** ★ ★

Almighty Lord, thank You for not yet judging America for all our wrongs and injustices. We have instead received Your unfailing and completely undeserved mercy and compassion. I thank You for this mercy even as I pray You will prompt us to repent, even as You continue in Your mercy.

★ ★ **Patriot's Promise** ★ ★

"The LORD is good; His mercy is everlasting, and His truth endures to all generations" (Psalm 100:5).

I proclaimed a fast . . . that we might humble ourselves before our God, to seek from
Him the right way for us.

So Help Me, God

EZRA 8:21

These short samples from presidential inaugural addresses reflect our nation's
dependence upon God:

*No people can be bound to acknowledge and adore the Invisible Hand which
conducts the affairs of men more than those of the United States.*

GEORGE WASHINGTON, APRIL 30, 1789

*I shall need, too, the favor of that Being in whose hands we are. . . . and to whose
goodness I ask you to join in supplications with me.*

THOMAS JEFFERSON, MARCH 4, 1805

*With malice toward none, with charity for all, with firmness in the right as God
gives us to see the right, let us strive . . . to bind up the nation's wounds . . . to do
all which may achieve and cherish a just and lasting peace among ourselves and
with all nations.*

ABRAHAM LINCOLN, MARCH 4, 1865

*The Almighty God . . . has given to our country a faith which has become the hope
of all peoples in an anguished world.*

FRANKLIN ROOSEVELT, JANUARY 20, 1945

*May He continue to hold us close as we fill the world with our sound . . . one people
under God, dedicated to the dream of freedom that He has placed in the human
heart, called upon now to pass that dream on to a waiting and hopeful world.*

RONALD REAGAN, JANUARY 21, 1985

★ ★ Patriot's Prayer ★ ★
Almighty God, bring us back to closer fellowship with You and Your Word.

★ ★ Patriot's Promise ★ ★
"There is no authority except from God, and the authorities that exist are appointed by God" (Romans 13:1).

August 23

God's Sovereign Control

The God of heaven will set up a kingdom which shall never be destroyed; and the kingdom shall not be left to other people; it shall break in pieces and consume all these kingdoms, and it shall stand forever.

DANIEL 2:44

Taken into captivity as a teenager and chosen to serve in the Babylonian government, Daniel stood before the exiled children of Israel—and among their godless captors—as a clear example of godly and upright behavior. As a prophet, Daniel encouraged the exiled Jews with the truth that their captivity would not last forever, but that their restoration would come at God's appointed time, foreshadowing the everlasting kingdom of God's chosen Messiah.

Like the prophet Daniel, General Robert E. Lee stood as a bright example of integrity, honor, character, and courage during one of America's darkest chapters. "My trust is in the mercy and wisdom of a kind Providence, who ordereth all things for our good," he wrote as he led the vastly outnumbered Army of Northern Virginia in America's Civil War. While his soldiers placed great confidence in his ability as a military leader, General Lee remained deeply humble: "I tremble for my country when I hear of confidence expressed in me. I know too well my weakness, that our only hope is in God."

★ ★ Patriot's Prayer ★ ★

Almighty Father, give me renewed assurance that You are in control of all that comes my way and that I may trust that You are my Protection and my Provider.

★ ★ Patriot's Promise ★ ★

"The LORD . . . will be with you, He will not leave you nor forsake you; do not fear nor be dismayed" (Deuteronomy 31:8).

Therefore you are no longer a slave but a son.

GALATIANS 3:28

Free to Worship

Born into slavery, Richard Allen (1760–1831) came to faith in Christ at age seventeen and started preaching at Methodist churches around Philadelphia. His owner allowed Allen to purchase his freedom for $2,000 by working for the Revolutionary forces, and he was one of the first blacks emancipated during the Revolutionary Era. For the following six years, Allen traveled the Methodist circuit in the mid-Atlantic states, preaching to black and white congregants alike.

In 1786, upon returning to Philadelphia, he preached at St. George's Methodist Church at 5:00 a.m. so his services would not interfere with the whites. His leadership attracted dozens of blacks, and with them came increased racial tension. Recognizing that blacks needed a place they could worship without restriction or harassment, Allen and a few others formed the Free African Society in 1787 and, in 1794, he started the Bethel African Methodist Episcopal Church.

Also in 1794, Allen and representatives from four other black Methodist congregations met at Bethel and organized the African Methodist Episcopal Church (AME), the first fully independent black denomination in America. Its motto has always been "God our father, man our brother, and Christ our redeemer."

A strong patriot, Allen supported the War of 1812 and denounced the notion of sending blacks to colonize in Africa: "This land which we have watered with our tears and our blood is now our mother country."

★ ★ Patriot's Prayer ★ ★

Lord, I commit my life to You afresh. Give me a fresh anointing to minister to those who are hurting, no matter how different they are from me.

★ ★ Patriot's Promise ★ ★

"Blessed is the nation whose God is the LORD" (Psalm 33:12).

August 25

A Godly Work Ethic

Whatever you do in word or deed, do all in the name of the Lord Jesus.

COLOSSIANS 3:17

Engrained in the American spirit is the work ethic of the Puritans, who believed that all of life is to be lived in relation to God. They therefore valued work as a vital part of their worship and service to God.

God Himself taught as about work and rest. He could have merely spoken creation into being, but He took six days and rested on the seventh. Created in God's image and with a purpose, man is to care for the world, work for six days, and rest on the seventh. The Puritans believed that the quality of our work reflects our personal character. So, whatever our trade or craft, we should do all to the glory of God: He is worthy of the best we can offer. The Sabbath offers opportunities for spirit-renewing worship.

This work ethic, with its spiritual roots, has enabled America to become the strongest economic powerhouse in the history of the world. This industrious spirit is not content to exist on government handouts, and it flies in the face of a pleasure-oriented society that exalts leisure above all else. As we work, we are to give our very best, "with goodwill doing service, as to the Lord, and not to men" (Ephesians 6:7).

★ ★ Patriot's Prayer ★ ★

Lord, may I be Your light where I work—doing everything for Your glory, working hard and honestly, avoiding conflicts, and serving others.

★ ★ Patriot's Promise ★ ★

"If anyone will not work, neither shall he eat" (2 Thessalonians 3:10).

If the Son makes you free,
you shall be free indeed.

JOHN 8:36

Protecting Basic Personal Freedoms

During the debates on the adoption of the US Constitution, some of its opponents argued that it failed to protect basic liberties. The Constitution spelled out the new government's delegated powers, but it did not define the citizens' rights or ensure that the federal government would never infringe on foundational civil rights.

James Madison introduced these ten amendments to the first US Congress in 1791, and they came into effect on December 15, 1791, after being ratified by three-fourths of the states. The Bill of Rights further defined the role of the federal government by identifying certain actions it would not do. Specifically, without the Bill of Rights, basic human rights—such as the freedom of religion and of speech, the freedom to assemble, the right to a free press, the right to keep and bear arms, the right to a speedy public trial—could have been denied or repressed. The Bill of Rights prohibits unreasonable search and seizure, cruel and unusual punishment, and compelled self-incrimination. In addition, the Bill of Rights reserves all powers not granted to the federal government to the citizenry or states.

★ ★ Patriot's Prayer ★ ★

Lord, thank You for the wisdom You provided our Founding Fathers. May those who lead us now preserve the basic rights set forth in the Constitution. Give leaders today wisdom so theirs, too, will be a legacy of freedom.

★ ★ Patriot's Promise ★ ★

"If anyone among you thinks he is religious, and does not bridle his tongue but deceives his own heart, this one's religion is useless" (James 1:26).

"I Have a Dream"

Every valley shall be exalted and every mountain and hill brought low.

ISAIAH 40:4

On August 28, 1963, Martin Luther King Jr.—a driving force in the effort to end segregation and racial discrimination—stood on the steps of the Lincoln Memorial and delivered these unforgettable words:

Now is the time to rise from the dark and desolate valley of segregation to the sunlit path of racial justice . . .

I have a dream that one day this nation will rise up and live out the true meaning of its creed: "We hold these truths to be self-evident: that all men are created equal."

I have a dream that one day on the red hills of Georgia the sons of former slaves and the sons of former slave owners will be able to sit down together at the table of brotherhood . . .

I have a dream that my four little children will one day live in a nation where they will not be judged by the color of their skin but by the content of their character. . . .

When we allow freedom to ring . . . we will be able to speed up that day when all of God's children, black men and white men, Jews and Gentiles, Protestants and Catholics, will be able to join hands and sing in the words of the old Negro spiritual, "Free at last! Free at last! Thank God Almighty, we are free at last!"

★ ★ Patriot's Prayer ★ ★

Lord, as You have brought right from wrong to strengthen this nation, use the trials in my life to strengthen my character.

★ ★ Patriot's Promise ★ ★

"No longer . . . a slave, but more than a slave—a beloved brother" (Philemon 1:16).

Pray without ceasing.

1 Thessalonians 5:17

The Lifeblood of Prayer

Thomas "Stonewall" Jackson (1824–1863), probably the most revered Confederate commander after General Robert E. Lee, said this:

> When we take our meals, there is the grace. When I take a draught of water, I always pause . . . to lift up my heart to God in thanks and prayer for the water of life. . . . When I break the seal of a letter just received, I stop to pray to God that He may prepare me for its contents and make it a messenger of good. When I go to my classroom and await the arrangement of the cadets in their places, that is my time to intercede with God for them.

★ ★ Patriot's Prayer ★ ★

Prayer, Holy Father, is the key to life lived in relationship to You. So I make a new commitment to You today: I will be more conscientious about praying like Stonewall Jackson prayed. As I intercede for others, guide my prayers for them according to Your will.

★ ★ Patriot's Promise ★ ★

Hear Jesus' amazing promise: "Whatever you ask in My name, that I will do, that the Father may be glorified in the Son" (John 14:13). We can't assume that God will straighten out our problems if we do not pray about them, and asking in Jesus' name and according to God's will is key.

August 29

Returning to God

"Behold, the days are coming," says the Lord GOD, "that I will send a famine on the land . . . a famine . . . of hearing the words of the LORD."

AMOS 8:11

The book of Amos was written when Israel's economic prosperity only thinly covered the greedy hearts of those who dealt heartlessly with the poor and disadvantaged among them. God called Amos, a farmer by trade, to urge the people of Israel to repent of their sin.

A similar challenge exists today for the people of America to return to God as she did during America's Great Awakening, a revival sparked largely by twenty-five-year-old George Whitefield's 1739–1740 preaching tour. His farewell sermon on August 30, 1769 on Boston Common drew 23,000 people—more than Boston's entire population:

> The door of mercy is not yet shut, there does yet remain a sacrifice for sin, for all that will accept of the Lord Jesus Christ. He will embrace you in the arms of His love. O turn to Him . . . tell Him how polluted you are, how vile, and be not faithless, but believing. Why fear ye that the Lord Jesus Christ will not accept of you? Your sins will be no hindrance, your unworthiness no hindrance; if your own corrupt hearts do not keep you back, nothing will hinder Christ from receiving of you . . . He will not send you away without His Spirit; no, but will receive and bless you.

★ ★ Patriot's Prayer ★ ★

O Lord, may America return to You. Prompt a national revival of sorrow for sin, repentance, and rededication to You—and let that revival begin in my heart.

★ ★ Patriot's Promise ★ ★

"In returning and rest you shall be saved; in quietness and confidence shall be your strength" (Isaiah 30:15).

The apostles and elders came together to consider this matter.

ACTS 15:6

"A Little Short of a Miracle"

Defining government as *of*, *by*, and *for* the people, the US Constitution was the first written constitution in the world. Enduring through more than two centuries of trial by bloodshed, fire, and tears, it has served as a model for many nations. . . .

On September 17, 1787, George Washington witnessed the signing of the US Constitution and later declared it as "little short of a miracle"—and for good reason. The leaders from the thirteen states were deeply divided on many fundamental issues, particularly on the extent to which the states would cede any power to a national government.

So remarkable was the consensus for a strong central government that Benjamin Franklin said, "I have so much faith in the general government of the world by Providence, that I can hardly conceive a transaction of such momentous importance . . . should be suffered to pass without being in some degree influenced, guided, and governed by that omnipotent, omnipresent, and beneficent Ruler."

Charles Pinckney, another of the framers, said, "Nothing less than that superintending hand of Providence, that so miraculously carried us through the war . . . could have brought [the Constitution] about so complete."

Alexander Hamilton expressed a similar view: "I sincerely esteem it a system, which, without the finger of God, never could have been suggested and agreed upon by such a diversity of interests."

★ ★ Patriot's Prayer ★ ★
Father, thank You for Your involvement in the forming of this great land's government and history. May we always look to You for guidance.

★ ★ Patriot's Promise ★ ★
"With God all things are possible" (Mark 10:27).

251

September

How can a young man cleanse his way? By
taking heed according to Your Word.

PSALM 119:9

Fisher Ames (1758–1808) was a Founding Father and a politician who helped
formulate the Bill of Rights. Consider His perspective on the importance of
reading God's Word:

> We have a dangerous trend beginning to take place in our educa-
> tion. We're starting to put more and more textbooks into our
> schools. . . . We've become accustomed of late of putting little books
> into the hands of children containing fables and moral lessons. . . .
>
> We are spending less time in the classroom on the Bible, which
> should be the principal text of our schools. . . . The Bible states these
> great moral lessons better than any manmade book.

★ ★ Patriot's Prayer ★ ★

God, help me to be more aware of what I read. May I not compromise my Christian testimony, values, or mind-set by reading those things I shouldn't. Help me
choose material that fosters in me pure thoughts and right ideas.

★ ★ Patriot's Promise ★ ★

As Psalm 119:114 says, "You are my hiding place and my shield; I hope in Your
word." God's Word serves as a shield of protection and a source of hope in this
dark and confused world.

September 1

McGuffey Readers

> Whatever things were written before were written for our learning.
>
> ROMANS 15:4

Considered the "Schoolmaster of the Nation," William Holmes McGuffey (1800–1873) published the first edition of his *McGuffey Reader* in 1836, one of the nation's first and most widely used series of textbooks in public education. It is estimated that at least 120 million copies of *McGuffey Readers* were sold between 1836 and 1960, placing its sales in a category with the *Bible* and *Webster's Dictionary.* In the preface of his *Eclectic Third Reader*, McGuffey wrote the following:

Selections [have been] drawn from the purest fountains of English literature.... Copious extracts made from the Sacred Scripture.

Upon a review of the work ... an apology may be due for not having still more liberally transferred to pages the chaste simplicity, the thrilling pathos, the living descriptions, and the matchless sublimity of the Sacred Writings.

From no source has the author drawn more copiously than from the Sacred Scriptures.... This certainly apprehends no censure. In a Christian country, that man is to be pitied, who, at this day, can honestly object to imbuing the minds of youth with the language and spirit of the Word of God.

★ ★ Patriot's Prayer ★ ★

Abba Father, use Your Word to guide me in my everyday life. May the language of Your Word guide my own even as the spirit of Your Word transforms my heart.

★ ★ Patriot's Promise ★ ★

John 12:48 promises that "He who rejects Me, and does not receive My words, has that which judges him—the word that I have spoken will judge him in the last day."

My people have been lost sheep. Their shepherds have led them astray.

JEREMIAH 50:6

Gone Astray

Many states have passed laws that allow the posting of our national motto, "In God We Trust," in public buildings and school classrooms. In 1992, for instance, the State of Kentucky passed Kentucky Revised Statute, Title XIII, Education, 158.195, regarding conduct of schools:

> Reading and posting in public schools of texts and documents on American history and heritage.—Local school boards may allow any teacher or administrator in a public school district of the Commonwealth to read or post in a public school building, classroom, or event any excerpts or portions of the National Motto, the National Anthem, the Pledge of Allegiance, the Preamble to the Kentucky Constitution, the Declaration of Independence, the Mayflower Pact, the writings, speeches, documents, and proclamations of the founding fathers and presidents of the United States, U.S. Supreme Court decisions, and acts of the U.S. Congress, including the published text of the Congressional Record.
>
> There shall be no content-based censorship of American history or heritage in the Commonwealth based on religious references in these writings, documents, and records.

How far astray have we gone that we have to pass such laws?

★ ★ Patriot's Prayer ★ ★

Lord, it is tragic that such laws need even be written, but thank You for those elected officials who know You and are willing to do the work.

★ ★ Patriot's Promise ★ ★

Proverbs 10:17 says, "He who keeps instruction is in the way of life, but he who refuses correction goes astray."

September 3

Why a Wall of Separation?

> This evil people . . . refuse to hear My words . . . and walk after other gods to serve them and worship them.
>
> JEREMIAH 13:10

The Founding Fathers began the First Amendment with these words: "Congress shall make no law respecting an establishment of religion, or prohibiting the free exercise thereof." For over 150 years, this mandate was understood to prohibit the establishment of a national religion by Congress, the preference of one religion over another, and the preference of religion over non-religion. Clearly, there was no hint that the amendment means to exclude people of faith or their values from impacting, participating in, or shaping government.

But in 1947 the *Everson v. Board of Education* decision took up Thomas Jefferson's "wall of church and state" metaphor, a phrase not even in the Constitution. Those words appeared in a letter thirteen years after the Constitution was adopted: "The First Amendment has erected a wall between church and state. That wall must be kept high and impregnable."

Since that case, religion has been silenced. Court decisions have declared verbal prayer in school unconstitutional, restricted religious speech, removed the Ten Commandments from public buildings—and the list goes on.

Soon after *Emerson*, another wall against religious freedom was built with the revision of the IRS tax code. Tax-exempt religious groups are now prohibited from even implicitly endorsing or opposing candidates for public office.

We need to take action to reestablish the primacy of faith in American life and maintain America as "one nation, under God."

★ ★ Patriot's Prayer ★ ★

Lord, help me courageously stand for the right to publicly practice my faith.

★ ★ Patriot's Promise ★ ★

"Be of good courage, and He shall strengthen your heart" (Psalm 27:14).

Every word of God is pure.

PROVERBS 30:5

Founding Father Dr. Benjamin Rush was one of the first to call for public schools. He understood the value of educated citizens:

I believe no man was ever early instructed in the truths of the Bible without having been made wiser or better.

If moral precepts alone could have reformed mankind, the mission of the Son of God into our world would have been unnecessary. He came to promulgate a system of doctrines, as well as a system of morals. The perfect morality of the Gospel rests upon ... the vicarious life and death of the Son of God. This sublime and ineffable doctrine ... fixes [moral obligation] upon the eternal and self-moving principle of LOVE. It concentrates a whole system of ethics in a single text of Scripture: "A new commandment I give unto you, that ye love one another, even as I have loved you." By withholding the knowledge of this doctrine from children, we deprive ourselves of the best means of awakening moral sensibility in their minds....

I lament that we ... take so little pains to prevent [crimes].... We neglect the only means of establishing and perpetuating our republican forms of government; that is, the universal education of our youth in the principles of Christianity by means of the Bible; for this divine book, above all others, favors that equality among mankind, that respect for just laws, and all those sober and frugal virtues which constitute the soul of republicanism.

★ ★ Patriot's Prayer ★ ★

Use me, Father, to share Christ's love with my family, church, community, and nation.

★ ★ Patriot's Promise ★ ★

"The humble He guides in justice" (Psalm 29:5).

September 5

The First Prayer in Congress

Fight against those who fight against me.

The first Congress of the United States met on September 7, 1774, when members were very concerned about Great Britain's recent attack on Boston. Reverend Jacob Duché, rector of Christ Church of Philadelphia, was summoned to lead the opening prayers. After reading Psalm 35, Reverend Duché prayed extemporaneously:

> O Lord our Heavenly Father, high and mighty King of kings and Lord of lords . . . look down in mercy, we beseech Thee, on these our American States, who have fled to Thee from the rod of the oppressor and thrown themselves on Thy gracious protection, desiring to be henceforth dependent only on Thee. To Thee have they appealed for the righteousness of their cause; to Thee do they now look up for that countenance and support, which Thou alone canst give. Take them, therefore, Heavenly Father, under Thy nurturing care; give them wisdom in council and valor in the field; defeat the malicious designs of our cruel adversaries. . . .
>
> Be Thou present, O God of wisdom, and direct the councils of this honorable assembly; enable them to settle things on the best and surest foundation. That the scene of blood may be speedily closed; that order, harmony, and peace may be effectually restored, and truth and justice, religion and piety, prevail and flourish amongst the people. . . . All this we ask in the name and through the merits of Jesus Christ, Thy Son and our Savior. Amen.

★ ★ Patriot's Prayer ★ ★

Heavenly Father, when I need direction, help my first reaction be to read Your Word and go to You in prayer.

★ ★ Patriot's Promise ★ ★

"You will find [the LORD] if you seek Him with all your heart" (Deuteronomy 4:29).

September 6

★ ★ ★
★ 258 ★
★ ★ ★

> Let every soul be subject to the governing authorities.
>
> ROMANS 13:1

Our Nation's Security

Congregational minister Benjamin Franklin Morris (1810–1867) authored *The Christian Life and Character of the Civil Institutions of the United States* in 1864. Consider this observation:

> These fundamental objects of the Constitution are in perfect harmony with the revealed objects of the Christian religion. Union, justice, peace, the general welfare, and the blessings of civil and religious liberty, are the objects of Christianity, and always secured under its practical and beneficent reign.
>
> The state must rest upon the basis of religion ... or itself must fall. But the support which religion gives to the state will obviously cease the moment religion loses its hold upon the popular mind.
>
> This is a Christian nation, first in name, and secondly because of the many and mighty elements of a pure Christianity which have given it character and shaped its destiny from the beginning. It is preeminently the land of the Bible, of the Christian Church, and of the Christian Sabbath. ... The chief security and glory of the United States of America has been, is now, and will be forever, the prevalence and domination of the Christian faith.

★ ★ Patriot's Prayer ★ ★

Lord, even when I may not agree with what our leaders are doing, keep me disciplined and faithful about praying for them. Guide every decision they make and give Your wisdom to every man and woman who leads us.

★ ★ Patriot's Promise ★ ★

Psalm 19:7–8 teaches that "the law of the LORD is perfect ... The statutes of the LORD are right."

Tyranny—Natural and Supernatural

I n 1774, the Massachusetts Provincial Congress set forth this resolution: Resistance to tyranny becomes the Christian and social duty of each individual.... Continue steadfast, and with a proper sense of your dependence on God, nobly defend those rights which heaven gave, and no man ought to take from us.

★ ★ Patriot's Prayer ★ ★

Today, Lord, I pray for the protection of this nation. May I do all that I can to maintain the rights and individual freedoms that You have granted us.

★ ★ Patriot's Promise ★ ★

This is a promise from Jesus Himself: "I will give you the keys of the kingdom of heaven, and whatever you bind on earth will be bound in heaven, and whatever you loose on earth will be loosed in heaven" (Matthew 16:19). When we find ourselves facing seemingly impossible situations, we can give them to God, and He will provide a way when there seems to be no way.

Judas Iscariot . . . became a traitor.

LUKE 6:16

Benedict Arnold

During the Revolutionary War, Benedict Arnold (1741–1801) was considered by many to be the best general in the Continental Army. Without his early contributions to the American cause, the patriots might have lost the war. Despite being imaginative, daring, and courageous, Benedict Arnold is instead remembered for his act of treason.

After marrying Peggy Shippen, a beautiful young British Loyalist, getting into deep debt, becoming frustrated over the lack of recognition he received, and being disgusted with congressional politics, Arnold negotiated with British commander Sir Henry Clinton and promised to deliver the well-fortified American stronghold at West Point and its 3,000 defenders for 20,300 sterling (about $1 million today), an act that would devastate the American cause.

Persuading George Washington to place the fort under his command, Arnold moved to execute his treacherous plan in September 1780. Fortunately, the plot was discovered just before the British attack, but Arnold escaped. Rewarded with a commission as a brigadier general in the British army, he served with the same dynamic energy and daring he had served the American cause, leading devastating attacks against his countrymen. After the war, he returned to England and later died there, virtually unknown.

Benedict Arnold abused his position of authority and trust, willingly betraying the American cause. He could have been one of the great heroes of the American Revolution, but is instead its greatest traitor.

★ ★ Patriot's Prayer ★ ★
Dear Lord, may I humbly serve and glorify You . . . and not the enemy.

★ ★ Patriot's Promise ★ ★
"Let us not grow weary while doing good, for in due season we shall reap if we do not lose heart" (Galatians 6:9).

261

"Let's Roll!"

Greater love has no one than this, than to lay down one's life for his friends.

JOHN 15:13

On the morning of September 11, 2001, United Flight 93 from Newark to San Francisco was hijacked by terrorists. With telephone confirmation that other planes had struck the Twin Towers of the World Trade Center, the passengers understood the hijackers' intent.

Thirty-two-year-old Todd Beamer picked up a seat-back phone and reached GTE supervisor Lisa Jefferson. He told her that he and others were going to "jump on" the hijacker guarding the passengers in the rear. Beamer asked her to pray the Lord's Prayer with him. He also made her promise to call his wife, Lisa, and tell her that he loved her and their two little boys.

Then, dropping the phone, Beamer said, "Jesus, help me." After reciting Psalm 23, he said, "Are you guys ready? Okay, let's roll." Those were the unforgettable last words Beamer said before he and others rushed the hijackers of United Airlines Flight 93. There were screams, then silence.

Brave American civilians rose against impossible odds and made the ultimate sacrifice. United Flight 93 crashed into a field near Shanksville, Pennsylvania, killing all forty-four aboard. Of the four hijacked planes that morning, United 93 was the only one that failed to hit the targeted site.

★ ★ Patriot's Prayer ★ ★
Dear Lord, thank You for the men and women and their families who sacrificially serve our country and often give their lives to protect our freedom.

★ ★ Patriot's Promise ★ ★
"Be strong and of good courage, do not fear nor be afraid of them; for the LORD your God . . . goes with you. He will not leave you nor forsake you" (Deuteronomy 31:6).

If I perish, I perish!

Esther 4:15

In *A Time for Heroes*, Lance Wubbels paid tribute to the patriotic heroes the world watched on September 11, 2001:

> It was a day of unthinkable horror and destruction, but it became a day for American heroes. Ordinary American citizens, suddenly caught in the crossfire of terrorism, put their lives on the line to preserve the lives of others. . . .
>
> They emerged as the truly mighty and valiant ones of Flight 93. Among the smoldering wreckage of the Pentagon, they stood with undimmed spirits as firefighters unfurled a gigantic flag from the roof of the burned-out structure. At Ground Zero, hundreds and thousands of people on dozens of fronts searched the mountain of unstable rubble in an epic battle to win back as many lives as could possibly be rescued.
>
> Most of them remain nameless to us, but their undaunted faces are engraved forever upon our hearts. They are the firefighters. . . . They are the police, paramedics, rescue workers, doctors, nurses, National Guard, Red Cross workers. And they are the janitors and security guards and office managers and the coworkers who said no to death and helped thousands escape who might have easily perished. . . .
>
> In a world where rock superstars, athletes, and celebrities have been elevated to hero status, we were given a lesson on true heroism and patriotism.

★ ★ Patriot's Prayer ★ ★

Father, please comfort those who lost loved ones in that 9-11 tragedy. Convict the wicked perpetrators and draw them to repentance . . . and to You.

★ ★ Patriot's Promise ★ ★

"Your God will come with vengeance . . . He will come and save you" (Isaiah 35:4).

263

America's Steel Resolve

All the men of Israel were gathered against the city, united together as one man.

JUDGES 20:11

When he addressed the American people on September 11, 2001, President George Bush said this:

The pictures of airplanes flying into buildings, fires burning, huge structures collapsing, have filled us with disbelief, terrible sadness, and a quiet, unyielding anger. These acts of mass murder were intended to frighten our nation into chaos and retreat. But they have failed; our country is strong.

A great people has been moved to defend a great nation. Terrorist attacks can shake the foundations of our biggest buildings, but they cannot touch the foundation of America. These acts shattered steel, but they cannot dent the steel of American resolve. . . .

Today, our nation saw evil, the very worst of human nature. And we responded with the best of America—with the daring of our rescue workers, with the caring for strangers and neighbors who came to give blood and help in any way they could.

This is a day when all Americans from every walk of life unite in our resolve for justice and peace. America has stood down enemies before, and we will do so this time. None of us will ever forget this day. Yet, we go forward to defend freedom and all that is good and just in our world.

★ ★ Patriot's Prayer ★ ★

Heavenly Father, give us wisdom and strength as we fight against evil in this world and for goodness, justice, and peace.

★ ★ Patriot's Promise ★ ★

Hear the promises implicit in this prayer: "According to Your mercy remember me, for Your goodness' sake, O LORD" (Psalm 25:7).

September 12

Our God whom we serve is able to deliver us
from the burning fiery furnace.

DANIEL 3:17

A Fireman's Prayer

When I am called to duty, God,
      Wherever flame may rage,
      Give me the strength to save some life,
      Whatever be its age.
Help me embrace a little child
      Before it is too late,
      Or save an older person from
      The horror of that fate.
Enable me to be alert
      And hear the weakest shout,
      And quickly and efficiently
      To put the fire out.
I want to fill my calling and
      To give the best in me,
      To guard my every neighbor
      And protect his property.
And if according to my fate,
      I am to lose my life,
      Please bless with Your protecting hand
      My children and my wife.
                Author Unknown

★ ★ Patriot's Prayer ★ ★

Dear God, I pray the you would be a shield around the fire fighters, police officers,
air traffic controllers, soldiers, and every other man and woman, here and abroad,
who protect and serve us.

★ ★ Patriot's Promise ★ ★

"The LORD is my strength and my shield; my heart trusted in Him, and I am
helped" (Psalm 28:7).

September 13

Hope

On September 14, 2001, three days after the September 11 attacks, Dr. Billy Graham led a national prayer service at Washington National Cathedral: This event reminds us of the brevity and the uncertainty of life. We never know when we too will be called into eternity. I doubt if even one of those people who got on those planes or walked into the World Trade Center or the Pentagon last Tuesday morning thought it would be the last day of their lives. It didn't occur to them. And that's why each of us needs to face our own spiritual need and commit ourselves to God and His will now.

Here in this majestic National Cathedral we see all around us symbols of the Cross. For the Christian . . . the Cross tells us that God understands our sin and our suffering, for He took upon Himself in the person of Jesus Christ our sins and our suffering. And from the Cross, God declares, "I love you. I know the heartaches and the sorrows and the pains that you feel. But I love you."

The story does not end with the Cross, for Easter points us beyond the tragedy of the Cross to the empty tomb. It tells us that there is hope for eternal life, for Christ has conquered evil and death, and hell. Yes, there is hope.

★ ★ Patriot's Prayer ★ ★

Thank You, Father, for the Cross and for the hope of the empty tomb.

★ ★ Patriot's Promise ★ ★

"Christ has redeemed us from the curse of the law, having become a curse for us (for it is written, *Cursed is everyone who hangs on a tree*)" (Galatians 3:13). What a great and hope-filled covenant promise for us!

September 14

We ask you . . . not to be soon shaken in mind or troubled, either by spirit or by word or by letter, as if from us, as though the day of Christ had come. Let no one deceive you by any means; for that Day will not come unless the falling away comes first, and the man of sin is revealed, the son of perdition.

2 THESSALONIANS 2:2–3

Although Paul's first letter to the Thessalonians addressed the coming day of the Lord, they had nevertheless fallen prey to false teaching, being persuaded that the day of the Lord had already begun. Paul wrote this epistle to correct the error and to encourage those believers whose faith was being tested by persecution.

Paul always moved quickly to deal with heresy before it could damage the churches. Standing on the authority of his apostleship, he did not ask anyone's permission to be straightforward about the truth of the gospel. Similarly, after the terrorist attacks of September 11, 2001, President George W. Bush said, "America will never seek a permission slip to defend the security of our country." He immediately announced a Global War on Terrorism: it started with the invasion of Afghanistan as the first step toward the overthrow of the Taliban regime.

★ ★ Patriot's Prayer ★ ★
Heavenly Father, please grant me the strength and courage to speak for that which is just and moral and right and true. Let me be unashamed of my faith and my Savior as the days of wickedness approach.

★ ★ Patriot's Promise ★ ★
God promised, "I will never leave you nor forsake you" (Hebrews 13:5).

September 15

Paying the Price of Liberty

> Every good gift and every perfect
> gift is from above.
>
> JAMES 1:17

In his 1837 farewell address, President Andrew Jackson issued this charge: But you must remember, my fellow citizens, that eternal vigilance by the people is the price of liberty, and that you must pay the price if you wish to secure the blessing.

You have no longer any cause to fear danger from abroad; your strength and power are well known throughout the civilized world, as well as the high and gallant bearing of your sons. It is from within, among yourselves—from cupidity, from corruption, from disappointed ambition and inordinate thirst for power—that factions will be formed and liberty endangered. It is against such designs, whatever disguise the actors may assume, that you have especially to guard yourselves. You have the highest of human trusts committed to your care. Providence has showered on this favored land blessings without number, and has chosen you as the guardians of freedom, to preserve it for the benefit of the human race. May He who holds in His hands the destinies of nations make you worthy of the favors He has bestowed and enable you, with pure hearts and pure hands and sleepless vigilance, to guard and defend to the end of time the great charge He has committed to your keeping.

★ ★ Patriot's Prayer ★ ★

Dear Lord, help me faithfully and vigilantly guard and defend the gift of liberty You have graciously bestowed upon this nation.

★ ★ Patriot's Promise ★ ★

God promises to protect those who trust in Him: "You who fear the LORD, trust in the LORD; He is their help and their shield" (Psalm 115:11).

September 16

★ 268 ★

Though He slay me, yet will I trust Him.

Job 13:15

God's Sovereignty

The heartaches and difficulties of Job are well known. Yet in the end, despite his unimaginable loss and intense suffering of the soul, Job recognized and bowed before God's unquestionable sovereignty. In the end Job declared, "I have heard of You by the hearing of the ear, but now my eye sees You" (42:5). Having seen God more accurately than ever, Job submitted to His lordship to a new degree, and God graciously restored all that was taken from him—and blessed him with even more.

In times of great stress and trial, God remains faithful. On September 16, 1775, Abigail Adams wrote to her husband, John Adams, about her decision to trust in God despite intense uncertainty:

> "Unto Him who mounts the whirlwind and directs the storm, I will cheerfully leave the ordering of my lot and whether adverse or prosperous days should be my future portion, I will trust in His right hand to lead me safely through, and after a short rotation of events, fix me in a state immutable and happy."

★ ★ Patriot's Prayer ★ ★

Help me, O Lord, even in the midst of my most difficult hours, to choose to trust in Your sovereignty and in Your love for me. Just as Job patiently waited to see You work on his behalf, so let me wait in trust for You to deliver me from my troubles.

★ ★ Patriot's Promise ★ ★

"Those who wait on the Lord shall renew their strength; they shall mount up with wings like eagles, they shall run and not be weary, they shall walk and not faint" (Isaiah 40:31).

September 17

Righteous Laws

You shall be holy to Me, for I the LORD am holy, and have separated you from the peoples, that you should be Mine.

LEVITICUS 20:26

When America's Founding Fathers wrapped up the Constitutional Convention in Philadelphia on September 18, 1787, they knew they had hammered out a system of government far different from any that then existed. This was a government based on the "Laws of Nature and of Nature's God" rather than on the arbitrary and unjust rule of man.

God created humans to lead upright and orderly lives, but in the fall we lost the God-given ability to consistently choose His path of righteousness and obedience. The book of Leviticus reflects God's plan to lead humanity back to righteousness, initially through a set of Old Testament laws and, later, through the righteousness of His only Son, Jesus Christ.

★ ★ Patriot's Prayer ★ ★

Dear God, may I walk this day according to Your law of love, because of my love for You. I do not trust in obedience to the law for my salvation, but in Your mercy and grace. Teach me to choose rightly—to choose to obey You—so that I might live abundantly within that mercy and grace.

★ ★ Patriot's Promise ★ ★

When we walk in obedience to the will of God, He will open doors of blessings before us that we never imagined we could enter into: "If you diligently obey the voice of the LORD your God, to observe carefully all His commandments which I command you today, . . . the LORD your God will set you high above all nations of the earth" (Deuteronomy 28:1).

Man is not justified by the works of the law but by faith in Jesus Christ, . . . for by the works of the law no flesh shall be justified.

GALATIANS 2:16

Freedom from the Law

As the book of Galatians reveals, the believers there had heard Paul preach and accepted Christ as their Lord and Savior by faith. They had begun, however, to surrender their priceless liberty by succumbing to a gospel of works. Paul wrote this forceful epistle to convince them to do away with that false gospel of works; he also argued the clear superiority of justification by faith. This is Paul's manifesto of justification by faith and his charge that no believer should ever trade away the resulting liberty.

The oppressive theology of certain Jewish legalizers, however, had caused Galatian believers to question and even surrender their freedom in Christ. Paul's stern warning to the Galatians is similar to President Abraham Lincoln's warning to the people of the United States: "America will never be destroyed from the outside. If we falter and lose our freedoms, it will be because we destroyed ourselves."

★ ★ Patriot's Prayer ★ ★

Lord, keep me from trading away my liberty in You for works of the flesh no matter how good they may seem. Also keep from my life those who are steeped in the religious bondage of "good works" as they would try to rob me of my joy in serving You out of love.

★ ★ Patriot's Promise ★ ★

Jesus proclaimed, "If the Son makes you free, you shall be free indeed" (John 8:36).

"The Moral Precepts of Jesus"

Then He opened His mouth and taught them.

MATTHEW 5:2

In a letter to Dr. Benjamin Rush in 1803, President Thomas Jefferson made this statement:

> The practice of morality being necessary for the well-being of society, He [God] has taken care to impress its precepts so indelibly on our hearts that they shall not be effaced by the subtleties of our brain. We all agree in the obligation of the moral precepts of Jesus, and nowhere will they be found delivered in greater purity than in His discourses.

★ ★ Patriot's Prayer ★ ★

Father, forgive my blunders and make my heart pure before You. Renew my strength in moral values and give me understanding of how to guard my mind against the wickedness of this world. Take hold of me, Lord, and don't let me go.

★ ★ Patriot's Promise ★ ★

God is so faithful to us. In fact, in 1 John 1:9, we are told that our faithful God will forgive our sins if we confess them to Him. The verse goes on to say that He will not only forgive us of our sins, but He will cleanse us of all unrighteousness.

[God has] heard the groaning of the children of Israel whom the Egyptians keep in bondage.

Exodus 6:5

The Emancipation Proclamation

Near the end of the Civil War, President Abraham Lincoln issued the two-part Emancipation Proclamation. On September 22, 1862, he declared the freedom of all slaves in any of the Confederate States of America that did not return to Union control by January 1, 1863. On January 1, 1863, Lincoln named the specific states where it applied. The Emancipation Proclamation committed the Union to ending slavery, and as the Union armies conquered the Confederacy, thousands of slaves were freed each day.

President Lincoln stated that the Bible—especially Exodus 6:5—moved him to issue this highly controversial proclamation. He later remarked, "I never, in my life, felt more certain that I was doing right, than I did in signing this paper."

Booker T. Washington remembered the day of freedom for his family when he was nine:

> After the reading [of the Emancipation Proclamation], we were told that we were all free and could go when and where we pleased. My mother, who was standing by my side, leaned over and kissed her children, while tears of joy ran down her cheeks. She explained to us what it all meant, that this was the day for which she had been so long praying, but fearing that she would never live to see.

★ ★ Patriot's Prayer ★ ★
Holy Father, thank You for bringing me out of sin and into the freedom of Your salvation.

★ ★ Patriot's Promise ★ ★
"The law of the Spirit of life in Christ Jesus has made me free from the law of sin and death" (Romans 8:2).

September 21

Faith That Works

> What does it profit, my brethren, if someone says he has faith but does not have works? Can faith save him? . . . Faith by itself, if it does not have works, is dead.
>
> JAMES 2:14, 17

The book of James has been called "the Proverbs of the New Testament" for its similarities to Old Testament wisdom literature, and its author's impassioned preaching against injustice has earned James the title "the Amos of the New Testament." Throughout this epistle, James teaches how true faith can impact everyday practical experience, emphasizing that true faith must manifest itself in works.

James would have commended Nathan Hale for being a man of action. When Hale heard about the British Siege of Boston in 1775, he declared, "Let us march immediately, and never lay down our arms until we obtain our independence." Later, having served as a spy in the Revolutionary War, Hale was captured by the British and hanged on September 22, 1776. This great American hero reportedly said to his captors, "I only regret that I have but one life to lose for my country." Nathan Hale willingly put his beliefs into action. That is the Christian faith's ultimate goal as well.

★ ★ Patriot's Prayer ★ ★

Heavenly Father, show me how to be involved in Your kingdom work. Use me to help the weak, lift up the downtrodden, comfort the grieving, and be the hand of Jesus by putting my faith into action each day.

★ ★ Patriot's Promise ★ ★

God has promised that if we demonstrate our faith in Him, He is pleased and He will reward those who diligently, by faith, seek after Him. "Without faith it is impossible to please [God], for he who comes to God must believe that He is, and that He is a rewarder of those who diligently seek Him" (Hebrews 11:6).

Do not fear; Zion, let not your hands be weak.

ZEPHANIAH 3:16

Facing Fear

In his first inaugural address on March 4, 1933, Franklin Delano Roosevelt, the thirty-second president of the United States (1933–1945), proclaimed the following to his nation, which had just entered the Depression:

> Let me assert my firm belief that the only thing we have to fear is fear itself—nameless, unreasoning, unjustified terror which paralyzes needed efforts to convert retreat into advance....
>
> Practices of the unscrupulous moneychangers stand indicted in the court of public opinion....They know only the rules of a generation of self-seekers. They have no vision, and where there is no vision the people perish [Proverbs 29:18]. The moneychangers have fled from their high seats in the temple of our civilization. We may now restore that temple to the ancient truths....
>
> We face arduous days that lie before us in the warm courage of national unity; with the clear consciousness of seeking old and precious moral values....
>
> We humbly ask the blessing of God. May He protect each and every one of us!

★ ★ Patriot's Prayer ★ ★

Lord, at times, I feel overwhelmed by fear. I fear the future, fear I'm going to fail, and fear I won't be able to take care of my family. Holy Spirit, fill me with Your presence, because whom shall I fear if You are there?

★ ★ Patriot's Promise ★ ★

According to 1 Corinthians 10:13, "God is faithful, who will not allow you to be tempted beyond what you are able, but with the temptation will also make the way of escape, that you may be able to bear it."

American Education

Gather the people together, men and women and little ones . . . that they may hear . . . and carefully observe all the words of this law.

DEUTERONOMY 31:12

Believing that the purpose of schools was to advance the Christian faith, Noah Webster, "The Father of American Education," said this in 1836:

> "In my view, the Christian religion is the most important and one of the first things in which all children, under a free government ought to be instructed. . . . The Christian religion must be the basis of any government intended to secure the rights and privileges of a free people."

Reflecting the philosophical shift that took place in America, John Dewey, the twentieth-century "Architect of Modern Education," said, "There is no God, and there is no soul. Hence, there are no needs for the props of traditional religion." The loss of these props and therefore of moral standards has opened the door to teen pregnancies, abortions, drug abuse, alcoholism, violence, and suicide.

If we believe that America will fail if it loses its religious foundation, we Christian believers must reclaim our Christian educational heritage. Instigating this crucial change begins with a willingness to become engaged in the battle.

★ ★ Patriot's Prayer ★ ★

Lord, the Founding Fathers believed that if our nation fails to believe in You, it will ultimately fail—and that's the path we're on. God of the impossible, please work a miracle in our schools and our nation.

★ ★ Patriot's Promise ★ ★

"Whoever says to this mountain, 'Be removed and be cast into the sea,' and does not doubt in his heart, but believes that those things he says will be done, he will have whatever he says" (Mark 11:23).

Your word is a lamp to my feet
and a light to my path.

PSALM 119:105

In colonial America, children learned to read from the Bible and the Bay Psalm Book. The first textbook for schoolchildren was *The New England Primer*, and it clearly taught children not only the ABCs but—as the next devotional shows in its entirety—basic biblical truths and lessons about life as well:

> A—In Adam's Fall, we sinned all.
> B—Heaven to find, the Bible mind.
> C—Christ crucify'd for sinners dy'd.

Included in the primer were the names of the Old and New Testament books, the Lord's Prayer, the Apostles' Creed, the Ten Commandments, the Westminster Assembly Shorter Catechism, and New England Puritan minister John Cotton's "Spiritual Milk for American Babes." The primer was the second best-selling book in the American colonies; the Bible was number one.

★ ★ **Patriot's Prayer** ★ ★

God, please give me the self-discipline I need. I want to hide Your Word in my heart—and abide in it—so that I am armed when temptations come and prepared to defend my faith when opportunities arise. My spirit is willing; my flesh is weak.

★ ★ **Patriot's Promise** ★ ★

"If you abide in My word, you are My disciples indeed. And you shall know the truth, and the truth shall make you free" (John 8:31–32).

September 25

The New England Primer

Teach [this song] to the children of Israel;
put it in their mouths.

DEUTERONOMY 31:19

Initially published between 1688 and 1690 by Benjamin Harris, *The New England Primer* was the first reader designed for the American colonies. The ninety-page work contained religious maxims, woodcuts, alphabetical assistants, catechisms, and moral lessons.

A In Adam's Fall
We sinned all.

B Heaven to find,
The Bible mind.

C Christ crucify'd
For sinners dy'd.

D The Deluge drown'd
The earth around.

E Elijah hid
By Ravens fed.

F The judgment made
Felix afraid.

G As runs the Glass,
Our Life doth pass.

H My Book and Heart
Must never part.

J Job feels the Rod,
Yet blesses God.

K Proud Korah's troop
Was swallowed up.

L Lot fled to Zoar
Saw fiery Shower
On Sodom pour.

M Moses was he
Who Israel's Host
Led thro' the Sea.

N Noah did view
The old world & new.

O Young Obadias,
David, Josias:
All were pious.

P Peter deny'd
His Lord and cry'd.

Q Queen Esther sues
And saves the Jews.

R Young pious Ruth
Left all for Truth.

S Young Sam'l dear
The Lord did fear.

T Young Timothy
Learnt sin to flee.

V Vashti for Pride,
Was set aside.

W Whales in the Sea
God's Voice obey.

X Xerxes did die
And so must I.

Y While youth do chear
Death may be near.

Z Zaccheus he
Did climb the Tree
Our Lord to see.

★ ★ Patriot's Prayer ★ ★

Thank You, Father, for every individual who has been a godly influence in my life.

★ ★ Patriot's Promise ★ ★

"Believe on the Lord Jesus Christ, and you will be saved" (Acts 16:31).

September 26

> The fear of the LORD is the
> beginning of knowledge.
>
> PROVERBS 1:7

The Root of Knowledge

In 1776, John Adams said, "It is religion and morality alone, which can establish the principles upon which freedom can securely stand." Men like Daniel Webster, Benjamin Franklin, Benjamin Rush, Samuel Adams, and George Washington agreed, religion must undergird that morality, and the education of young minds was key.

Not surprisingly, preachers and churches founded most of America's oldest universities:

- At Harvard University (founded in 1636), the primary goal of every student's "life and studies is, to know God and Jesus Christ which is eternal life (John 17:3), and therefore lay Christ . . . as the only foundation of all sound knowledge and learning." Harvard's original seal proclaimed, "Truth for Christ and the Church."
- The College of William and Mary was founded in 1693 to supply the church of Virginia "with a seminary of ministers" that the "Christian faith may be propagated."
- Yale College (1701) aimed to have "every student . . . consider the main end of his study . . . to know God in Jesus Christ and answerably to lead a godly, sober life."
- King's College—Columbia University—purposed to "inculcate upon [students'] tender minds the great principles of Christianity and morality."
- A founding statement at Princeton reads, "Cursed is all learning that is contrary to the Cross of Christ."

★ ★ Patriot's Prayer ★ ★

Thank You, Jesus, that I am forgiven and free from the curse of the grave.

★ ★ Patriot's Promise ★ ★

Jesus "wiped out the handwriting of requirements that was against us . . . having nailed it to the cross" (Colossians 2:14).

September 27

The Star-Spangled Banner

[The LORD] rescued us from our enemies, for
His mercy endures forever.

PSALM 136:24

During the War of 1812, the British navy fiercely bombarded Fort McHenry from the Baltimore harbor. On September 13, 1814, a young American lawyer named Francis Scott Key watched the relentless bombing throughout the night, then silence followed. Had the fort been forced to surrender? In the first rays of sunlight, Key saw the American flag waving proudly. Inspired, he began writing "Defence of Fort McHenry." This poem was set to a popular tune, renamed "The Star-Spangled Banner," and made the national anthem by a congressional resolution on March 3, 1931. It expresses one man's deep gratitude for America's freedom and God's blessings, as this lesser known verse clearly reflects:

> O! thus be it ever, when freemen shall stand
> Between their loved home and the war's desolation!
> Blest with victory and peace, may the heav'n-rescued land
> Praise the Power that hath made and preserved us a nation.
> Then conquer we must, when our cause it is just,
> And this be our motto: "In God is our trust."
> And the star-spangled banner in triumph shall wave
> O'er the land of the free and the home of the brave!

★ ★ Patriot's Prayer ★ ★

Thank You for keeping this nation safe and protecting us from harm. Call us back to You that we may live with You as our trust.

★ ★ Patriot's Promise ★ ★

"He has put a new song in my mouth—praise to our God; many will see it and fear, and will trust in the LORD " (Psalm 40:3).

> [Jesus] gave Himself for us, that He might . . . purify for Himself His own special people, zealous for good works.
>
> TITUS 2:14

A Chosen People, A Purified Church

S amuel Sullivan Cox (1824–1889), congressman and US ambassador to the Ottoman Empire, revered the Lord:

> There was a poignancy in my heart when I saw the old church, where I so often worshipped, razed to the ground. Was it not there I attended my first Sunday school? There it was that I learned my Bible verses . . .
>
> Those early memories were cut in durable stone. Tarnished by worldliness, dusted with the activities of life, they have pursued me through the various vicissitudes of professional, literary, and political life. They became the nucleus of studies in college; the very coat of mail in the struggles against selfishness and skepticism . . . they prefigured and preordained my choice of spiritual belief against the delusive sophistries of new philosophies and mere material science.
>
> They have enabled me . . . to perceive in all the atoms, forms, and forces of nature and the phenomena of mind, the truth and benignity of the great scheme of human redemption, which is founded on the veracity of Christ, and becomes, with lapsing years, more beautiful with the white radiance of an ennobling spirituality.

★ ★ Patriot's Prayer ★ ★

Thank You, dear God, for Your plan for my redemption and the opportunity to share that truth about Christ.

★ ★ Patriot's Promise ★ ★

Jesus "loved the church and gave Himself for her, that He might sanctify and cleanse her . . . that He might present her to Himself a glorious church, not having spot or wrinkle or any such thing . . . holy and without blemish" (Ephesians 5:25–27).

September 29

God's Compassion

I will sacrifice to You with the voice of thanksgiving; I will pay what I have vowed.
Salvation is of the LORD.

JONAH 2:9

When God called the prophet Jonah to preach repentance to the wicked people of Nineveh, Jonah ran the other way. After spending three harrowing days in the belly of a big fish, Jonah agreed to go to Nineveh. When the people heard his call to repentance, they openly received the truth about their sin and turned to God. The book of Jonah illustrates the Lord's eagerness to extend His forgiveness and mercy to even the most undeserving of sinners.

During the dark days of the Civil War, President Abraham Lincoln appealed to God's mercy when he proclaimed a National Fast Day for March 30, 1863. Mr. Lincoln admonished the American people to "rest humbly in the hope authorized by the Divine teachings, that the united cry of the nation will be heard on high and answered with blessing no less than the pardon of our national sins and the restoration of our now divided and suffering country to its former happy condition of unity and peace."

★ ★ Patriot's Prayer ★ ★

O Lord, thank You that You are willing to forgive everyone who repents and asks for Your forgiveness—and I am one of those. I rejoice that Your love includes me.

★ ★ Patriot's Promise ★ ★

Scripture's promise of salvation for all reveals the limitlessness of God's mercy: "As far as the east is from the west, so far has He removed our transgressions from us" (Psalm 103:12).

October

Acting with Courage

Do you not know that your body is the temple of the Holy Spirit . . . and you are not your own? For you were bought at a price; therefore glorify God in your body and in your spirit.

1 Corinthians 6:19–20

The well-entrenched pagan lifestyle of the decadent Corinthian culture exerted a profound influence upon young Christians in that Greek city. When the apostle Paul founded a Christian church there, the believers faced factions, lawsuits, immorality, questionable practices, abuse of the Lord's Supper, and misuse of spiritual gifts. The apostle courageously responded to each of these challenging matters.

Like Paul in his church leadership, US presidents face a variety of problems that require momentous decisions and involve significant risks. In October 1962, for instance, President John F. Kennedy faced the Soviet construction of an intermediate-range ballistic missile site in Cuba. If the United States attacked, the result might be nuclear war with the Soviets, but doing nothing would mean the ever-present threat of close-range nuclear weapons. Through negotiations with the Russians, Kennedy averted the crisis. President Kennedy observed, "There are risks and costs to a program of action. But they are far less than the long-range risks and costs of comfortable inaction."

★ ★ Patriot's Prayer ★ ★

Merciful Father, I am guilty of "comfortable inaction"—sins of omissions—as well as outright wrong action—sins of commission. Give me courage to face and confess my sin, so that I may know Your forgiveness and grace.

★ ★ Patriot's Promise ★ ★

"If we confess our sins"—of omission as well as commission—"[God] is faithful and just to forgive us our sins and to cleanse us from all unrighteousness" (1 John 1:9).

Now when they began to sing and to praise, the LORD set ambushes against the people . . . who had come against Judah; and they were defeated.

2 CHRONICLES 20:22

When the Continental Army fought to defend the new nation's independence, they adapted a hymn by the Boston church composer William Billings, which became the song of the American Revolution.

Let tyrants shake their iron rod,
> And slavery clank her galling chains,
> We fear them not, we trust in God,
> New England's God forever reigns.

Howe and Burgoyne and Clinton too,
> With Prescott and Cornwallis join'd,
> Together plot our overthrow,
> In one infernal league combin'd.

When God inspir'd us for the fight,
> Their ranks were broke, their lines were forc'd,
> Their ships were shatter'd in our sight
> Or swiftly driven from our coast.

The foe comes on with haughty stride,
> Our troops advance with martial noise,
> Their vet'rans flee before our youth,
> And gen'rals yield to beardless boys.

What grateful offerings shall we bring?
> What shall we render to the Lord?
> Loud Hallelujahs let us sing,
> And praise His name on ev'ry chord.

★ ★ Patriot's Prayer ★ ★

May we never forget, Lord, that our blessings and freedom come from You.

★ ★ Patriot's Promise ★ ★

"Come, let us worship . . . for He is our God, and we are the people of His pasture" (Psalm 95:6–7).

285

October 2

William Penn's "Holy Experiment"

> You yourselves are taught by
> God to love one another.
>
> 1 THESSALONIANS 4:9

William Penn (1644–1718), the founder of Pennsylvania, was imprisoned in England several times for his Quaker faith. While imprisoned in the Tower of London, he wrote the classic book *No Cross, No Crown*, in which appears this compelling statement:

> *No pain, no palm; no thorns, no throne; no gall, no glory; no cross, no crown.*

In 1682, Penn established the Pennsylvania colony as a land of religious freedom, granting religious freedom and tolerance to every denomination. He printed advertisements in six different languages and sent them across Europe. Soon Quakers, Mennonites, Lutherans, Dunkards (Church of the Brethren), Amish, Moravians, Huguenots (French Protestants), Catholics, and Jews from England, Sweden, Wales, Germany, Scotland, Ireland, and Holland began arriving to take part in his "holy experiment." To emphasize his goal of Christians working together, he named their city "Philadelphia," which is Greek for "City of Brotherly Love." He maintained that religion is not to be limited to some Sunday ritual, but should be an integral aspect of everyday life, characterized by people getting along with one another.

★ ★ Patriot's Prayer ★ ★

I ask You, Father, to fill my heart to overflowing with Your love. Enable me to love those who have beliefs different from mine, who have angered me, and even those who have hurt me.

★ ★ Patriot's Promise ★ ★

In Psalm 84:11, God promises to show us His love: "The LORD will give grace and glory; no good thing will He withhold from those who walk uprightly."

October 3

The soldiers' plan was to kill the prisoners . . . But the centurion . . . kept them from their purpose.

ACTS 27:42–43

A Policeman's Prayer

When I start my tour of duty, God,
    Wherever crime may be,
    As I walk the darkened streets alone,
    Let me be close to Thee.
Please give me understanding
    With both the young and old.
    Let me listen with attention
    Until their story's told.
Let me never make a judgment
    In a rash or callous way,
    But let me hold my patience . . .
    Let each man have his say.
Lord, if some dark and dreary night,
    I must give my life,
    Lord, with Your everlasting love
    Protect my children and my wife.

Author Unknown

★ ★ Patriot's Prayer ★ ★

Lord, give police officers and other law enforcement officials insight and discernment, so that, like the Acts 27 centurion, they might prevent evil and effectively protect those needing protection. And please protect them as they risk their lives for others.

★ ★ Patriot's Promise ★ ★

"Whoever desires to become great among you, let him be your servant" (Matthew 20:26).

287

The Body of Christ

> By grace you have been saved through faith, and that not of yourselves; it is the gift of God, not of works, lest anyone should boast.
>
> EPHESIANS 2:8–9

The believers in Ephesus were rich beyond measure in Christ, yet they were living as beggars simply because they were ignorant of their great spiritual wealth. In the wonderful book that bears their name, Paul began by describing the vast spiritual blessings they have received in Christ (chapters 1–3). He continued in chapters 4–6 with how a Christian learns to live a life rooted in that spiritual wealth.

Reflecting these spiritual blessings are the "inalienable rights" described in the Declaration of Independence. John Dickinson, a Pennsylvania Quaker and a signer of the US Constitution, wrote this in the very year that the Constitution was adopted:

> "Kings or parliaments could not give the rights essential to happiness—we claim them from a higher source—from the King of kings and the Lord of all the Earth. They are not annexed to us by parchments or seals. They are created in us by the decrees of Providence, which establish the laws of our nature. They are born with us; and cannot be taken from us by any human power."

★ ★ Patriot's Prayer ★ ★

Lord Jesus, keep me from ever surrendering the great riches of Your love and blessings, purchased for me at so great a price on Calvary.

★ ★ Patriot's Promise ★ ★

Paul wrote, "We are [God's] workmanship, created in Christ Jesus for good works, which God prepared beforehand that we should walk in them" (Ephesians 2:10).

I will cleanse you from all your filthiness and from all your idols. I will give you a new heart and put a new spirit within you; I will take the heart of stone out of your flesh and give you a heart of flesh.

EZEKIEL 36:25–26

A New Heart

George Bancroft, Secretary of the Navy in 1845 under President James Polk, wrote that, for eternal salvation to come to all people, "it was requisite that the Divine Being should enter the abodes and hearts of men and dwell there" and that He should be known "not as a distant Providence of boundless power and uncertain and inactive will, but as God present in the flesh."

From Babylon, exiled with the nation of Judah, the prophet Ezekiel offered a similar message of hope for God's children. Sin and rebellion had caused the glory of the Lord to depart from the people of Israel, but God promised to return with a fresh wind of His Spirit. God would replace the despair and hopelessness of His exiled children with a double portion of His glory: He would give them a new heart to know and love Him.

★ ★ Patriot's Prayer ★ ★
Each day, dear Lord, let me be reminded that true life comes only through the indwelling power of Your Holy Spirit. Help me not to grieve the Spirit by my thoughts or actions, but to surrender my heart to His full control.

★ ★ Patriot's Promise ★ ★
"When [the Holy Spirit], the Spirit of truth, has come, He will guide you into all truth" (John 16:13). We are never alone: God's Spirit is with us.

October 6

The Constitution of the United States

> Hear, O Israel, the statutes and
> judgments . . . that you may learn
> them and be careful to observe them.
>
> DEUTERONOMY 5:1

The US Constitution has been the supreme law of the nation since it was adopted on September 17, 1787. All thirteen states ratified the Constitution by May 29, 1790, and the first US Congress ratified ten amendments, which became known as the Bill of Rights. Our Constitution, the oldest of any existing nation, occupies the central place in United States law and political culture.

The Constitution provides the framework of the United States government, outlining the three main branches—legislative, judicial, and executive; carefully limiting the delegated powers each branch may exercise; and reserving numerous rights for the individual states.

In the preamble, our Founders wrote, "We the people of the United States," specifying that the power to govern belongs to the people and that the people have created the government to protect their rights and promote their welfare.

Much has been made of the Constitution's silence on the subject of God or faith. The consensus of the Framers was that religious matters are best left to the individual citizens and their state government. Most state constitutions already defined the relationship between religion and civil government. For the federal government to enter into matters regarding religion would have been to encroach upon state jurisdiction.

★ ★ Patriot's Prayer ★ ★

Thank You for the wisdom that You gave to the framers of the Constitution and may we be effective stewards of the rights they outlined.

★ ★ Patriot's Promise ★ ★

"All kings shall fall down before Him; all nations shall serve Him" (Psalm 72:11).

I have fought the good fight.

What We Owe This Land

Eddie Rickenbacker (October 8, 1890–July 23, 1973) was an American fighter ace in France during World War I, a Medal of Honor recipient, and later a pioneer in air transportation. Hear what motivated him:

> I pray to God every night of my life to be given the strength and power to continue my efforts to inspire in others the interest, the obligation, and the responsibilities that we owe to this land for the sake of future generations—for my boys and girls—so that we can always look back when the candle of life burns low and say, "Thank God, I have contributed my best to the land that contributed so much to me."

★ ★ Patriot's Prayer ★ ★

Preserve this nation, merciful Father! And help me do my part to make it a great country. I pray for the leaders who have been elected to office, that they will do what is right for this great nation.

★ ★ Patriot's Promise ★ ★

"I have fought the good fight, I have finished the race, I have kept the faith. Finally, there is laid up for me the crown of righteousness" is the promise of 2 Timothy 4:7–8. By God's grace, the life that we live here on earth can culminate in a heavenly crown. What a reward that will be!

God's Pursuing Love

Hear the word of the LORD, you children of Israel, for the LORD brings a charge against the inhabitants of the land: "There is no truth or mercy or knowledge of God in the land."

HOSEA 4:1

The Old Testament prophet Hosea loved his unfaithful spouse, living out for us a heartbreaking illustration of the faithful love God has for us His people even when we turn from Him. Just as Hosea pursued his adulterous wife, so God pursues His people in order to show them—us—His love and forgiveness.

Charles Colson, founder of Prison Fellowship, experienced a firsthand encounter with this pursuing love of God. As a high-powered attorney and member of President Richard Nixon's White House inner circle, Colson was considered one of the most powerful men in Washington, D.C. His hard-nosed tactics as Mr. Nixon's political "hatchet man" also made him one of the most hated. But when the consequences of the infamous Watergate scandal sent him to federal prison, the cynical and self-sufficient Colson was confronted with something he could not earn and did not deserve—the love and mercy of God.

★ ★ Patriot's Prayer ★ ★

I am humbled, O Lord, that You pursued me even when I was lost in sin. Your love is too great for my understanding, and it is only by faith that I dare to claim it. Thank You for loving me this day and all the days forward.

★ ★ Patriot's Promise ★ ★

"God demonstrates His own love toward us, in that while we were still sinners, Christ died for us" (Romans 5:8).

October 9

Saviors shall come to Mount Zion to judge the mountains of Esau, and the kingdom shall be the LORD's.

OBADIAH 1:21

Repentance and Restoration

"Though force can protect in emergency," declared Dwight David Eisenhower, America's thirty-fourth president, "only justice, fairness, consideration, and cooperation can finally lead men to the dawn of eternal peace."

As a spokesperson for God, the Old Testament prophet Obadiah spoke directly to the issues of justice and fairness. God's people had a long-standing feud with the neighboring nation of Edom, even though the two peoples were distant blood relatives. When Judah was conquered by Babylon, Edom not only rejoiced but actually looted Judah, captured those trying to escape, and turned them over to their enemies. Obadiah condemned Edom's treachery and arrogance, declaring that God would destroy them for coming against His people. Obadiah, however, also spoke of the future restoration of Israel through God's own faithfulness.

★ ★ Patriot's Prayer ★ ★
Father in heaven, deliver America from our pride and arrogance—and forgive us. And, Father, help me examine my own heart that I may confess and be free of such pride and arrogance and any other attitude and behavior which is not pleasing in Your sight.

★ ★ Patriot's Promise ★ ★
God loves His own and, by His Spirit, provides His personal protection in times when evildoers come against them: "He who is in you is greater than he who is in the world" (1 John 4:4).

293

Hope in God

Who is a God like You . . . ? He does not retain His anger forever, because He delights in mercy.

MICAH 7:18

The powerful Assyrian empire demanded Israel's surrender. When God's people did not submit, the Assyrians destroyed the capital city of Samaria and took many Hebrews into exile. God's judgment came because His people had rejected Him and His law. Micah, however, offered hope to the faithful few who had kept the word of the Lord, assuring them that God would one day restore their nation.

Founder and governor of the Massachusetts Bay Colony and author of *A Model of Christian Charity*, John Winthrop referred to Micah in his 1630 writings:

> To provide for our posterity, is to follow the counsel of Micah, to do justly, to love mercy, to walk humbly with our God. For this end, we must be knit together in this work as one man. We must hold a familiar commerce together in each other in all meekness, gentleness, patience, and liberality. We must delight in each other; make others' conditions our own; rejoice together, mourn together, labor and suffer together, always having before our eyes our commission and community in the work, as members of the same body. So shall we keep the unity of the spirit in the bond of peace.

★ ★ Patriot's Prayer ★ ★

Lord God, show me today how I might do justly, love mercy, and walk humbly before You. I long to please You and show Christ to others.

★ ★ Patriot's Promise ★ ★

"Turn to Me with all your heart . . . Return to the LORD your God, for He is gracious and merciful" (Joel 2:12–13).

He shall speak peace to the nations.

ZECHARIAH 9:10

Christopher Columbus

Christopher Columbus (1451–1506) was an Italian navigator and explorer whose voyages across the Atlantic Ocean ushered in the first period of sustained contact between Europe and the Americas. When he sailed from Spain in 1492, his motives may have been many—to tap into the wealth of the Orient, to weaken the powerful Ottoman Turks, and definitely to serve his Lord. A devout Catholic, Columbus felt his name, *Christopher*, which means "Christ-bearer," was evidence of his destiny. He thought he found assurance in the Scriptures for a call to sail the globe with the Christian message. Psalm 107:23–24, for instance, promises that "those who go down to the sea in ships, who do business on great waters, they see the works of the LORD, and His wonders in the deep."

Describing his motive, Columbus stated:

> "With a hand that could be felt, the Lord opened my mind to the fact that it would be possible . . . and He opened my will to desire to accomplish that project. . . . The Lord purposed that there should be something miraculous in this matter of the voyage to the Indies."

As Pulitzer Prize-winning biographer Samuel Eliot Morison wrote, "This conviction that God destined him to be an instrument for spreading the faith was far more potent than the desire to win glory, wealth, and worldly honors, to which he was certainly far from indifferent."

★ ★ Patriot's Prayer ★ ★

Dear Lord, guide me on this journey of life just as You guided Columbus.

★ ★ Patriot's Promise ★ ★

"The steps of a good man are ordered by the LORD, and He delights in his way" (Psalm 37:23).

October 12

Our Stronghold

The book of Nahum was written approximately one hundred years after God had called Nineveh to repentance through the preaching of the prophet Jonah. As the years passed, Assyrian leaders once again hardened their hearts against God's people, and the Lord used them to bring a terrible judgment against the city of Nineveh. In this event, the nation of Judah saw a God who is all-powerful, holy, just, merciful, and always true to His Word. Nahum assured the people that evil would not last forever and that God would fulfill His plan and bring permanent restoration to Israel.

In the long struggle for civil rights, Martin Luther King Jr. held on to the hope that equality and justice would finally come for all Americans:

"I refuse to accept the view that mankind is so tragically bound to the starless midnight of racism and war that the bright daybreak of peace and brotherhood can never become reality. I believe that unarmed truth and unconditional love will have the final word."

★ ★ Patriot's Prayer ★ ★

Dear Lord, You have never failed to keep Your Word, You have never turned Your face from me, and You have never withheld Your hand of mercy when I have reached to heaven for Your help. I thank You for Your everlasting faithfulness.

★ ★ Patriot's Promise ★ ★

"The LORD knows the way of the righteous, but the way of the ungodly shall perish" (Psalm 1:6).

Seek the LORD, all you meek of the earth who have upheld His justice. Seek righteousness, seek humility. It may be that you will be hidden in the day of the LORD's anger.

ZEPHANIAH 2:3

In 1843, historian Emma Willard, who founded the first women's school of higher education, wrote this:

> "The government of the United States is acknowledged by the wise and good of other nations, to be the most free, impartial, and righteous government of the world; but all agree, that for such a government to be sustained for many years, the principles of truth and righteousness, taught in the Holy Scriptures, must be practiced. The rulers must govern in the fear of God, and the people obey the laws."

In Zephaniah's day, the civil and religious leaders of Judah had grown corrupt, and idolatry was widespread. The prophet wrote to the people of Judah to warn them of impending judgment and the coming "day of the LORD" (1:14–15). But he tempered the message of judgment with one of mercy, declaring that God is also gracious and compassionate. What began as a prophecy of doom concluded in triumph as Zephaniah spoke of God's unending love and righteousness.

★ ★ Patriot's Prayer ★ ★

O Lord, even in judgment You have shown mercy to those who seek it from You. I ask You to continue to show mercy and patience to America as I pray that our nation returns to You.

★ ★ Patriot's Promise ★ ★

"Behold, the LORD's hand is not shortened, that it cannot save; nor His ear heavy, that it cannot hear" (Isaiah 59:1).

October 14

The Biblical Basics of Marriage

> A man shall leave his father and mother and be joined to his wife, and the two shall become one flesh.
>
> MATTHEW 19:5

The Bible is clear: "A man shall leave his father and mother and be joined to his wife, and they shall become one flesh" (Genesis 2:24). God's creation and uniting of Adam and Eve, male and female, set in place the foundation of human civilization. Jesus also taught that marriage is an institution established by God and designed as a lifelong covenant relationship between a man and woman (Matthew 19:1–6).

God commanded Adam and Eve to "be fruitful and multiply; fill the earth and subdue it" (Genesis 1:28). In fact, God's design for procreation demanded the union of a man and woman. Ideally, children are born into a secure home with a father and a mother who love, nurture, and teach them to love and serve the Lord and, incidentally, to become responsible citizens. God's plan is that a man and a woman raise children within the institution of marriage.

Preserving the traditional family is vital to America's future. We must join together to maintain the God-ordained truth that marriage is one man and one woman committed to each other for life. Beyond being a basic unit of society, the family is a sacred institution.

★ ★ Patriot's Prayer ★ ★

Thank You, Lord, for my husband/wife. Marriage is hard work. Help us never give up and enable us to keep You at the center of our marriage and our home.

★ ★ Patriot's Promise ★ ★

"Marriage is honorable among all, and the bed undefiled; but fornicators and adulterers God will judge" (Hebrews 13:4).

Teach the children of Israel all the statutes which the LORD has spoken.

LEVITICUS 10:11

Noah Webster on Education

"Father of American Scholarship and Education," Noah Webster (October 16, 1758–May 28, 1843) gave us the very first *American Dictionary of the English Language*. In it, he defined *education* as "the bringing up, as of a child; instruction; formation of manners." He went on to say, "To give children a good education in manners, arts, and science is important; to give them a religious education is indispensable."

Webster believed a well-educated citizenry was essential to the preservation of freedom. Convinced that "information is fatal to despotism," he wrote textbooks that covered moral formation and civic education, as well as spelling and grammar. He wrote:

> An attempt to conduct the affairs of a free government with wisdom and impartiality, and to preserve the just rights of all classes of citizens, without the guidance of Divine precepts, will certainly end in disappointment. God is the supreme moral Governor of the world He has made . . . If men will not submit to be controlled by His laws, He will punish them by the evils resulting from their own disobedience. . . .
>
> In my view, the Christian religion is the most important and one of the first things in which all children, under a free government ought to be instructed. . . . The Christian religion must be the basis of any government intended to secure the rights and privileges of a free people.

★ ★ Patriot's Prayer ★ ★

Father, help me teach my children about secular affairs as well as Your Word—and provide godly leaders in our school systems.

★ ★ Patriot's Promise ★ ★

"Train up a child in the way he should go, and when he is old he will not depart from it" (Proverbs 22:6)

★ 299 ★

October 16

Christian, Explorer, and American Hero

Fear God and keep His commandments.

ECCLESIASTES 12:13

Born on July 14, 1732, and growing up in Virginia's Shenandoah Valley, Daniel Boone became best known for exploring the new American West.

Early in 1775, Virginia governor Patrick Henry commissioned Boone to explore the mountainous area we now know as Kentucky. When he discovered the Kentucky River, he built a fort on its banks and named it Boonesboro. Stories about his great adventures in the Kentucky wilderness, many involving warring Indians, have made courage and heroism synonymous with his name.

In 1778, for instance, during the American Revolution, Boone was captured by the Shawnee Indians and taken to Detroit. While he was there, he heard about a British plot to attack his settlement at Boonesboro. After a courageous escape he traveled by foot and horseback—nearly four hundred miles in five days—to save the fort from the British.

In an October 17, 1816 letter to his sister-in-law, Daniel Boone wrote this: "The religion I have is to love and fear God, believe in Jesus Christ, do all the good to help my neighbor and myself that I can, do as little harm as I can help, and trust on God's mercy for the rest."

★ ★ Patriot's Prayer ★ ★

Heavenly Father, thank You for the courageous men and women who have helped shape, guide, and protect this great nation that we call America. May their bravery and Christian convictions be apparent in my life as well.

★ ★ Patriot's Promise ★ ★

"Be strong and very courageous . . . do not turn from [God's law] . . . that you may prosper wherever you go" (Joshua 1:7).

They all glorified God for what had been done.

ACTS 4:21

The Divine Origin of Jesus

David Torquemada (1813–1891), a US Navy admiral and later the superintendent of US Naval Academy in Annapolis, Maryland, shared this observation: When one sees how much has been done for the world by the disciples of Christ and those professing the Christian religion, he must be astonished to find anyone who hesitates to believe in the Divine origin of Jesus and the wonderful works He performed, all of which are so beautifully portrayed by the Author of the work under consideration; and no man or woman of real intelligence would hesitate to believe that it is only through Christ that sinners can be saved, unless their vanity is so great that they are capable of saving themselves without an intermediary.

★ ★ Patriot's Prayer ★ ★

O God, I pray for missionaries across this country and around the world. Protect them and keep them from harm. Give them courage to remain in Your service and bless their efforts with a bountiful kingdom harvest. How beautiful are the feet of those who preach the good news of Jesus Christ (see Isaiah 52:7)!

★ ★ Patriot's Promise ★ ★

In Isaiah 52:7–8 God promises to bless those who preach the good news of peace and salvation.

October 18

State-Funded Ministers

Let the cost be paid at the king's expense.

EZRA 6:8

The State of Massachusetts paid the salaries of the Congregational ministers in that state until 1833. Other states had cut official ties to a church before that change came to Massachusetts.

★ ★ Patriot's Prayer ★ ★

I would like to pray today, Father, for my pastor. I know he feels burdened from time to time by all the worries and duties that come with dealing with church matters. On this day, please help him feel Your presence more than ever. Keep my pastor in Your continuous care and bless his family, that they may prosper.

★ ★ Patriot's Promise ★ ★

Romans 10:14–15 says, "And how shall they hear without a preacher? And how shall they preach unless they are sent? As it is written: 'How beautiful are the feet of those who preach the gospel of peace, who bring glad tidings of good things!'" God considers beautiful every person who preaches His gospel, and He promises to bless them.

Beware lest you be consumed by one another!

GALATIANS 5:15

A Constitution for Moral People

John Adams (1735–1826) is one of America's Founding Fathers, and he served as the second president of the United States. Read what he wrote in an October 1798 letter to the Massachusetts militia:

> We have no government armed with power capable of contending with human passions unbridled by morality and religion. Avarice, ambition, revenge, or gallantry would break the strongest cords of our Constitution as a whale goes through a net. Our Constitution was made only for a moral and religious people. It is wholly inadequate to the government of any other.

★ ★ Patriot's Prayer ★ ★

Thank You, dear Father, for the love You have shown me and this nation. I pray that You continue to bless us, help the economy grow stronger, and lead us to a point of such high standards that the world will notice that You truly do have Your hand upon us.

★ ★ Patriot's Promise ★ ★

Matthew 7:12 is the basis of the Golden Rule: "Therefore, whatever you want men to do to you, do also to them, for this is the Law and the Prophets." If we follow this rule, God will see that our moral values will raise our society to a new level.

"The Bible Came with Them"

The word of God . . . lives and abides forever.

1 Peter 1:23

Daniel Webster (1782–1852) was a leading American statesman during the nation's Antebellum Period. In 1843, he spoke of the Founding Fathers' regard for the Bible in an address celebrating the completion of the Bunker Hill Monument:

> The Bible came with them. And it is not to be doubted, that to free and universal reading of the Bible, in that age, men were much indebted for right views of civil liberty.
>
> The Bible is a book of faith, and a book of doctrine, and a book of morals, and a book of religion, of special revelation from God; but it is also a book which teaches man his own individual responsibility, his own dignity, and his equality with his fellowman.

★ ★ Patriot's Prayer ★ ★

Dear God, You have given me Your Word to learn from and live by. Today and every day, please give me insight into the Scriptures I read and then help me to apply that truth to my life.

★ ★ Patriot's Promise ★ ★

Second Timothy 3:16 is clear: "All Scripture is given by inspiration of God, and is profitable for doctrine, for reproof, for correction, for instruction in righteousness." God promises that His Word will teach us how to live.

For this reason I left you in Crete, that you should set in order the things that are lacking, and appoint elders in every city as I commanded you.

TITUS 1:5

Titus, a young pastor, faces the difficult assignment of setting in order the church at Crete. Paul wrote advising him to appoint elders, men of proven spiritual character in their homes and businesses, to do the work of the church. In addition, men and women, young and old, each are shown to have vital functions to fulfill in the church if they are to be living examples of the doctrine they profess to believe.

Martin Luther King Jr., the great civil rights leader of the twentieth century, is credited with saying, "Our lives begin to end the day we become silent about things that matter." If King did not say it, he certainly lived it. Likewise, Paul told Titus that he could not be silent about the greatest matter in human history, because "the grace of God that brings salvation has appeared to all men" (2:11). Paul stated that Titus should "speak these things, exhort, and rebuke with all authority. Let no one despise you" (2:15).

★ ★ Patriot's Prayer ★ ★
Father in Heaven, please grant me the wisdom to know when I am to speak for You and the courage to do so without fear or timidity.

★ ★ Patriot's Promise ★ ★
"My soul finds rest in God alone; my salvation comes from him. He alone is my rock and my salvation; he is my fortress, I will never be shaken" (Psalm 62:1–2 NIV).

October 22

"Give Me Liberty or Give Me Death"

While they promise them liberty, they themselves are slaves of corruption; for by whom a person is overcome, by him also he is brought into bondage.

2 PETER 2:19

On March 23, 1775, Patrick Henry spoke the now-famous phrase "Give me liberty or give me death!" to arouse the Second Virginia Convention to arms against the tyranny of Great Britain. In that speech, the fiery patriot noted that "we have done everything that could be done to avert the storm which is now coming upon us."

During the critical years of 1765–1776, the American colonies had been forced to endure taxation without representation, searches and seizures without probable cause, the confiscation of firearms, and on and on. The colonial leaders had tried to remain loyal to the Crown and reconcile their differences, but they were finally compelled to break away in revolt.

In the Declaration of Independence, the Founding Fathers set forth their reasons for separating from England. The Declaration gives a detailed list of legal offenses that England had left unresolved, but the Founders saw these as more than isolated wrongs. Rather, our forefathers saw these wrongs as a part of a predetermined plan to take away their religious liberties and reestablish the Church of England to rule over their hearts and souls, thus enslaving the colonies. In that light, one better understands the power of Patrick Henry's fiery words.

★ ★ Patriot's Prayer ★ ★

Dear Lord, guide my path that I might obey You—and work within me that I will obey wholeheartedly. I want to be faithful and true to You.

★ ★ Patriot's Promise ★ ★

"Obey My voice, and I will be your God, and you shall be My people" (Jeremiah 7:23).

When Abram heard that his brother was taken captive, he armed his three hundred and eighteen trained servants.

Genesis 14:14

The Right to Keep and Bear Arms

According to the Second Amendment to the US Constitution, "a well-regulated militia being necessary to the security of a free State, the right of the People to keep and bear arms shall not be infringed."

Having fled persecution, the Puritans required every family to own a gun, carry it in public, and train children in its use. In 1619, Virginia required everyone to bear arms. Connecticut law in 1650 required every male above the age of sixteen to possess "a good musket or other gun, fit for service."

America's early laws were very clear: citizens were responsible for defending themselves and protecting their freedoms. Thomas Jefferson said, "The strongest reason for the people to retain the right to bear arms is, as a last resort, to protect themselves against tyranny in government." At the time, there was no concept of a professional army, paid to defend the colonies.

Furthermore, for the most part, the colonial churches believed that to revolt against tyrants like King George was to obey God. This conviction, perhaps having its roots in the Old Testament accounts of Israel's wars for freedom, sparked a powerful fire that impassioned the citizenry. Americans continue to value their right to bear arms.

★ ★ Patriot's Prayer ★ ★

Lord, please guard my family; keep us under Your wing. I praise You, our Defense, our Fortress.

★ ★ Patriot's Promise ★ ★

If a person walks with righteousness, "his place of defense will be the fortress of rocks; bread will be given him, his water will be sure" (Isaiah 33:16).

October 24

"The Whole Hope of Human Progress"

The path of the just is like the shining sun.

PROVERBS 4:18

William Henry Seward (1801–1872), the Secretary of State who served under Presidents Abraham Lincoln and Andrew Johnson and who negotiated the purchase of Alaska from Russia, stated this conviction:

> I do not believe human society, including not merely a few persons in any state, but whole masses of men, ever have attained, or ever can attain, a high state of intelligence, virtue, security, liberty, or happiness without the Holy Scriptures; even the whole hope of human progress is suspended on the ever-growing influence of the Bible.

★ ★ Patriot's Prayer ★ ★

Dear Father, I pray that Your Word be "hidden in my heart that I may not sin against You" (Psalm 119:11). Yet I confess, Lord, that it's difficult for me to find time to read the Bible. Help me to develop a better schedule: I truly long to have a regular quiet time with You and Your Word.

★ ★ Patriot's Promise ★ ★

God considers His Word holy, so His Revelation 22:18 promise to those who water down or change His Word is no surprise: "I testify to everyone who hears the words of the prophecy of this book: If anyone adds to these things, God will add to him the plagues that are written in this book."

October 25

Trust in the LORD with all your heart, and lean not on your own understanding; in all your ways acknowledge Him, and He shall direct your paths.

PROVERBS 3:5–6

A True American Servant

Mitchell Paige received the Medal of Honor for his actions at the Battle of Guadalcanal. On October 26, 1942, for hours after all the Marines in his platoon were killed or wounded, Paige operated four machine guns, single-handedly stopping an entire Japanese regiment. Had that position fallen and the Japanese regained the airfield the Marines had taken, the outcome of World War II may have been significantly different.

Why had Paige been willing to put his life on the line for his country? He spoke of his childhood education and being so steeped in the traditions of America that he felt part of our glorious heritage: "My undying love of country, and my strong loyalty to the Marines fighting by my side, gave me no choice but to fight on unswervingly throughout my battles, utilizing my God-given ability to make use of what I had been taught and learned."

And his mother had taught him well, including in the lunch she had made him for his two-hundred-mile walk to the nearest Marine Corps recruiting station the note, "Trust in the Lord, son, and He will guide you always."

Mitchell Paige was a true American servant. . . and America is blessed and proud to have had hundreds of thousands of valiant soldiers like him.

★ ★ Patriot's Prayer ★ ★
Thank You for the many role models in my life, Lord, and for family, for friends, for patriots.

★ ★ Patriot's Promise ★ ★
"From the Lord you will receive the reward of the inheritance; for you serve the Lord Christ" (Colossians 3:24).

309

"The Government of God"

The government will be upon His shoulder.

ISAIAH 9:6

Lyman Beecher (1775–1863) was a renowned Presbyterian clergyman in New England who later became president of Lane Theological Seminary. Read his thoughts below:

> The government of God is the only government which will hold society, against depravity within and temptation without; and this it must do by the force of its own law written upon the heart.
>
> This is that unity of the Spirit and that bond of peace which can alone perpetuate national purity and tranquility—that law of universal and impartial love by which alone nations can be kept back from ruin. There is no safety for republics but in self-government, under the influence of a holy heart, swayed by the government of God.

★ ★ Patriot's Prayer ★ ★

Lord Jesus, give us Americans love for one another in this great land. Let me give a helping hand when it is needed. If I see someone who is hurting, Lord, give me the wisdom to know what to do.

★ ★ Patriot's Promise ★ ★

Romans 13:1 says, "Let every soul be subject to the governing authorities. For there is no authority except from God, and the authorities that exist are appointed by God." Therefore, we can rest assured that no matter the government control, God is ultimately in control.

Eye has not seen, nor ear heard . . . the things which God has prepared for those who love Him.

1 CORINTHIANS 2:9

A Strong Entrenchment

Dr. James McHenry (1753–1816), one of the signers of the Constitution, served as a member of the Continental Congress and as US Secretary of War. In 1813, he became the president of a Bible Society in Baltimore, Maryland. He recognized how important the Bible is to society:

> Public utility pleads most forcibly for the general distribution of the Holy Scriptures. The doctrine they preach, the obligations they impose, the punishment they threaten, the rewards they promise, the stamp and image of divinity they bear, which produces a conviction of their truths, can alone secure to society, order and peace, and to our courts of justice and constitutions of government, purity, stability and usefulness.
>
> In vain, without the Bible, we increase penal laws and draw entrenchments around our institutions. Bibles are strong entrenchments. Where they abound, men cannot pursue wicked courses and at the same time enjoy quiet conscience. . . .
>
> It is a book of counsel and directions, fitted to every situation in which man can be placed. It is an oracle which reveals to mortals the secrets of heavens and the hidden will of the Almighty.

★ ★ Patriot's Prayer ★ ★

Lord, may I always turn to the Scriptures for guidance, hope, and truth—and may Your Spirit work so that, as a nation, we open, study, and obey Your Word.

★ ★ Patriot's Promise ★ ★

The prayer of Psalm 119:133—"Direct my steps by Your word" —implicitly promises God's guidance to those of us who look to Him.

October 28

A Witness for the Lord

He has filled them with skill to
do all manner of work.

EXODUS 35:35

Harriet Powers (October 29, 1837–January 1, 1910) was an African-American slave folk artist and quilt maker from rural Georgia. Only two of her quilts have survived—Bible Quilt 1886 and Bible Quilt 1898—and they are nationally recognized as masterworks of American folk art. Considered among the finest examples of nineteenth-century Southern quilting, her work is on display at the National Museum of American History in Washington, D.C., and the Museum of Fine Arts in Boston, Massachusetts.

Using traditional appliqué techniques and piecework, her quilts reflect both African and African-American influences. The panel-storied quilts consist of numerous pictorial squares, with each depicting a celestial phenomenon or a biblical story, such as Adam and Eve naming the animals in the Garden of Eden, Cain killing his brother Abel, and the baptism of Christ. The vivid art of Harriet Powers clearly tells a story—God's story. It is thought that Powers could neither read nor write, but she had learned the Bible stories from singing spirituals and hearing sermons.

★ ★ Patriot's Prayer ★ ★

Lord, may Your Word influence everything that I do today in my work, my home, my family, and my community. And, just as Harriet Powers's quilts are, may all that I do, each and every day, be a witness for You.

★ ★ Patriot's Promise ★ ★

God's promises offer hope: "Forever, O LORD, Your word is settled in heaven. Your faithfulness endures to all generations" (Psalm 119:89–90).

You shall love . . . your neighbor as yourself.

JESUS IN LUKE 10:27

On Civil Liberty

Noah Webster (1758–1843) was an American lexicographer, spelling reformer, textbook and political writer, word enthusiast, and editor. He has been called the "Father of American Scholarship and Education." His public school textbook *History of the United States*, published in 1832, includes the following passage:

> Almost all the civil liberty now enjoyed in the world owes its origin to the principles of the Christian religion. . . .
>
> The religion which has introduced civil liberty is the religion of Christ and His apostles, which enjoins humility, piety, and benevolence; which acknowledges in every person a brother, or a sister, and a citizen with equal rights. This is genuine Christianity, and to this we owe our free constitutions of government.
>
> The moral principles and precepts contained in the Scriptures ought to form the basis of all of our civil constitutions and laws. . . . All the miseries and evils which men suffer from vice, crime, ambition, injustice, oppression, slavery, and war, proceed from their despising or neglecting the precepts contained in the Bible.

★ ★ Patriot's Prayer ★ ★

Gracious heavenly Father, Your Word is, indeed, the true compass of what is good and right. Enable me to show the love, humility, and generosity that You call us Christians to show others. And I pray this nation would return to the principles found in Your Word.

★ ★ Patriot's Promise ★ ★

First John 4:8 says, "He who does not love does not know God, for God is love." The promise is that our love for others reveals our knowledge of God. May He use us to draw others to Him.

October 30

A Sure Foundation

Whoever comes to Me, and hears My sayings and does them . . . is like a man building a house, who dug deep and laid the foundation on the rock. And when the flood arose, the stream beat vehemently against that house, and could not shake it, for it was founded on the rock.

JESUS IN LUKE 6:47–48

Did you know that Founding Father James Madison was responsible for our three-part government? Maybe you did. But did you know that his inspiration for that design came from Isaiah 33:22?

For the LORD is our Judge [judicial branch],
The LORD is our Lawgiver [legislative branch],
The LORD is our King [executive branch];
He will save us.

Now consider this snapshot from April 18, 1775: Founding Fathers John Adams and John Hancock were at the home of Reverend Jonas Clarke, a pastor as well as a militia leader in Lexington. That night silversmith and patriot Paul Revere warned them of the British soldiers who were approaching—and approach they did. The next morning British Major Pitcairn shouted to the assembled minutemen, "Disperse, ye villains! Lay down your arms in the name of George the Sovereign King of England." Hear the immediate response of John Adams and John Hancock: "We recognize no Sovereign but God, and no King but Jesus!"

James Madison, John Adams, John Hancock, and others built this land on Christian principles, for God's glory and the people's good.

★ ★ **Patriot's Prayer** ★ ★

Father God, please use me in my community, my state, and even this great country to rebuild our nation so that people who look at the US will see that we, like our forefathers, recognize only God as sovereign and Jesus alone as our King.

★ ★ **Patriot's Promise** ★ ★

"Let Your mercy, O LORD, be upon us, just as we hope in You" (Psalm 33:22).

November

Good Soldiers

Endure hardship as a good soldier of Jesus Christ. No one engaged in warfare entangles himself with the affairs of this life, that he may please him who enlisted him as a soldier.

2 TIMOTHY 2:3–4

As Paul wrote his final epistle, 2 Timothy, he realized that his days on earth were quickly drawing to a close. He therefore sought to challenge and strengthen his somewhat timid but faithful associate in his difficult ministry in Ephesus. In spite of Paul's bleak personal circumstances, he passionately encouraged Timothy to remain steadfast in the fulfillment of his divinely appointed task.

Paul's poignant words to Timothy—"the time of my departure is at hand" (2 Timothy 4:6) —were echoed by Ronald Reagan in his November 1994 letter to the American people revealing his Alzheimer's diagnosis:

"In closing, let me thank you, the American people, for giving me the great honor of allowing me to serve as your president. When the Lord calls me home, whenever that day may be, I will leave with the greatest love for this country of ours and eternal optimism for its future. I now begin the journey that will lead me into the sunset of my life. I know that for America there will always be a bright dawn ahead."

★ ★ Patriot's Prayer ★ ★

I pray with the psalmist, Lord, teach me to number my days, that I may gain a heart of wisdom (see Psalm 90:12).

★ ★ Patriot's Promise ★ ★

"[God] shall give His angels charge over you, to keep you in all your ways" (Psalm 91:11–12). Nothing can take your life until it is your time, and that moment is appointed by God Himself.

For the leaders of this people cause them to err,
and those who are led by them are destroyed. . . .
For all this His anger is not turned away, but His
hand is stretched out still.

Isaiah 9:16–17

Benjamin Rush, a signer of the Declaration of Independence, wrote the following in a letter to Thomas Jefferson:

> I have always considered Christianity as the strong ground of republicanism. The spirit is opposed, not only to the splendor, but even to the very forms of monarchy, and many of its precepts have for their objects republican liberty and equality as well as simplicity, integrity, and economy in government. It is only necessary for republicanism to ally itself to the Christian religion to overturn all the corrupted political and religious institutions in the world.

★ ★ Patriot's Prayer ★ ★

Righteous Father, I pray for the men and women in political leadership that they may turn to You when they need to make decisions. Please move upon the hearts of those who legislate and those who vote for them. May our country turn to You now more wholeheartedly than ever.

★ ★ Patriot's Promise ★ ★

Hear this charge to believers: "I exhort first of all that supplications, prayers, intercessions, and giving of thanks be made for all men, for kings and all who are in authority, that we may lead a quiet and peaceable life in all godliness and reverence" (1 Timothy 2:1–2). The promise is that when we pray for our leaders, we will live a better life.

November 2

A Call to Praise

We never saw anything like this!

WITNESSES TO A HEALING MIRACLE IN MARK 2:12

Known as the "Father of American Poets," William Cullen Bryant (1794–1878) was also longtime editor of the *New York Evening Post.* Hear his bold stand for Jesus:

> The very men who, in the pride of their investigations into the secrets of the internal world, turn a look of scorn upon the Christian system of belief, are not aware how much of the peace and order of society, how much the happiness of households, and the purest of those who are the dearest to them, are owing to the influence of that religion extending beyond their sphere. . . .
>
> In my view, the life, the teachings, the labors, and the sufferings of the blessed Jesus, there can be no admiration too profound, no love of which the human heart is capable too warm, no gratitude too earnest and deep of which He is justly the object.

★ ★ Patriot's Prayer ★ ★

Lord, I cannot express my gratitude for Your gift of Jesus and the salvation from my sins that He provided for me on the cross. Thanks to this amazing sacrifice, I live in the abundant life of the heart and anticipate a glorious eternal life in heaven. May my life today reflect my profound gratitude.

★ ★ Patriot's Promise ★ ★

The life-saving promise of Romans 10:9 is straightforward: "If you confess with your mouth the Lord Jesus and believe in your heart that God has raised Him from the dead, you will be saved."

November 3

Do you still hold fast to your integrity?

JOB'S WIFE IN JOB 2:9

William Bross (1813–1890) was a successful American journalist and co-publisher of the *Chicago Tribune*. In an interview, he discussed his success:

What maxims have had a strong influence on your life and helped your success?

The Proverbs of Solomon and other Scriptures. They were quoted a thousand times by my honored father and caused an effort to do my duty each day, under a constant sense of obligation to my Savior and fellow man.

What do you consider essential elements of success for a young man entering upon such a profession as yours?

Sterling, unflinching integrity in all matters, public and private. Let everyone do his whole duty, both to God and man. Let him follow earnestly the teachings of the Scriptures and eschew infidelity in all its forms.

What, in your observation, have been the chief causes of the numerous failures in the life of business and professional men?

Want of integrity, careless[ness] of the truth, reckless[ness] in thought and expression, lack of trust in God, and a disregard of the teachings of His Holy Word, bad company, and bad morals in any of their many phases.

★ ★ Patriot's Prayer ★ ★

Dear Lord, enable me to recognize and then do what is right in Your sight today. Help me live as one who esteems integrity, truth, and trust in You and Your Word.

★ ★ Patriot's Promise ★ ★

According to Proverbs 10:9, "he who walks with integrity walks securely."

November 4

Voting

Since the founding of our nation, voting has been considered one of the core responsibilities of citizenship. In 1781, Samuel Adams—the "Father of the American Revolution" and signer of the Declaration of Independence—said this about voting:

> Let each citizen remember at the moment he is offering his vote that he is not making a present or a compliment to please an individual— or at least that he ought not so to do; but that he is executing one of the most solemn trusts in human society for which he is accountable to God and his country.

★ ★ Patriot's Prayer ★ ★

Heavenly Father, thank You for the opportunity and freedom to vote. What an honor! I pray that You would guide and direct my every decision as I stand in the voting booth. Help me to cast my vote for the person who stands for liberty, freedom, and respect for human life.

★ ★ Patriot's Promise ★ ★

Proverbs 16:1 tells us, "The preparations of the heart belong to man, but the answer of the tongue is from the LORD." God will show us what is proper and right if we seek His advice.

November 5

They have despised the law of the LORD.

AMOS 2:4

In 1802 Judge Nathaniel Freeman charged the Massachusetts grand juries as follows:

> The laws of the Christian system, as embraced by the Bible, must
> be respected as of high authority in all our courts, and it cannot be
> thought improper for the officers of such government to acknowl-
> edge their obligation to be governed by its rule.... [Our govern-
> ment] originating in the voluntary compact of a people who in that
> very instrument profess the Christian religion, it may be considered,
> not as republic Rome was, a pagan, but a Christian republic.

★ ★ Patriot's Prayer ★ ★

I worship You, Lord, and thank You for this nation. I thank You that You have
smiled down on us and been merciful to us. I am grateful for the times when we
have seen the fulfillment of Your miraculous and powerful promises.

★ ★ Patriot's Promise ★ ★

As the writer of Proverbs noted, "When the righteous are in authority, the people
rejoice; but when a wicked man rules, the people groan" (29:2). God has shown us
that when we put into office people who are true to His principles, we can rejoice.

November 6

Priorities

In 1966, Senator Robert F. Kennedy described what happens when citizens join together in a righteous cause:

> Few will have the greatness to bend history itself, but each of us can work to change a small portion of events, and in the total of all those acts will be written the history of this generation. . . . It is from numberless diverse acts of courage and belief that human history is shaped. Each time a man stands up for an ideal, or acts to improve the lot of others, or strikes out against injustice, he sends forth a tiny ripple of hope, and crossing each other from a million different centers of energy and daring, those ripples build a current that can sweep down the mightiest walls of oppression and resistance.

Freed from Babylonian exile, the children of Israel returned to their land and enthusiastically began to rebuild the temple. But the strenuous work, fear, and other hardships turned their initial joy into despondency, and they put the project aside. With the temple still unfinished sixteen years later, the prophet Haggai told the people that they had put their own priorities above God's. When they repented, put God first, and completed the temple, God blessed them with joy and prosperity.

★ ★ Patriot's Prayer ★ ★

Father, forgive me for those times I've put aside work You've called me to and turned my attention to foolish things. I want to live according to Your will and Your priorities.

★ ★ Patriot's Promise ★ ★

"Seek first the kingdom of God and His righteousness, and all these things shall be added to you" (Matthew 6:33).

November 7

My help comes from the LORD, who
made heaven and earth.

PSALM 121:2

Confederate Robert E. Lee is among the most celebrated generals in Ameri-can history, admired equally for his character and his military prowess. One historian has written, "What he seemed, he was—a wholly human gentleman, the essential elements of whose positive character were two and only two, simplicity and spirituality."

We get a glimpse of Lee's character in this greeting to his wife written on Christmas Day 1862:

> My heart is filled with gratitude to Almighty God for His unspeak-able mercies with which He has blessed us in this day...What should have become of us without His crowning help and protection? Oh, if our people would only recognize it and cease from vain self-boasting and adulation, how strong would be my belief in final success and happiness to our country! For in Him alone I know is our trust and safety....
>
> What a cruel thing is war; to separate and destroy families and friends, and mar the purest joys and happiness God has granted us in this world; to fill our hearts with hatred instead of love for our neighbors...
>
> My heart bleeds at the death of every one of our gallant men.

Lee's words underscore President Lincoln's ironic summary of the Civil War: "Each invokes [God's] aid against the other."

★ ★ Patriot's Prayer ★ ★

Great is Your healing mercy when brother turns against brother, and I praise You, Lord, that You will always be merciful.

★ ★ Patriot's Promise ★ ★

"Jesus Christ is the same yesterday, today, and forever" (Hebrews 13:8).

November 8

Freedom Must Be Practiced

For this is the will of God . . . as free, yet not using liberty as a cloak for vice, but as bondservants of God.

1 PETER 2:15–16

Through the years, Americans have commented on the value and preservation of freedom. Here is a sampling:

We must be free not because we claim freedom, but because we practice it.

WILLIAM FAULKNER

Have we too much freedom? Have we so long ridiculed authority in the family, discipline in education, rules in art, decency in conduct, and law in the state that our liberation has brought us close to chaos in the family and the school, in morals, arts, ideas, and government? We forgot to make ourselves intelligent when we made ourselves free.

WILL DURANT

We proclaim ourselves as indeed we are: the defenders of freedom, wherever it continues to exist in the world. But we cannot defend freedom abroad by deserting it at home.

EDWARD R. MURROW

Injustice anywhere is a threat to justice everywhere.

MARTIN LUTHER KING JR.

No one is free when others are oppressed.

UNKNOWN

★ ★ Patriot's Prayer ★ ★

Help me, Lord, to remember that with freedom comes great responsibility. Teach me to live not just freely, but responsibly and according to Your Word and principles.

★ ★ Patriot's Promise ★ ★

"Where the Spirit of the Lord is, there is liberty" (2 Corinthians 3:17).

He shall bruise your head, and you
shall bruise His heel.

GENESIS 3:15

"The Battle Hymn of the Republic"

In November 1861, after visiting a Union Army camp, Julia Ward Howe wrote
the poem that came to be called "The Battle Hymn of the Republic."

Mine eyes have seen the glory of the coming of the Lord:
> He is trampling out the vintage where the grapes of wrath are stored;
> He hath loosed the fateful lightning of His terrible swift sword:
> His truth is marching on.

I have seen Him in the watch-fires of a hundred circling camps,
> They have builded Him an altar in the evening dews and damps;
> I can read His righteous sentence by the dim and flaring lamps:
> His day is marching on.

I have read a fiery gospel writ in burnished rows of steel:
> "As ye deal with my contemners, so with you my grace shall deal;
> Let the Hero, born of woman, crush the serpent with His heel,
> Since God is marching on."

He has sounded forth the trumpet that shall never call retreat;
> He is sifting out the hearts of men before His judgment-seat:
> Oh, be swift, my soul, to answer Him! be jubilant, my feet!
> Our God is marching on.

In the beauty of the lilies Christ was born across the sea,
> With a glory in His bosom that transfigures you and me:
> As He died to make men holy, let us die to make men free,
> While God is marching on.

★ ★ Patriot's Prayer ★ ★

My Lord, may we as a nation seek You first so we do not repeat the sins of our past.

★ ★ Patriot's Promise ★ ★

"You should keep all His commandments . . . that you may be a holy people to the
LORD your God" (Deuteronomy 26:18–19).

November 10

A Prayer for Our Nation

The LORD your God will bless you just as He promised you.

DEUTERONOMY 15:6

Born in a poor Russian Jewish ghetto, Irving Berlin immigrated to America with his parents when he was five, settling in New York's Lower East Side. He became one of the most prolific American songwriters in history. In 1918 he originally wrote "God Bless America," and he revised it in 1938 as war and the Nazis were threatening Europe. The lyric takes the form of a prayer for God's blessing and peace for the nation. Singer Kate Smith introduced the revised "God Bless America" during her radio broadcast on Armistice Day (now called Veteran's Day) 1938, and the song was an immediate hit. Even now it is considered an unofficial national anthem of the United States.

> While the storm clouds gather far across the sea,
> Let us swear allegiance to a land that's free,
> Let us all be grateful for a land so fair,
> As we raise our voices in a solemn prayer.
> God bless America, land that I love.
> Stand beside her and guide her
> Through the night with the light from above.
> From the mountains, to the prairies,
> To the oceans white with foam,
> God bless America, my home sweet home.

★ ★ Patriot's Prayer ★ ★

I pray, Almighty God, that You will continue to bless America. May we, also Lord, be a blessing to You—and let that blessing begin with me.

★ ★ Patriot's Promise ★ ★

Hear the promise of Psalm 29:11—"The LORD will give strength to His people; the LORD will bless His people with peace."

November 11

So I shall not see him?"

"Known Only to God"

In November 1921, after the end of World War I, the Tomb of the Unknowns was built in Arlington Cemetery, Virginia. It contains the remains of unidentified American soldiers from World Wars I and II, the Korean Conflict, and the Vietnam War (through 1998), and it represents the missing and unknown service members who died so our country could remain free. The Tomb gives the families of these brave Americans a place to grieve and pray, and it has been guarded continuously, twenty-four hours a day, seven days a week, since July 1937, by specially trained Tomb Guards, who ensure these heroes rest in peace.

The Tomb's inscription reads:
Here Rests
In Honored Glory
An American Soldier
Known But To God.

★ ★ Patriot's Prayer ★ ★
Lord, I thank You that You know every part of me. I thank You that You love me enough pay the price of my salvation by dying for me.

★ ★ Patriot's Promise ★ ★
In Luke 12:7, Jesus reminds us that "the very hairs of your head are all numbered." Since God knows the very number of hairs on our heads, we must indeed be most precious to Him.

The Heart of Democracy

To God our Savior, who alone is wise, be glory and majesty . . . now and forever.

JUDE 25

The Mayflower Compact was America's first significant governmental document, signed on November 11, 1620, by the forty-one adult male Pilgrims on the *Mayflower*. This document established the powerful idea of self-government through laws made by the people, an idea at the heart of democracy:

> In the name of God, Amen. We, whose names are underwritten. . . . Having undertaken for the Glory of God, and Advancement of the Christian Faith, and the Honour of our King and Country, a voyage to plant the first colony in the northern parts of Virginia; do by these presents, solemnly and mutually in the Presence of God and one of another, covenant and combine ourselves together into a civil Body Politick, for our better Ordering and Preservation, and Furtherance of the Ends aforesaid; And by Virtue hereof to enact, constitute, and frame, such just and equal Laws, Ordinances, Acts, Constitutions and Offices, from time to time, as shall be thought most meet and convenient for the General good of the Colony; unto which we promise all due submission and obedience . . .

★ ★ Patriot's Prayer ★ ★

Lord, those individuals who first settled this nation did so to spread the Christian faith. Please give us Christians today the same kind of courage and strength to spread the gospel of Jesus Christ around the world.

★ ★ Patriot's Promise ★ ★

The risen Jesus commanded us to share the news of His resurrection victory over sin and death (Matthew 28:18). What a glorious truth to be privileged to share with others!

There lay Sisera, dead with the
[tent] peg in his temple.

JUDGES 4:22

Women in the Revolutionary War

During the Revolutionary War, it was not unusual to see women on the battlefield, particularly as camp followers who performed vital chores like cooking, doing laundry, carrying water, loading weapons, and nursing the wounded.

Margaret Corbin accompanied her husband, John, when he joined the Continental Army. During the Battle of Fort Washington in 1776, an artillery bombardment fatally wounded John as he manned one of the two cannons. Seeing him dead, Margaret took his place, firing the cannon until she was severely wounded. She became the first woman to receive a pension from Congress.

Deborah Sampson Gannett was the first known American woman to impersonate a man in order to fight for freedom. Participating in several skirmishes, she took musket balls in her thigh and suffered a huge cut on her forehead. Her identity was discovered when she came down with a malignant fever. After the war, Sampson received a pension that matched that of the men who fought.

Women served as spies, alerting American troops to enemy movement, carrying messages, and transporting contraband. George Washington chose Ann Simpson Davis to carry messages to his generals when the army was in eastern Pennsylvania. An accomplished horsewoman, Davis slipped unnoticed through areas occupied by the British army. She received a letter of commendation from General Washington.

The bravery of these, and many unnamed women throughout American history, cannot be measured. Just as Jael helped the Israelites win victory over Sisera, women have played a vital role in protecting this nation.

★ ★ Patriot's Prayer ★ ★
Lord, grant me the courage to serve wherever You call me to serve.

★ ★ Patriot's Promise ★ ★
"I will be with you" through rising rivers, rushing waters, and raging fires (Isaiah 43:2).

November 14

Women in the Civil War

She hid the messengers whom Joshua
sent to spy out Jericho.

JOSHUA 6:25

During the Civil War, hundreds of women served in the infantry, cavalry, and artillery for both the Union and Confederate armies. Many took on male disguises, and all endured hardships and dangers while serving with distinction.

In 1862 Sarah Rosetta Wakeman enlisted in the New York State Volunteers under the name "Lyons Wakeman" After performing guard duty in Virginia, her regiment marched 700 miles to Louisiana where they repelled a Confederate attack.

Rosetta contracted dysentery and died in 1864. Her identity remained undiscovered for more than a century until her letters home surfaced. The headstone at her Louisiana grave reads "4006 Lyons Wakeman, N.Y."

In those letters, Rosetta wrote about the battlefield, her pride at being a soldier, and her faith: "I don't feel afraid . . . I don't believe there are any Rebel bullets made for me yet. . . . But if it is God's will for me to fall in the field of battle, it is my will to go and never return home."

Confederate soldier Rose Rooney signed on to serve as cook and laundress. After her unit became Company K of the 15th Louisiana, she is reported to have run through a field of heavy fire to tear down a rail fence, allowing a battery of Confederate artillery to stop a Union charge.

★ ★ Patriot's Prayer ★ ★

Almighty God, thank You for soldiers—women and men—who are willing to fight for our freedom. Strengthen, protect, and bless them.

★ ★ Patriot's Promise ★ ★

"Though I walk through the valley of the shadow of death . . . Your rod and Your staff, they comfort me" (Psalm 23:4).

Everyone who practices righteousness
is born of Him.

1 John 2:29

A Churchless Nation

Consider these comments made in 1917 by Theodore Roosevelt, twenty-sixth president of the United States:

> The most perfect machinery of government will not keep us as a nation from destruction if there is not within us a soul. No abounding material prosperity shall avail us if our spiritual senses atrophy. The foes of our own household shall surely prevail against us unless there be in our people an inner life which finds its outward expression in a morality not very widely different from that preached by the seers and prophets of Judea when the grandeur that was Greece and the glory that was Rome still lay in the future. . . .

[George] Washington said:

> "Morality is a necessary spring of popular government" . . . The result [of the French Revolution's effort to abolish not only Christianity but religion] was a cynical disregard of morality and a carnival of cruelty and bigotry, committed in the name of reason and liberty, which equaled anything ever done by Torquemada and the fanatics of the Inquisition in the name of religion and order. . . . A churchless community, a community where men have abandoned and scoff at or ignore their Christian duties, is a community on the rapid downgrade.

★ ★ Patriot's Prayer ★ ★

Lord, our nation is "on the rapid downgrade," but we are not beyond Your all-powerful, redemptive reach. Please, merciful and faithful Lord, save us!

★ ★ Patriot's Promise ★ ★

"The Lord your God . . . keeps covenant and mercy for a thousand generations with those who love Him and keep His commandments" (Deuteronomy 7:9).

331

God's Invaluable Word

[God] enlarges nations, and guides them.

JOB 12:23

In 1917 Woodrow Wilson, the twenty-eighth president of the United States, led America into World War I. The following excerpt from a 1911 speech sets forth his view of God's Word:

> There are great problems before the American people.... I should be afraid to go forward if I did not believe that there lay at the foundation of all our schooling and of all our thought this incomparable and unimpeachable Word of God.... The providence of God is the foundation of affairs, and ... only those can guide, and only those can follow, who take this providence of God from the sources where it is authentically interpreted....
>
> The happiness of seeing a great company of people like this gathered [for] Sunday school is the happiness of knowing that there are they who seek light and who know that the lamp from which their spirits can be kindled is the lamp that glows in the Word of God.
>
> Every Sunday school should be a place where this great book is not only opened, is not only studied, is not only revered, but is drunk of as if it were a fountain of life, is used as if it were the only source of inspiration and of guidance. No great nation can ever survive its own temptations and its own follies that does not indoctrinate its children in the Word of God.

★ ★ Patriot's Prayer ★ ★

Lord, when I try to resolve problems on my own, situations don't turn out well. I need You and Your Word to guide me.

★ ★ Patriot's Promise ★ ★

"O Lord GOD, You are God, and Your words are true" (2 Samuel 7:28).

Freedom's Defense

*T*he soldier's heart, the soldier's spirit, the soldier's soul are everything. Unless the soldier's soul sustains him, he cannot be relied upon and will fail himself, his commander, and his country in the end.

GENERAL GEORGE C. MARSHALL

Wars may be fought with weapons, but they are won by men. It is the spirit of the men who follow and of the man who leads that gains that victory.

GENERAL GEORGE S. PATTON

God grants liberty only to those who love it and are always ready to guard and defend it.

DANIEL WEBSTER

This nation will remain the land of the free only so long as it is the home of the brave.

ELMER DAVIS

A man who won't die for something is not fit to live.

MARTIN LUTHER KING JR.

The liberties of our country, the freedom of our civil Constitution, are worth defending at all hazards; and it is our duty to defend them against all attacks. We have received them as a fair inheritance from our worthy ancestors: they purchased them for us with toil and danger and expense of treasure and blood, and transmitted them to us with care and diligence.

SAMUEL ADAMS

★ ★ Patriot's Prayer ★ ★

Almighty Father, please continue to give us brave men and women who are willing to sacrifice everything in defense of our country.

★ ★ Patriot's Promise ★ ★

"Do not be afraid . . . the battle is not yours, but God's" (2 Chronicles 20:15).

333

The Gettysburg Address

Five hundred thousand choice men of Israel fell slain.

2 CHRONICLES 13: 17

The Battle of Gettysburg (July 1–3, 1863) resulted in over 51,000 deaths, the largest number of casualties in the Civil War. Abraham Lincoln's November 19, 1863 address at the dedication of the Soldiers' National Cemetery in Gettysburg, is regarded as one of the greatest speeches in American history:

> Fourscore and seven years ago our fathers brought forth on this continent a new nation, conceived in liberty and dedicated to the proposition that all men are created equal. Now we are engaged in a great civil war, testing whether that nation or any nation so conceived and so dedicated can long endure. We are met on a great battlefield of that war. We have come to dedicate a portion of that field as a final resting-place for those who here gave their lives that that nation might live. . . . It is for us the living rather to be dedicated here to the unfinished work which they who fought here have thus far so nobly advanced. It is rather for us to be here dedicated to the great task remaining before us . . . that we here highly resolve that these dead shall not have died in vain, that this nation under God shall have a new birth of freedom, and that government of the people, by the people, for the people shall not perish from the earth.

★ ★ Patriot's Prayer ★ ★

Lord, thank You for this nation and for those who have given their lives to gain and protect our freedom. Bless those who are currently serving.

★ ★ Patriot's Promise ★ ★

"The LORD your God, who goes before you, He will fight for you" (Deuteronomy 1:30).

Trust in the LORD with all your heart.

PROVERBS 3:5

Our Nation's Coins and Currency

O ur nation's coins have not always had "In God We Trust" stamped on them. The motto was placed on United States coins largely because of increased religious sentiment during the Civil War. From Treasury Department records, the first suggestion that God be recognized on US coinage can be traced to a letter addressed to the Secretary of Treasury Salmon P. Chase from a small-town Pennsylvania minister in 1861.

As a result, in a letter dated November 20, 1861, Secretary Chase instructed James Pollock, Director of the Mint at Philadelphia, to prepare a motto: "Dear Sir: No nation can be strong except in the strength of God, or safe except in His defense. The trust of our people in God should be declared on our national coins."

"In God We Trust" first appeared on the 1864 two-cent coin. An Act of Congress passed on March 3, 1865, allowed the Mint Director, with the Secretary's approval, to place the motto on all gold and silver coins that "shall admit the inscription thereon."

Legislation approved July 11, 1955, made the appearance of "In God We Trust" mandatory on all coins and paper currency of the United States. Since 1955, all United States coins and currency have carried the motto "In God We Trust." By an act of Congress, July 30, 1956, "In God We Trust" became the national motto of the United States.

★ ★ Patriot's Prayer ★ ★
Father, teach us—as individuals and as a nation—to trust in You.

★ ★ Patriot's Promise ★ ★
"In all your ways acknowledge Him, and He shall direct your paths" (Proverbs 3:6).

The Colonies' First Book

Be filled with the Spirit, speaking to one another
in psalms and hymns and spiritual songs.

EPHESIANS 5:18–19

When the Pilgrim Fathers arrived at Plymouth, Massachusetts, in 1620, the influence of the Bible and their Christian faith on their lives and literature came with them. A mere twenty years later, *The Bay Psalm Book* (originally titled *The Whole Booke of Psalmes Faithfully Translated into English Metre*) was printed in Cambridge, Massachusetts. It was the first book entirely written in the colonies and printed here as well. The first printing press in New England was imported specifically for this volume.

The early residents of the Massachusetts Bay Colony, dissatisfied with earlier translations of the psalms, hired "thirty pious and learned Ministers" to undertake a new translation. The project reflected the Puritans' values and priorities: they wanted a faithful translation of God's Word that an entire congregation could sing. Given the harsh living conditions of those early years, the successful translation and publication of this volume was a remarkable achievement.

The Bay Psalm Book, in use for well over a century, and *The New England Primer* were, next to the Bible, the most commonly owned books in seventeenth-century New England.

★ ★ Patriot's Prayer ★ ★

Heavenly Father, thank You for the influence Your Word has had on this nation. I pray that You raise up another generation of Americans that will be passionate for Your Word and committed to building their lives and guiding this nation according to its truth.

★ ★ Patriot's Promise ★ ★

Psalm 147:1 says, "Praise the LORD! For it is good to sing praises to our God." Consider the good that God does in our hearts—providing peace, perspective, hope, comfort—whenever we offer Him praise and thanks.

Give thanks to him and praise his name.

PSALM 100:4 NIV

"Our Sincere and Humble Thanks"

In 1921 Dr. J. C. Fitzpatrick noticed a curious document being auctioned off at an art gallery in New York—and he bought it for $300 for the Library of Congress. What Fitzpatrick purchased was George Washington's Thanksgiving Proclamation, dating back to 1789. How had it gotten lost—and stayed lost—for 130 years? The document was probably mixed in with private papers when the US Capitol moved from New York to Washington DC. Below is an excerpt:

> I do recommend and assign Thursday, the 26th day of November next, to be devoted by the people of these States to the service of that great and glorious Being who is the beneficent author of all the good that was, that is, or that will be; that we may then all unite in rendering unto Him our sincere and humble thanks for His kind care and protection of the people of this country previous to their becoming a nation; for the signal and manifold mercies and the favorable interpositions of His providence in the course and conclusion of the late war; for the great degree of tranquility, union, and plenty which we have since enjoyed; for the peaceable and rational manner in which we have been enable to establish constitutions of government for our safety and happiness ... and, in general, for all the great and various favors which He has been pleased to confer upon us.

★ ★ Patriot's Prayer ★ ★

Merciful God, even as we thank You for blessing this nation, we—as President Washington himself did—pray that you will "pardon our national and other transgressions . . ."

★ ★ Patriot's Promise ★ ★

"Humble yourselves . . . that [God] may lift you up" (1 Peter 5:6 NIV).

November 22

Feed the Hungry

If your enemy is hungry, feed him.

ROMANS 12:20

Henry Ward Beecher (1813–1887) was a leading American clergyman, editor, and abolitionist. He shared this observation:

> Christianity works while infidelity talks. She feeds the hungry, clothes the naked, visits and cheers the sick, and seeks the lost, while infidelity abuses her and babbles nonsense and profanity. "By their fruits ye shall know them."

Mr. Beecher also wrote this:

> The Bible is God's chart for you to steer by, to keep you from the bottom of the sea, and to show you where the harbor is, and how to reach it without running on the rocks or bars.

★ ★ Patriot's Prayer ★ ★

Merciful God, give me an opportunity to help someone today. Help me recognize that opportunity when it comes my way. May I be generous and compassionate to those who need me to be. Give me a loving heart.

★ ★ Patriot's Promise ★ ★

"Cast your bread upon the waters, for you will find it after many days" (Ecclesiastes 11:2). In this verse, God commands us to be generous and promises that He will reward our generosity.

For all things are for your sakes, that grace, having spread through the many, may cause thanksgiving to abound to the glory of God.

2 CORINTHIANS 4:15

On October 3, 1863, in the midst of the Civil War, President Abraham Lincoln called Americans to a National Day of Thanksgiving and Praise: No human counsel hath devised nor hath any mortal hand worked out these great things. They are the gracious gifts of the Most High God, who, while dealing with us in anger for our sins, hath neverthe-less remembered mercy. It has seemed to me fit and proper that they should be solemnly, reverently, and gratefully acknowledged as with one heart and one voice by the whole American People. I do therefore invite my fellow citizens . . . to set apart and observe the last Thursday of November next, as a day of Thanksgiving and Praise to our beneficent Father who dwelleth in the Heavens.

And I recommend . . . they do also, with humble penitence for our national perverseness and disobedience, commend to His tender care all those who have become widows, orphans, mourners, or sufferers in the lamentable civil strife in which we are unavoidably engaged, and fervently implore the interposition of the Almighty Hand to heal the wounds of the nation and to restore it as soon as may be consistent with the Divine purposes to the full enjoyment of peace, harmony, tranquility, and Union.

★ ★ Patriot's Prayer ★ ★
Merciful God in heaven, I offer my thanks to You for Your bountiful blessings to my country, my family, and me.

★ ★ Patriot's Promise ★ ★
"Thanks be to God, who gives us the victory [over death] through our Lord Jesus Christ" (1 Corinthians 15:57).

339

A Thankful Nation

In his 1815 Thanksgiving Day proclamation, President James Madison reminded his audience:

> No people ought to feel greater obligations to celebrate the goodness of the Great Disposer of Events of the destiny of Nations than the people of the United States. . . . And to the same Divine Author of Every Good and Perfect Gift we are indebted for all those privileges and advantages, religious as well as civil, which are so richly enjoyed in this favored land.

★ ★ Patriot's Prayer ★ ★

Lord, only You can fill the emptiness in my heart. Sometimes I feel very lonely, but I know that You are with me all the time. You never leave me alone. Your presence with me—now, that's a good gift from You, Lord.

★ ★ Patriot's Promise ★ ★

What a great promise we find in James 1:25—"He who looks into the perfect law of liberty and continues in it, and is not a forgetful hearer but a doer of the work, this one will be blessed in what he does."

It is more blessed to give than to receive.

ACTS 20:35

T he evidence of God's grace," said the Presbyterian revivalist Charles G. Finney, "was a person's benevolence toward others," and this principle was borne out in the Second Great Awakening (1800–1830s) in the United States. From the extraordinary energies generated by the evangelical movement, numerous benevolent societies emerged. All of them were voluntary and passionately Christian; many had no ties to any single religious group. Most were interdenominational, and cooperative enterprises often took place among the societies.

John Beck, for instance, devised the evangelistic Mississippi Valley Plan in 1826. He went first to the Baptist General Convention and the American Home Missionary Society (1826) and convinced them that every missionary could sell Bibles for the American Bible Society (1816), distribute tracts for the American Tract Society (1825), and start Sunday schools for the American Sunday School Union (1824). The agencies adopted the plan, and as a result, 23,000 Bibles and $18,000 worth of tracts were shipped to Ohio and Kentucky in 1830 alone.

Subscribing to the Founding Fathers' views, members of this evangelical movement saw religion as a "necessary spring" for republican government: these benevolent societies were helping to form the virtuous citizenry of which the Founders spoke. The American Home Missionary Society assured its supporters in 1826 that "we are doing the work of patriotism no less than Christianity."

★ ★ Patriot's Prayer ★ ★
Lord, show me where You would have me share the love and compassion of Christ with someone today.

★ ★ Patriot's Promise ★ ★
"Give, and it will be given to you: good measure, pressed down, shaken together, and running over" (Luke 6:38).

November 26

Blessings and Responsibilities

Thus says the LORD: "I will return to Zion, and dwell in the midst of Jerusalem."

ZECHARIAH 8:3

God's richest blessings carry with them certain responsibilities, as Benjamin Harrison, America's twenty-third president, was well aware of. Hear some thoughts from his 1889 talk:

> No other people have a government more worthy of their respect and love, or a land so magnificent in extent, so pleasant to look upon, and so full of generous suggestion to enterprise and labor. God has placed upon our head a diadem and has laid at our feet power and wealth beyond definition or calculation. But we must not forget that we take these gifts upon the condition that justice and mercy shall hold the reins of power and the upward avenues of hope shall be free to all people.

In the book of Zechariah, God spoke through the prophet to exhort the people to finish rebuilding the temple in Jerusalem. Zechariah reminded them that one day the Messiah's glory would fill that temple, but such future blessings hinged on their present obedience. When the children of Israel entered into the project with renewed zeal, Zechariah declared that they would be blessed because Yahweh would remember His covenant with their forefathers.

★ ★ Patriot's Prayer ★ ★

Lord, Your Word teaches that my body is Your temple. Help me to bring into subjection those habits and acts that would result in sickness and disease. Help me be a good steward of my body and thereby glorify You.

★ ★ Patriot's Promise ★ ★

"You are the Temple of God and . . . the Spirit of God dwells in you" (1 Corinthians 3:16).

The glory of the LORD appeared.

NUMBERS 16:42

Blessed by His Providence

In his 1805 inaugural address, President Thomas Jefferson said this:
I shall need, too, the favor of that Being in whose hands we are, who led our forefathers, as Israel of old, from their native land and planted them in a country flowing with all the necessities and comforts of life, who has covered our infancy with His Providence and our riper years with His wisdom and power, and to whose goodness I ask you to join with me in supplications that He will so enlighten the minds of your servants, guide their councils and prosper their measures, that whatever they do shall result in your good, and shall secure to you the peace, friendship, and approbation of all nations.

★ ★ Patriot's Prayer ★ ★

Creator God, grant us Your favor in this land. And, like those who celebrated the first Thanksgiving, may we always lift up our thanks to You who have been so good to this nation. I lift my praise and thanks to You.

★ ★ Patriot's Promise ★ ★

Hear the psalmist's joy: "Oh, give thanks to the LORD, for He is good! For His mercy endures forever" (1 Chronicles 16:34). When we give thanks to the Lord, God guarantees His mercy and favor.

November 28

America, Never Forget!

Israel has forgotten his Maker.

Carlos Rómulo (1899–1985), a Philippine general renowned for his heroic activities during World War II, issued this charge to us Americans:

> Never forget, Americans, that yours is a spiritual country. Yes, I know you're a practical people. Like others, I've marveled at your factories, your skyscrapers, and your arsenals. But underlying everything else is the fact that America began as a God-loving, God-fearing, God-worshipping people.

★ ★ Patriot's Prayer ★ ★

Lord, liberate the minds of unbelievers that they may recognize the true foundation of our great land. May I be a witness to Your glory on earth. You are the Author and Finisher of my faith. Use me to help others come to faith in You.

★ ★ Patriot's Promise ★ ★

Psalm 103:2 says, "Bless the LORD, O my soul, and forget not all His benefits." The psalm lists some of those benefits, which result in the promise that our youth will be renewed like the eagle (v. 5). When we remember God's goodness to us—and may we never forget—we can soar spiritually.

Your word is a lamp to my feet and a
light to my path.

PSALM 119:105

Rooted in God's Word

Until the American Revolution, America's Bibles were shipped over from
England. In 1777, that supply was cut off, and supplies dwindled. Reason-
ing that "the use of the Bible is so universal and its importance so great," Congress
resolved to import 20,000 copies of the Bible.

When that resolution was not acted upon, Robert Aitken of Philadelphia published a New Testament in 1777 and followed it with three additional editions. In
early 1781, he petitioned Congress and received approval to print the entire Bible.
This first American printing of the English Bible in 1782 has come to be called
the "Bible of the Revolution."

American historian W. P. Strickland shared this point:

> "Who, in view of this fact, will call in question the assertion that this
> is a Bible nation? Who will charge the government with indifference
> to religion when the first Congress of the States assumed all the
> rights and performed all the duties of a Bible society long before
> such an institution had an existence in the world?"

★ ★ Patriot's Prayer ★ ★

Because we as a nation are rooted in Your Word, Lord, we are generous to other
countries and we work to see that *all* may experience life, liberty, and the pursuit
of happiness. Any goodness in our nation is because we were founded on Your
Word.

★ ★ Patriot's Promise ★ ★

Deuteronomy 4:29 says, "You will find [God] if you seek Him with all your heart
and with all your soul." Such seeking and finding will help us restore our land.

December

He was despised and rejected by men, a man of sorrows, and familiar with suffering.

Isaiah 53:3 NIV

Valley Forge, December 1777

After severe defeats in the fall of 1777, twelve thousand members of the Continental Army encamped at Valley Forge, living in tents and struggling to survive the winter's bitter cold. Nine out of ten soldiers had no shoes, food and firewood ran short, and supplies couldn't be bought because paper money wasn't worth anything. General Washington pleaded with Congress for supplies. More than two thousand soldiers died that winter from pneumonia, typhoid, and dysentery.

Over one hundred years later, attorney and orator Henry Armitt Brown paid tribute to the sacrifices and sufferings of these brave men:

> Danger shall not frighten nor temptation have power to seduce them. Doubt shall not shake their love of country nor suffering overcome their fortitude. The powers of evil shall not prevail against them, for they are the Continental Army, and these are the hills of Valley Forge! . . .
>
> Their trials here secured the happiness of a continent; their labors have born fruit in the free institutions of a powerful nation; their examples give hope to every race and clime; their names live on the lips of a grateful people; their memory is cherished in their children's hearts, and shall endure forever.

★ ★ Patriot's Prayer ★ ★

O God, trials are not easy, but You promise to help me face any situation. Thank You—and may what I go through strengthen me and glorify You.

★ ★ Patriot's Promise ★ ★

"Blessed is the man who endures temptation; for when he has been approved, he will receive the crown of life which the Lord has promised to those who love Him" (James 1:12).

December 1

On Moral Decay

Then God saw . . . that they turned
from their evil way.

JONAH 3:10

General Douglas MacArthur, Supreme Commander of the Allied Forces in the
Pacific during World War II, said this in December 1951:

> In this day of gathering storms, as moral deterioration of political
> power spreads its growing infection, it is essential that every spiritual
> force be mobilized to defend and preserve the religious base upon
> which this nation is founded; for it has been that base which has been
> the motivating impulse to our moral and national growth. History
> fails to record a single precedent in which nations subject to moral
> decay have not passed into political and economic decline. There has
> been either a spiritual reawakening to overcome the moral lapse or
> a progressive deterioration leading to ultimate national disaster.

★ ★ Patriot's Prayer ★ ★

I know, Father, that our nation needs You now more than ever. I pray today for
our leaders. Open their hearts to Your Word and to Your will. Please give us a
reawakening to Your ways and to Your purpose for our country. Restore to us the
knowledge of the principles upon which this nation was founded.

★ ★ Patriot's Promise ★ ★

In 2 Chronicles 7:14, God assures us that if we humble ourselves, pray, and turn
from our wickedness, He will heal our land. What glory awaits us if we obey Him.

Hope deferred makes the heart sick.

PROVERBS 13:12

"The Last Best Hope"

In December 1862, President Lincoln concluded his second annual message to Congress with this:

> In giving freedom to the slave, we assure freedom to the free—honorable alike in what we give and what we preserve. We shall nobly save—or meanly lose—the last best hope of earth. Other means may succeed; this could not fail. The way is plain, peaceful, generous, just—a way which if followed the world will forever applaud and God must forever bless.

★ ★ Patriot's Prayer ★ ★

Thank You, dear Lord, that all people in this country are free. May we never allow anything or anyone to change that. You have been generous to this nation and have blessed it and for that we are humbly grateful.

★ ★ Patriot's Promise ★ ★

Consider the second part of Proverbs 13:12: "Hope deferred makes the heart sick, but when the desire comes, it is a tree of life." When we have hope based in God, He promises that it will sustain us.

December 3

Houses of Worship

On December 4, 1800, Congress approved the use of the Capitol building for religious services, and this practice lasted until well after the Civil War and Reconstruction. Even after dozens of churches were established in the city, religious services continued at the Capitol.

Thomas Jefferson, who recommended "a wall of separation between church and state," attended church services in the House of Representatives. Throughout his presidency (1801–1809), he permitted voluntary and nondiscriminatory church services in executive branch buildings. (Preachers from every Protestant denomination appeared, and Catholic priests began officiating in 1826.) Apparently, Jefferson's concern for "separation" meant he opposed an official state-sponsored church, rather than excluding religion from government.

Jefferson's successor, James Madison, also attended church at the Capitol, as did many more presidents through Abraham Lincoln. It was also common for many members of Congress to attend those services, and often the floor of the House was filled. From 1807 to 1857, interdenominational services—overseen by chaplains appointed by the House and Senate—were held in what is now Statuary Hall.

In addition to this service, several individual churches met in the Capitol each week for their own services. Church services were also held in the Supreme Court Chamber as well as the Senate Chamber.

★ ★ Patriot's Prayer ★ ★

Father, may our freedom *of* religion not be interpreted as freedom *from* religion. Please protect our freedom of worship and our freedom to speak openly of You.

★ ★ Patriot's Promise ★ ★

"Whoever resists the authority resists the ordinance of God, and those who resist will bring judgment on themselves" (Romans 13:2).

Remember His covenant forever.

1 CHRONICLES 16:15

The First Expression of Americanism

In his National Day of Prayer Proclamation on December 5, 1974, President Gerald Ford quoted President Dwight Eisenhower's 1955 declaration:

> Without God there could be no American form of government, nor an American way of life. Recognition of the Supreme Being is the first—the most basic—expression of Americanism. Thus, the Founding Fathers of America saw it, and thus with God's help, it will continue to be.

★ ★ Patriot's Prayer ★ ★

Heavenly Father, I know that, as a nation, we need You now more than ever. I lift Your name up in praise today for the blessings You have bestowed on this country. I pray that people across the country will turn to You, for You are the ultimate Source of freedom and hope.

★ ★ Patriot's Promise ★ ★

In Isaiah 43:2, God gives us this wonderful promise: "When you pass through the waters, I will be with you; and through the rivers, they shall not overflow you. When you walk through the fire, you shall not be burned, nor shall the flame scorch you." God made a covenant promise to His people that He will continue to protect and bless us as long as we hold to His commandments.

Missions

Therefore I judge that we should not trouble
those from among the Gentiles
who are turning to God.

ACTS 15:19

In December 1803, upon the recommendation of President Thomas Jefferson, the US Congress ratified a treaty between the United States and the Kaskaskia Indian tribe. It included the following provision:

> And whereas the greater part of the said tribe have been baptized and received into the Catholic Church, to which they are much attached, the United States will give annually, for seven years, one hundred dollars toward the support of a priest of that religion, who will engage to perform for said tribe the duties of his office, and also to instruct as many of their children as possible, in the rudiments of literature, and the United States will further give the sum of three hundred dollars, to assist the said tribe in the erection of a church.

★ ★ Patriot's Prayer ★ ★

Heavenly Father, I pray Your protection and favor on the missionaries who serve You today. May we American believers never ignore Your call to preach the gospel to every nation.

★ ★ Patriot's Promise ★ ★

Galatians 3:28 teaches that "there is neither Jew nor Greek, there is neither slave nor free, there is neither male nor female; for you are all one in Christ Jesus."

Be strong and of good courage.

Joshua 1:6

Rising to the Occasion

By 1940, most of mainland Europe had fallen to Nazi aggression, and Stalin was rapidly building up one of history's largest ground armies to defend Russia. Japan had signed a ten-year military pact with Germany and Italy, confident they would eventually rule the world.

When the Japanese attacked Pearl Harbor on December 7, 1941, Americans volunteered by the hundreds of thousands to fight. Between the two opposing military alliances—Allies and the Axis powers—over 100 million military personnel engaged in the worldwide fighting. Over 60 million people—about 20 million soldiers and 40 million civilians—were killed, making it the deadliest war in history.

By June 6, 1944—D-Day—12 million Americans were in uniform, and over 16 million Americans would eventually fight in World War II. The war effort dominated the nation's industry, representing over 40 percent of the gross national product. By December 1944, over 6.5 million women had been added to the nation's work force in just five years. Valiant Marines planted the flag on Iwo Jima in February 1945, and on September 2, the Japanese signed the surrender agreement. Over 400,000 of America's young people gave their lives in this war.

Overcoming the long years of economic depression in the 1930s, then defeating Nazism and Japanese imperialism, and undertaking the Herculean task of remaking the postwar-US, this courageous generation of Americans rose to the occasion when they needed to.

★ ★ **Patriot's Prayer** ★ ★
Lord God, You call us to love You and obey You. If I don't do well personally; we don't do well as a nation. Help us be faithful to You.

★ ★ **Patriot's Promise** ★ ★
"Great is Your faithfulness" (Lamentations 3:23).

353

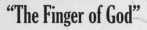

"The Finger of God"

> The LORD delivered to me two tablets of stone written with the finger of God.
>
> DEUTERONOMY 9:10

Founding Father Alexander Hamilton (1755–1804) was one of America's first Constitutional lawyers and author of fifty-one of the eighty-five *Federalist Papers*. After the Constitutional Convention of 1787, Hamilton made this comment about the proceedings:

> For my own part, I sincerely esteem it a system which without the finger of God, never could have been suggested and agreed upon by such a diversity of interests.

★ ★ Patriot's Prayer ★ ★

I don't want to go anywhere or do anything without You, dear God. Keep Your finger on my life no matter if I'm at work, with my family, or at church. Help me live one day at a time and not run ahead of Your will, step too quickly, and get off course.

★ ★ Patriot's Promise ★ ★

God wants us to have the Holy Spirit's transforming, guiding, and convicting power in our lives. In Luke 11:13, Jesus promises that we will receive the Holy Spirit simply by asking.

He is like a man building a house, who dug deep and laid the foundation on the rock.

Luke 6:48

Theodore Frelinghuysen (1787–1862), a US senator and the president of Rutgers College, wrote this:

> Let [the Bible] find its way into every cottage until the whole mass of our population shall yield to its elevating power; and under the benignant smiles of Him who delights to bless the Word, our government, the last hope of liberty, will rest on foundations against which the winds and waves shall beat in vain.

★ ★ Patriot's Prayer ★ ★

Lord, Your Word is a lamp to my feet and a light to my path. My life is in Your hands. Praises for You are on my lips. Joy in You is forever in my heart.

★ ★ Patriot's Promise ★ ★

In Hebrews 4:12 we read that "the word of God is living and powerful, and sharper than any two-edged sword, piercing even to the division of soul and spirit, and of joints and marrow, and is a discerner of the thoughts and intents of the heart." God promises us that His Word is not dormant or dead. It is living and alive today, transforming hearts and changing lives.

Free . . . to Help Others

The LORD saw that the affliction of Israel was very bitter . . . there was no helper for Israel.

2 KINGS 14:26

Having herself escaped from slavery, Harriet Tubman (1820–1913) repeatedly risked her life to free slaves using the network of antislavery activists and safe houses known as the Underground Railroad. She said this to her biographer Sarah H. Bradford:

> I had crossed de line of which I had so long been dreaming. I was free; but dere was no one to welcome me to de land of freedom, I was a stranger in a strange land, and my home after all was down in de old cabin quarter, wid de ole folks, and my brudders and sisters. But to dis solemn resolution I came; I was free, and dey should be free also; I would make a home for dem in de North, and de Lord helping me, I would bring dem all dere. Oh, how I prayed den, lying all alone on de cold, damp ground; "Oh, dear Lord," I said, "I haint got no friend but you. Come to my help, Lord, for I'm in trouble!"
>
> 'Twant me, 'twas the Lord. I always told Him, "I trust to You. I don't know where to go or what to do, but I expect You to lead me," and He always did.

★ ★ Patriot's Prayer ★ ★
Lead me, O Great God, to the place where You would have me serve You by serving Your people.

★ ★ Patriot's Promise ★ ★
Job 36:12 promises, "If they do not obey, they shall perish by the sword, and they shall die without knowledge."

Let the whole earth be filled with His glory.

PSALM 72:19

To God Be the Glory!

To celebrate the victorious conclusion of the Revolutionary War, Governor John Hancock of Massachusetts issued a Proclamation for a Day of Thanksgiving on December 11, 1783:

> Whereas ... these United States are not only happily rescued from the danger and calamities to which they have been so long exposed, but their freedom, sovereignty, and independence ultimately acknowledged.
>
> And whereas ... the interposition of Divine Providence in our favor hath been most abundantly and most graciously manifested, and the citizens of these United States have every reason for praise and gratitude to the God of their salvation.
>
> Impressed therefore with an exalted sense of the blessings by which we are surrounded, and of our entire dependence on that Almighty Being from whose goodness and bounty they are derived; I do by and with the Advice of the Council appoint Thursday the eleventh day of December next to be religiously observed as a day of Thanksgiving and Prayer, that all the people may then assemble to celebrate ... that He hath been pleased to continue to us the Light of the blessed Gospel; ... That we also offer up fervent supplications . . . to cause pure religion and virtue to flourish ... and to fill the world with His glory.

★ ★ Patriot's Prayer ★ ★

Heavenly Father, use me as Your light and a spokesperson for Your truth—and may You be glorified!

★ ★ Patriot's Promise ★ ★

Colossians 3:4 says, "When Christ who is our life appears, then you also will appear with Him in glory."

357

Son of Man and Son of God

The Son of Man has come to seek and to save that which was lost.

LUKE 19:10

Dr. Luke penned the gospel that bears his name with the compassion of a family physician, carefully documenting the perfect humanity of Jesus Christ. Luke built this gospel narrative on the foundation of historical reliability, emphasizing Jesus' ancestry, birth, and early life before moving chronologically through His earthly ministry. Growing belief and growing opposition develop side by side, with the opposition finally sending the Son of Man to His death on the cross. But Jesus' resurrection ensured that His purpose of saving the lost is fulfilled.

Christianity welcomes close examination, that the inquirer might "know the certainty" of its truths (Luke 1:4). Alexander Hamilton, a signer of the Constitution and one of America's first constitutional lawyers, made such an investigation. This is his conclusion: "I have carefully examined the evidences of the Christian religion, and if I was sitting as a juror upon its authenticity, I would unhesitatingly give my verdict in its favor. I can prove its truth as clearly as any proposition ever submitted to the mind of man."

★ ★ Patriot's Prayer ★ ★

Dear Lord Jesus, I do not question what Your Word proclaims about You, yet I am glad that even secular history reports Your birth, life, death, and resurrection.

★ ★ Patriot's Promise ★ ★

Jesus' stories of the Lost Sheep, the Lost Coin, and the Lost Son found in Luke 15 vividly teach the gospel message: God through Christ has come to seek people lost in their sins and save them.

These [signs] are written that you may believe that Jesus is the Christ, the Son of God, and that believing you may have life in His name.

JOHN 20:31

Son of God and Son of Man

Many people regard John's account of Jesus' life as the greatest and most powerful of the four Gospels. John sets forth Jesus in His deity for the specific purpose of bringing his readers to saving faith in Him and eternal life. John's gospel is topical, not primarily chronological, and it revolves around seven miracles and seven "I am" statements of Christ. Where the gospel of Luke presents Jesus and the Son of Man" in John we see Him as the Son of God.

In 1646, according to the university "Rules and Precepts," students entering Harvard University agreed that "the main end of his life and studies" was stated specifically in John 17:3—"This is eternal life, that they may know You, the only true God, and Jesus Christ whom You have sent." In those days, a Harvard education regarded knowing Christ as the "only foundation of all sound knowledge and learning."

★ ★ Patriot's Prayer ★ ★

Dear Jesus, Son of God, thank You for leaving Your throne in heaven to die on the cross as payment for my sins. Thank You for my salvation and for the promise of salvation for all who will believe.

★ ★ Patriot's Promise ★ ★

John 3:16 is the gospel message in its clearest and simplest form: "God so loved the world that He gave His only begotten Son, that whoever believes in Him should not perish but have everlasting life."

★★★ 359 ★★★

Watchmen on the Walls

Below are the unforgettable words President John F. Kennedy was to deliver in a luncheon speech on November 22, 1963, the day he was assassinated in Dallas, Texas:

> We in this country, in this generation are, by destiny rather than choice, the watchmen on the walls of world freedom. We ask, therefore, that we may be worthy of our power and responsibility, that we may exercise our strength with wisdom and restraint, and that we may achieve in our time and for all time the ancient vision of "peace on earth, good will toward men." That must always be our goal. For as was written long ago, "Except the LORD keep the city, the watchman waketh but in vain" (Psalm 127:1 KJV).

★ ★ Patriot's Prayer ★ ★

Freedom is such a blessing, O Lord. Help us watch over it and keep it not only for this moment, but for the generations to come. Let freedom ring in our hearts forever and ever as a blessing to people everywhere.

★ ★ Patriot's Promise ★ ★

Second Kings 9:17 speaks of a watchman standing on the tower looking for any potential threats. Seeing Jehu and his vast army coming, the watchman called out, "I see some troops coming" (NIV). When we stand as a watchman looking to protect our freedom, God will reveal to us any threat against it.

Before I formed you in the womb I knew you.

JEREMIAH 1:5

The Value of Human Life

Our Founding Fathers held to the biblical principle that human life is precious and that our Creator God endowed every man, woman, and child with the right to "life, liberty, and the pursuit of happiness." The inherent dignity and matchless value of every life, apparently from conception until death, was self-evident truth.

When God as Creator is removed from our nation's value system, however, our rights as citizens become subject to the relative values of those in position to make or change the laws. The weakest and most vulnerable among us will first suffer at the hands of those who will determine what rights we do and do not have. God's moral law that protects the innocent and the vulnerable will be superseded by the selfish pursuits and moral license of mere man.

Every human being, born or unborn, deserves equal protection by the law, and the value of life is not conditional upon that life's usefulness to others or to the state. Neither scientific progress nor the desire to help others can justify the sacrifice of any human being's life, whether by abortion, euthanasia, or any new form of biotechnology. We believers must actively defend the sanctity of human life.

★ ★ Patriot's Prayer ★ ★

Merciful God, we as a nation too easily ignore the little ones who lose their lives every day to abortion. Show me what You would have me do to defend the unborn.

★ ★ Patriot's Promise ★ ★

"As the body without the spirit is dead, so faith without works is dead also" (James 2:26).

December 15

Boston's Tea Party

The LORD has made bare His holy arm.

ISAIAH 52:10

The Stamp Act of 1765 and the Townshend Acts of 1767 angered American colonists: the British government was imposing taxes on the colonies even though the colonies were not represented in Parliament. In March 1770, British soldiers killed five American colonists. Early in 1773, the men of Marlborough, Massachusetts, declared this unanimously:

> Death is more eligible than slavery. A free-born people are not required by the religion of Jesus Christ to submit to tyranny, but may make use of such power as God has given them to recover and support their laws and liberties. . . . [We] implore the Ruler above the skies, that He would make bare His arm in defense of His Church and people, and let Israel go.

On December 16, 1773, a band of Boston patriots calling themselves the Sons of Liberty threw 342 chests of tea from a British East India Company ship into the waters of Boston Harbor. The British government responded by closing the port of Boston, enacting additional laws that were known as the "Intolerable Acts," and charging John Hancock, Samuel Adams, Joseph Warren, and Benjamin Church with the "Crime of High Treason." At the very least, the Boston Tea Party rallied the support for revolutionaries in the thirteen colonies and sparked the Revolution.

★ ★ Patriot's Prayer ★ ★

Thank You, heavenly Father, for brave Americans who have fought and do fight for my freedom. Show me my role in fighting to protect these freedoms.

★ ★ Patriot's Promise ★ ★

Hear the end of the Isaiah promise quoted above: "All the ends of the earth shall see the salvation of our God."

Moses said to the people, "Do not be afraid. Stand still, and see the salvation of the LORD, which He will accomplish for you today. For the Egyptians whom you see today, you shall see again no more forever. The LORD will fight for you, and you shall hold your peace."

EXODUS 14:13–14

The American Spirit

On December 17, 1620, a small group of Pilgrims who had left England in search of greater freedom to worship God dropped the anchor of the *Mayflower* at Plymouth Harbor in what is now Massachusetts. These were some of the very first individuals and families in whose soul burned what we call the "American spirit."

Their flight from oppression mirrored a much earlier Exodus, when God led the children of Israel out of the bondage and oppression of Egypt and into the land He had promised their forefather Abraham. The book of Exodus recounts how through His mercy—extended to those who were protected by a lamb's blood—God delivered His people, took them to a place of liberty, and promised them great success if they obeyed His Word and lived according to His will.

★ ★ Patriot's Prayer ★ ★

Lord, thank You for the blood of the Lamb, Jesus Christ, who through His death and resurrection has provided a way for all people to come to enjoy liberty from sin and its eternal consequences.

★ ★ Patriot's Promise ★ ★

"If the Son makes you free, you shall be free indeed" (John 8:36).

"Emancipate! Enfranchise! Educate!"

> You in Your mercy have led forth the people whom You have redeemed.
>
> EXODUS 15:13

On December 18, 1865, the Thirteenth Amendment abolished slavery, a process that had begun with President Abraham Lincoln's Emancipation Proclamation in 1862. At Lincoln's request, Presbyterian minister Henry Highland Garnet preached in the House of Representatives on February 12, 1865 to commemorate that proclamation. It was the first time a black American spoke in the Capitol, and he delivered these powerful words:

> Augustine, Constantine, Ignatius, Polycarp, Maximus, and the most illustrious lights of the ancient church denounced the sin of slaveholding. . . . Thomas Jefferson said . . . "There is preparing, I hope, under the auspices of heaven, a way for a total emancipation." The sainted Washington said . . . "It is among my first wishes to see some plan adopted by which slavery in this country shall be abolished by law". . . . Patrick Henry said, "We should transmit to posterity our abhorrence of slavery." So also thought [this] Congress. . . .
>
> Let the gigantic monster perish. Yes, perish now, and perish forever! . . . Let slavery die . . .
>
> Illustrious rulers of this great nation! . . . You have said, "Let the Constitution of the country be so amended that slavery and involuntary servitude shall no longer exist in the United States, except in punishment for a crime" . . . Favored men—and honored of God as His instruments—speedily finish the work which He has given you to do. Emancipate! Enfranchise! Educate! And give the blessings of the Gospel to every American citizen!

★ ★ Patriot's Prayer ★ ★

Thank You, Lord, for making *all* men and women free. Help me appreciate and protect the freedoms You have granted.

★ ★ Patriot's Promise ★ ★

"There is neither Jew nor Greek, there is neither slave nor free, there is neither male nor female; for you are all one in Christ Jesus" (Galatians 3:28).

He who looks into the perfect law of
liberty . . . and is a doer of the work,
this one will be blessed.

JAMES 1:25

Religion and Democracy
circa 1831

In 1831, French nobleman Alexis de Tocqueville spent nine months traveling
America, spending most of his time in Boston, New York, and Philadelphia. He
interviewed people from every walk of life and then shared these amazing observations in *Democracy in America*:

> Upon my arrival in the United States, the religious aspect of the country
> was the first thing that struck my attention. . . . In France I had almost
> always seen the spirit of religion and the spirit of freedom pursuing
> courses diametrically opposed to each other; but in America I found
> that they were intimately united, and that they reigned in common over
> the same country. . . .
>
> There is no country in the whole world in which the Christian
> religion retains a greater influence over the souls of men than in
> America . . . its influence is most powerfully felt over the most
> enlightened and free nation of the earth.
>
> Religion in America takes no direct part in the government of society,
> but it must nevertheless be regarded as the foremost of the political
> institutions of that country. . . .
>
> The Americans combine the notions of Christianity and of liberty so
> intimately in their minds, that it is impossible to make them conceive the
> one without the other.

★ ★ Patriot's Prayer ★ ★
Heavenly Father, forgive us for straying from our Christian roots. Call us back to
Your principles and the liberty we find there.

★ ★ Patriot's Promise ★ ★
"Creation itself also will be delivered from the bondage of corruption into the
glorious liberty of the children of God" (Romans 8:21). We do not have to live at
the mercy of the corruption of this world.

December 19

The Value of God's Word

Behold . . . the feet of him who brings good
tidings, who proclaims peace!

NAHUM 1:15

Consider this statement by John Jay (1745–1829), the first chief justice of the US Supreme Court:

> By conveying the Bible to people . . . we thereby enable them to learn that man was originally created and placed in a state of happiness, but, becoming disobedient, was subjected to the degradation and evils which he and his posterity have since experienced. The Bible will also inform them that our gracious Creator has provided for us a Redeemer, who has made atonement "for the sins of the whole world," and . . . has opened a way for our redemption and salvation; and that these inestimable benefits are of the free gift and grace of God, not of our deserving, nor in our power to deserve.

★ ★ Patriot's Prayer ★ ★

Kind and gracious Father, thank You for sending Jesus to this earth to live a sinless life, to teach us about You, and then to die on our behalf as payment for our sin. Most of all, though, thank You that He was resurrected, that He now lives, and that He is coming again soon.

★ ★ Patriot's Promise ★ ★

In Luke's Christmas story, the angels appear to the shepherds and say, "Do not be afraid, for behold, I bring you good tidings of great joy which will be to all people" (2:10). These tidings were the announcement that Jesus was born in Bethlehem. God had promised His Son to all people, to save them from their sins, and just as He fulfilled that promise, He will fulfill every promise He has made.

[The wise men from the East] saw the young Child with Mary His mother, and fell down and worshiped Him.

MATTHEW 2:11

Celebrating the Birth of Jesus

In the 1985 case of *Lynch v. Donnelly*, Chief Justice Warren Earl Burger delivered the Supreme Court's opinion: the city of Pawtucket, Rhode Island, did not violate the Constitution by displaying a Nativity scene. Noting that presidential orders and congressional proclamations have designated Christmas as a national holiday in religious terms for two centuries and in the Western world for twenty centuries, he wrote this:

> There is an unbroken history of official acknowledgment by all three branches of government of the role of religion in American life.... The Constitution does not require a complete separation of church and state. It affirmatively mandates accommodation, not merely tolerance, of all religions and forbids hostility towards any.... Anything less would require the "callous indifference" we have said was never intended by the Establishment Clause. Indeed, we have observed, such hostility would bring us into a "war with our national tradition as embodied in the First Amendment's guaranty of the free exercise of religion."

★ ★ Patriot's Prayer ★ ★

Thank You, Lord, for humbling Yourself, for giving up Your throne and coming to this earth as a helpless child, born to a young virgin. May we as a nation always have the freedom to celebrate the saving miracle of Your birth.

★ ★ Patriot's Promise ★ ★

It's one of many Old Testament promises fulfilled in Jesus: "For unto us a Child is born, unto us a Son is given . . . His name will be called Wonderful, Counselor, Mighty God, Everlasting Father, Prince of Peace" (Isaiah 9:6).

December 21

The "Unspeakable Gift"

Thanks be to God for His indescribable gift!

2 CORINTHIANS 9:15

John Sherman (1823–1900) is the longtime American political leader noted for having introduced the Sherman Anti-Trust Act (1879) in an effort to curb the monopolies of big businesses. Hear his convictions about God's written Word and living Word:

> I appreciate the Holy Bible as the highest gift of God to man, unless it be the "unspeakable Gift" of Jesus Christ as the Savior of the world. It is the Divine assurance that our life does not end with death, and it is the strongest incentive to honorable, charitable Christian deeds.

★ ★ Patriot's Prayer ★ ★

Thank You, Lord, for the greatest gift of all, Jesus Christ. I praise You for Him who opened for us the door to eternal life and heaven. Thank You also for the Bible and what it means to me.

★ ★ Patriot's Promise ★ ★

"For the wages of sin is death, but the gift of God is eternal life in Christ Jesus our Lord." Romans 6:23 promises us eternal life if we accept Jesus Christ as our Savior and Lord.

Out of you shall come forth to Me the
One to be Ruler in Israel.

Micah 5:2

Inexplicable Evidences

Robert Morris Page (1903–1992), the physicist known as the "Father of US
Radar," sets forth this apologetic for the Christian faith:

> The authenticity of the writings of the prophets . . . is established
> by such things as the prediction of highly significant events far in
> the future that could be accomplished only through a knowledge
> obtained from a realm that is not subject to the laws of time as we
> know them.
>
> One of the great evidences is the long series of prophecies
> concerning Jesus the Messiah. These prophecies extend hundreds
> of years prior to the birth of Christ. They include a vast amount
> of detail concerning Christ Himself, His nature and the things He
> would do when He came—things which to the natural world, or the
> scientific world, remain to this day completely inexplicable.

★ ★ Patriot's Prayer ★ ★

Thank You, dear God, for the prophets of old. They spoke faithfully for You,
giving Your people hope and—as You fulfilled these prophecies—stronger faith in
Your sovereignty and faithfulness. Thank You for evidence of Your hand in history.

★ ★ Patriot's Promise ★ ★

Hear God's promise of old: "But you, Bethlehem Ephrathah, though you are little
among the thousands of Judah, yet out of you shall come forth to Me the One to
be Ruler in Israel, whose goings forth are from of old, from everlasting" (Micah
5:2). Just as God promised us One out of Bethlehem, Jesus was born there, born
to save us from our sins.

December 23

"In the Beginning God . . ."

> In the beginning God created.
>
> GENESIS 1:1

Apollo 8, the first manned mission to circle the Moon, entered lunar orbit on Christmas Eve, December 24, 1968. That evening, during the ninth lunar orbit, the three astronauts—Frank Borman, Jim Lovell, and William Anders—broadcast pictures of the Earth and Moon as seen from Apollo 8.

A NASA official had called Borman and said, "We want you to say something appropriate." The Apollo 8 team chose Genesis 1:1–10 KJV.

William Anders began: "We are now approaching lunar sunrise and, for all the people back on Earth, the crew of Apollo 8 has a message that we would like to send to you. 'In the beginning God created the heaven and the earth.'"

Jim Lovell picked up the creation account a few verses later: "'And God called the light Day, and the darkness he called Night. And the evening and the morning were the first day.'"

After he finished reading about God's creation of heaven on the second day, Frank Borman read about God creating the dry land and the sea and ended with this: "From the crew of Apollo 8, we close with good night . . . Merry Christmas—and God bless all of you . . . on the good Earth.'"

★ ★ Patriot's Prayer ★ ★

Thank You, Creator God, for this magnificent universe that reveals Your glory. Help me to be an advocate on Your behalf against those who wish to erase all traces of "God as Creator" in our nation.

★ ★ Patriot's Promise ★ ★

"Remember your Creator" (Ecclesiastes 12:6), for doing so leads to wisdom and purpose in life.

For all the law is fulfilled in one word, even in this: "*You shall love your neighbor as yourself.*"

GALATIANS 5:14

Angel of the Battlefield

Born on Christmas Day 1821, in the small town of Oxford, Massachusetts, Clara Harlowe Barton was the youngest of five children. Her father made his living through farming and horse breeding, and her mother stayed busy as a homemaker. As Clara grew, so did her desire to become a nurse, and her father encouraged her:

> As a patriot, he had me serve my country with all I had, even with my life if need be . . . and as a Christian he charged me to honor God and love mankind.

At the outbreak of the American Civil War, Clara tirelessly nursed the wounded soldiers of the Union Army. In 1864, she was put in charge of all the Union hospitals until the war's end. Afterward, she played a major role in the founding of the American Red Cross and served as its first president from 1881 through 1904, when she retired at age 83. This American servant had truly earned the name "Angel of the Battlefield."

★ ★ Patriot's Prayer ★ ★

Father in heaven, help me this Christmas Day and every day to show the love of the Christ-child to all who cross my path. Thank You for sending Your Son to be my Savior.

★ ★ Patriot's Promise ★ ★

As the angel's words indicate— "Do not be afraid, for behold, I bring you good tidings of great joy which will be to all people" (Luke 2:10)—the birth of Jesus was for all people who will accept His love and forgiveness.

The December 25– July 4 Link

As you therefore have received Christ Jesus the Lord, so walk in Him, rooted and built up in Him and established in the faith.

COLOSSIANS 2:6–7

On the sixty-first anniversary of the signing of the Declaration of Independence, John Quincy Adams, the sixth president of the United States, proclaimed the following:

> Why is it that, next to the birthday of the Savior of the world, your most joyous and most venerated festival returns on this day? Is it not that, in the chain of human events, the birthday of the nation is indissolubly linked with the birthday of the Savior? That it forms a leading event in the progress of the Gospel dispensation? Is it not that the Declaration of Independence first organized the social compact on the foundation of the Redeemer's mission upon earth? That it laid the cornerstone of human government upon the first precepts of Christianity and gave to the world the first irrevocable pledge of the fulfillment of the prophecies announced directly from heaven at the birth of the Savior and predicted by the greatest of the Hebrew prophets six hundred years before.

★ ★ Patriot's Prayer ★ ★

Dear Lord, as the great men who founded this nation knew well, the greatest gift that America has for the world is the Gospel of Jesus Christ. Strengthen and enable us to continue to share this message of hope around the globe.

★ ★ Patriot's Promise ★ ★

Look again at Colossians 2:6–7. Being strongly rooted in Jesus, we will not be easily influenced or deceived by enemies of Christian truth.

Watch therefore, for you do not know what hour your Lord is coming.

JESUS IN MATTHEW 24:42

The book of Joel offers both good news and bad, and the prophet's call to repentance is as timely today as it was when it was first penned.

A recent plague of locusts gave Joel imagery for his warning. He calls to mind—as if the people of Israel could have forgotten—the ruined fields, the parched ground, the failed wheat and barley crops, the dried up grape vine, and the withered fig, pomegranate, palm, and apple trees (Joel 1:10–12). The prophet goes on to warn that this dreadful experience will seem like nothing compared to the judgment that is to come.

But Joel does more than just warn the people of Judah of the coming destruction for their sin and rebellion against God. The prophet also promises God's restoration and deliverance to all who repent of their sinful ways, change their behavior, and call upon Him as Lord:

> I will pour out My Spirit on all flesh . . .
> I will pour out My Spirit in those days.
> Joel 2:28–29

Like our Hebrew ancestors, twenty-first century believers also need to repent of our sinful ways, change our behavior, and call upon Jesus Christ as Lord.

★ ★ Patriot's Prayer ★ ★

Let me live, dear Lord, so that I honor Jesus Christ in my daily behavior and words as I anticipate His return. Pour Your Holy Spirit upon me that He might cause me to walk uprightly before Thee.

★ ★ Patriot's Promise ★ ★

"The LORD God is a sun and shield; the LORD will give grace and glory; no good thing will He withhold from those who walk uprightly" (Psalm 84:11).

Trust and Determination

The Lord GOD will help me . . . therefore
I have set My face like a flint.

ISAIAH 50:7

Abraham Lincoln, the sixteenth president of the United States (1861–1865), shared these words in a special message to Congress at the beginning of the Civil War:

Having thus chosen our course, without guile and with pure purpose, let us renew our trust in God and go forward without fear and with manly hearts.

★ ★ **Patriot's Prayer** ★ ★

Today, O God, I renew my trust in You, the Sovereign Master of the universe as well as my Savior and Friend. I will fear no one because I know that You are with me.

★ ★ **Patriot's Promise** ★ ★

Read the promise of Zephaniah 2:11: "The Lord will be awesome to them, for He will reduce to nothing all the gods of the earth; people shall worship Him, each one from his place, indeed all the shores of the nations." God pledges His faithfulness to us all. The Lord is awesome!

All things are possible to him who believes.

MARK 9:23

When you read the paper or listen to the news these days, what prompts the word *impossible* to come to mind? The Middle East? The economy? The war against terrorism? The national budget?

Generations of Americans have faced the seemingly impossible. The settlers faced the unknown wilderness, hunger, disease, and death. In addition, the pioneers heading west had to deal with buffalo herds, prairie fires, stagecoach bandits, and tornados.

Facing the impossible is a fact of life, anytime and anywhere. The early residents of Ohio acknowledged not only the impossibilities of life but the One for whom noting is impossible. This is the motto of the State of Ohio:

WITH GOD ALL THINGS ARE POSSIBLE

★ ★ Patriot's Prayer ★ ★
Strengthen my faith and forgive my unbelief, O Lord.

★ ★ Patriot's Promise ★ ★
Mark 9:23—"If you can believe, all things are possible to him who believes"—are the words of Jesus, spoken to a father who brought his little boy to Him to be healed. Jesus promised the man that if he would only believe in His power, nothing could stand in the way of his son's healing. This promise still stands today.

December 29

By God's Grace

> "Be strong and of good courage; do not be afraid, nor be dismayed, for the LORD your God is with you wherever you go."
>
> JOSHUA IN JOSHUA 1:9

As one year draws to a close and the beginning of another fast approaches, we do well to remember the goodness and faithfulness that God has blessed us with throughout this past year . . .

It is also encouraging to look back and see how our faithful God has graciously blessed and protected our nation. Hear these statements from some leaders of our young nation:

This nation was founded not by religionists, but by Christians; not on religion, but on the gospel of Jesus Christ.

PATRICK HENRY

We recognize no Sovereign but God, no king but Jesus.

JOHN ADAMS AND JOHN HANCOCK

God who gave us life gave us liberty. And can the liberties of a nation be thought secure when we have removed their basis?

THOMAS JEFFERSON

To the distinguished character of patriot it should be our highest glory to add the more distinguished character of Christian.

GEORGE WASHINGTON

May we honor God as well as our Founding Fathers by strengthening our nation according to these truths our wise forefathers set forth more than two hundred years ago.

★ ★ Patriot's Prayer ★ ★

You are King of kings, Sovereign and eternal, God of grace, and it is only by Your grace that this nation has lasted for more than two centuries. Use me to help recover America's commitment to You and Your ways.

★ ★ Patriot's Promise ★ ★

"You, O Lord, are a God full of compassion, and gracious, longsuffering and abundant in mercy and truth" (Psalm 86:15).

December 30

May the Lord . . . establish your hearts
blameless in holiness before our God
and Father at the coming of our Lord
Jesus Christ with all His saints.

1 THESSALONIANS 3:12–13

When Paul had to leave the Thessalonians prematurely, he sent Timothy to check on their progress in the faith. Relieved by Timothy's positive report, Paul wrote this warm epistle of commendation, exhortation, and consolation. He closed with instructions regarding the return of the Lord, whose Second Coming means hope and comfort for believers both living and dead.

President Ronald Reagan frequently invoked the words of George Washington, who said that religion and morality were "indispensable supports" to the prosperity of our political system. During a radio address in December 1983, Mr. Reagan described one of his favorite paintings, which shows George Washington praying at Valley Forge. He said the painting "personified a people who knew it was not enough to depend on their own courage and goodness; they must also seek help from God, their Father and their Preserver." Similarly, Paul exhorted the Thessalonian believers to put on "the breastplate of faith and love, and as a helmet the hope of salvation" (5:8) as they stood for Christ.

★ ★ **Patriot's Prayer** ★ ★

Lord Jesus, I thank You for the promise of Your coming again. What joy comes with anticipating that great day!

★ ★ **Patriot's Promise** ★ ★

"The Lord Himself will descend from heaven . . . The dead in Christ will rise first. Then we who are alive and remain shall be caught up together with them in the clouds to meet the Lord in the air. And thus we shall always be with the Lord" (1 Thessalonians 4:16–17). Come quickly, Lord!

December 31

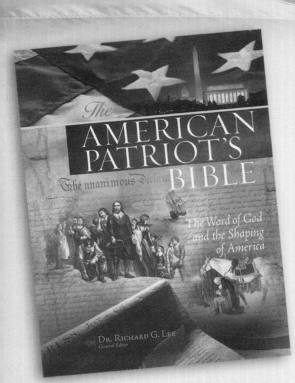

Discover.
Experience,
Examine.

THE WORD OF GOD AND THE SHAPING OF AMERICA

The American Patriot's Bible
978-1-4041-1405-0

THE AMERICAN PATRIOT'S BIBLE
connects the teachings of the Bible with
the history of the Unites States while
applying it to today's culture. Beautiful
full-color insert pages spotlight
America's greatest thinkers, leaders,
and events that present the rich heritage and future of our great nation.

Sometimes history does repeat itself.

THOMAS NELSON
Since 1798
For other products and live events,
visit us at: thomasnelson.com

Available Wherever Books & Bibles are sold.
For more information visit www.americanpatriotsbible.com.

In God We Still Trust Booklet
978-1-4185-4153-8

IN
God
WE STILL
TRUST
BOOKLET

Discover how our Christian roots are profoundly evident with many of our historic national leaders. This beautifully illustrated 4-color book includes excerpted articles from *The American Patriot's Bible* spotlighting America's greatest thinkers, leaders, and events that present the rich heritage and future of our great nation.

Blessed is the nation whose God is the Lord.

PSALM 33:12

THOMAS NELSON
Since 1798

For other products and live events,
visit us at: thomasnelson.com

* In reference to the April 3 devotional on page 97:

Shields of Strength

I am convinced that nothing can ever separate me from my Fathers love
Romans 8:38

There Is No End
To A Fathers Love

TIME
TAFL

ROM
8:37

In all things I am more than a conqueror through Christ who loves me.

Shields of Strength

I will be strong and courageous. I will not be terrified, or discouraged; for the Lord my God is with me wherever I go.
Joshua 1:9

United States of America
One Nation Under God

Prayer
Dear Lord Jesus,
I realize I am a sinner,
I repent for my sins,
and right this moment
I receive You as my
Lord and Savior. Amen

Shields of Strength

I will be strong and courageous. I will not be terrified, or discouraged; for the Lord my God is with me wherever I go.
Joshua 1:9

If you would like to review other designs and receive a free Shields of Strength catalog,
please call **1.800.326.7882** or visit **www.shieldsofstrength.com.**

"There is one in the Oval Office, others in the pockets of congressmen and senators, and, aside from the official insignias they wear, it is the emblem most often carried by members of the military in Afghanistan and Iraq."
—STEPHEN MANSFIELD, Author